DOBERMANNS
TODAY

JIMMY RICHARDSON

RINGPRESS

RINGPRESS

Published by Ringpress Books Ltd,
POBox 8, Lydney, Gloucestershire GL15 6YD

Discounts available for bulk orders
Contact the Special Sales Manager at
the above address. Telephone 01594 563800

ISBN 1 86054 050 3

Printed and bound in Singapore
by Kyodo Printing Co

CONTENTS

ACKNOWLEDGMENTS

I am grateful to have been given the opportunity of writing this book, which I hope will prove to be both educational and of some interest.

I am grateful to Peggy Dawson for writing the chapter on the history of the Breed; to Alan Ridout for his chapter on Obedience Training, and to Judy Doniere for her chapter on the Dobermann in the USA. I am also grateful to Peter Diment for converting my freehand sketches into works of art for the Breed Standard chapter. Thanks must also go to Brian Blades for supplying information on Dobermanns in South Africa and Han Zwan for information from Holland.

I am especially grateful to the many Dobermann owners who so willingly answered my requests for photographs. Unfortunately, lack of space has meant that not all the photographs, and not all the text submitted, could be included.

JIMMY RICHARDSON
June 1995

Chapter One

HISTORY OF THE DOBERMANN

By PEGGY DAWSON

To those of us who are captive to the breed, the name Dobermann is pure magic! Truly it is the dog of mystery, whose origins are shrouded in speculation. It's a sad fact that Herr Dobermann kept no records of the dogs he chose to breed from. There's a strong possibility that the old black and tan smooth-haired German Pinscher was used, or very likely the Beauceron, for when one studies this dog the similarities to the Dobermann become apparent, including the fact that the Beauceron has double dewclaws on the hind legs, and, I believe, in the early days, these were occasionally produced by our own breed. Perhaps the black and tan 'butcher's dog' played a part (this dog may also have been a forebear of the Rottweiler), but who knows? There have been so many theories put forward, and yet it's a puzzle that is impossible to unravel at the present time. Maybe at a future date some wondrous discovery will come to light, and then all will be revealed! However, in the meantime we are left to guess and speculate.

THE ORIGINAL BREEDERS

Frederick Louis Dobermann was born in 1834, and apparently enjoyed a variety of occupations – dog catcher, carcass cutter, night-watchman, and tax collector; but again, no clear-cut facts emerge. He would certainly have attended the annual Dog Market (Hundemarkt), where dogs of different categories were put up for sale, which took place in the market square of his home town, Apolda, Thuringia, Germany, in the early part of the year. This was a time for festivity after the hard winter months, with beer, sausages, and music much in evidence. So, quite apart from the buying and selling of dogs, it appears that a good time was had by all concerned!

The Dobermannpinscher was officially recognised in Germany in 1900, and, as a matter of interest, the first Breed Standard required the height of a male to be 55cm to 65cm (21.6 to 25.6 inches) at the shoulder, and a female 48cm to 55cm (18.9 to 21.6 inches). Keeping in mind the present Breed Standard requirements, this gives some indication of the progress of the Breed during this century – though one should always keep in mind the fact that the Dobermann is classed as a medium-sized dog.

After the death of Herr Dobermann in 1894, the development of the Breed was continued by Herr Otto Goeller. According to Philipp Gruenig, cross breedings with the Manchester Terrier were recorded at the turn of the century, and about six years later with the Greyhound, and again with the Manchester Terrier. It is believed that the Manchester Terrier was used to give a darker eye and improve the quality of the coat. One of the earliest pedigrees where it's possible to give a two-generation ancestry, was that of the black and tan bitch bred by Goswin Tischler – Glora von Groenland (later v.d. Nidda), who was born May 3rd 1900.

Lord v. Groenland
Troll v. Groenland
Tilly v. Groenland

Flora v. Groenland

Luchs v. Groenland
Tilly II v. Groenland
Tilly v. Groenland

This bitch was to become the dam of Sieger Leporello vom Main – reputed to be a dog of exceptional beauty, who was whelped on August 28th 1902.

Harking back to the cross breedings at the turn of the century – if you study the picture of Graf Wedigo v. Thueringen (Sg. Graf Belling v. Thueringen x Sgn. Freya v. Thueringen), born August 25th 1901, and then compare it with the picture of Fedor v. Aprath (Tell v. Kirchweyhe x Thina v. Aprath), a brown dog whelped on May 6th 1906, you will notice the difference in appearance.

Graf Wedigo v. Thueringen, born in 1901.

Fedor v. Aprath, born 1906.

GROWING POPULARITY

Although the Dobermann quickly gained popularity in America, South Africa, and Europe – especially in Holland where the Dutch Dobermann Club was formed as early as 1906 – the same did not apply to the UK, where I believe, less than a dozen were imported before the outbreak of the Second World War. One of these imports, a bitch named Ossi v. Stresow, made quite an impact, as she was featured in an article in *The Sunday Express* of June 24th 1928, headed 'The Most Romantic Dog in The World'. 'Ossi' belonged to the well-known author and cookery expert Elizabeth Craig, and was described in the article thus: 'She more than fulfils the highest ideals of the man who first produced the breed. She is as perfect as a dog can be.' It is quite obvious that 'Ossi' was a wonderful ambassadress for the breed.

1948 was an important year for the Dobermann in the UK. The Dobermann Pinscher Club (later to become The Dobermann Club) was formed, with Sir Noel Curtis-Bennet KCVO as President;

Mr A.T.A. (Fred) Curnow as Chairman; Mr L. Hamilton Renwick as Vice Chairman; and Mrs. Julia Curnow as Honorary Secretary and Treasurer. And four Dobermanns arrived from Europe!

THE GERMAN STUD BOOK
Before elaborating on the early European imports, I'd like to mention the Auchtbuch (Stud Book) published in Germany some years after the war. This contains the details of Dobermanns registered between 1945 and 1948 and it also states the number of pups that were whelped. It's a sad fact that some of the pups born towards the end of the war, and just afterwards, failed to survive. It's also true that occasionally one comes across a registration where, perhaps, the following is written: 'This bitch is six years of age. Her papers were destroyed by bombing. Two famous judges have stated that she is a first class Dobermann.' What an unhappy time that was for all of us – mankind and dogs alike!

UK IMPORTS
Now to those imports! Derb and Beka von der Brunoburg were imported from Germany by Fred Curnow. Beka was born on February 19th 1945, a black and tan bitch, bred by Herr Carl Wienenkotter:

Wltsg. Troll v.d. Engersburn SchH1

Frido v. Raufelsen SchH1

Rsgn. Jessy v.d. Sonnenhohe SchH1

Beka v.d. Brunoburg

Rsg. Artus v. Gurstenlager SchH1

Unruh v. Sandberg

Wltsgn. Alfa v. Hollingen SchH11

Derb v.d. Brunoburg was born on October 21st 1945, a black and tan male; he came from a large litter, ten pups in all, seven dogs, three bitches. He was sired by Axel Germania (Frido v. Raufelsen SchH1 x Fanny v. Pfeddersheim SchH111), but his dam was Unruh v. Sandberg, the same as 'Beka'. A mating between these two imports produced seven puppies, one of whom, Alpha of Tavey (later Cartergate Alpha of Tavey) was owned by Miss Eva Would, and became the foundation of the Cartergate line. 1948 also saw the arrival in the UK of Birling Bruno v. Ehrgarten, imported from Switzerland by Mr L. Hamilton Renwick. This black and tan male was born on May 20th 1946, bred by Mr W. Lenz:

Astor v. Hollingen SchH1

Dulo v. Bernau

Citta v. Laimatof

Birling Bruno v. Ehrgarten

Blitz v. Burgweiher

Blanka v. Lindenbaum

Dolli v. Holzeiken

It was a mating between Birling Britta v.d. Heerhof (imported from Holland by Mr L. Hamilton Renwick in 1949) and Birling Bruno v. Ehrgarten that produced the first Dobermann male champion in the UK, Ch. Wolfox Birling Rogue.

Now to Pia v.d. Dobberhof. Fred Curnow imported her from Holland, in whelp to Benno v.d. Schwedenhecke. She was actually born during the war, on November 27th 1943 and was a black and tan bitch, bred by Mr. J. A. Hofma:

                                    Artus v. Konigshalt
                        Brando v. Berggreef
                                    Heide v. Simmenau
     Pia v.d. Dobberhof
                                    Int. Ch. Waldo v.d. Wachtparade
                        Alie v.d. Heerhof
                                    Agnes

Pia produced two puppies in quarantine, Bruno (Brunno) of Tavey, and Don of Tavey. 'Bruno' was to become the sire of eight champions, one of whom, Ch. & Ob. Ch. Jupiter of Tavey CDex., is the only Dobermann, up to the present day, to become a dual champion in the UK. 'Bruno' also sired the first-ever Dobermann champion in the UK, Ch. Elegant of Tavey. Both 'Jupiter' and 'Elegant' were out of Prinses Anja v't Scheepjeskerk CDex., who was imported from Holland in 1950 by Mrs Julia Curnow. This black and tan bitch, born on July 3rd 1948, was to have a strong influence on the Breed. She became the dam of five champions.

Prinses Anja was bred by Miss N. van Amsterdam, and, I believe, originally belonged to the world-renowned Mrs V. Knijff-Dermout (van Neerlands Stam). Her sire, the black and tan Int. Ch. Graaf Dagobert v. Neerlands Stam, was born on Christmas Day 1946. He was a powerful dog, who won a total of twenty-seven International Champion Awards.

                                    Ch. Waldo v.d. Wachtparade
                    Int. Ch. Graaf Dagobert. v. Neerlands Stam
                                    Roeanka v'h Rhederveld
     Prinses Anja v't Scheepjeskerk
                                    Bucko v.d. Heerhof
                    Alindia v't Scheepjeskerk
                                    Andranette v. Rio de la Plata

Through her paternal grand-dam, Roeanka v'h Rhederveld, it is possible to trace Prinses Anja's ancestry back to Angola v. Grammont – a brown bitch, whelped in Holland on July 15th 1917. According to Philipp Gruenig, she was the most beautiful bitch of her time, and her appearance was so bewitching that one could never tire of looking at her.

WORKING TESTS CHAMPIONS
Kennel Club records for the year 1949 show the arrival from Germany of Ulf v. Margaretenhof and Donathe v. Begertal. These two Dobermanns were to have an enormous influence on the working potential of the Breed. Ulf v. Margaretenhof, a black and tan male, was born on June 30th 1946, bred by Herr Max Thurling:
                                    Horst v.d. Bismarcksaule SchH11
                    Oz. Sgr. Hasso v.d. Neckarstrasse SchH111
                                    Rsgn. Freya v. Rauhfelsen SchH1
     W/T Ch. Ulf v. Margaretenhof CDex. UDex. TDex. PDex.
                                    Arras v. Wilhelmhorst
                    Toska v. Margaretenhof
                                    Senta v. Margaretenhof

This photo, taken in the early 1950s, shows Fred and Julia Curnow, Sgt. Harry Darbyshire and WT Ch. Ulf v Margaretenhof. Ulf was born in July 1945, bred by Max Thurling, and imported by the Chief Constable of the Surrey Constabulary.

Ulf was given to the Surrey Police Dog Section, where he was handled by Sgt. Harry Darbyshire, who, as a matter of interest, was later to become Vice Chairman of The Dobermann Pinscher Club. Ulf proved himself an outstanding working dog and, by winning the Police Dog Trials in June 1949 and July 1950, he became the Breed's first UK Working Trials Champion. In fact, such was his meteoric progress in the working trials world that he was described by Sgt. Harry Darbyshire as 'The Bombshell of 1949'!

Donathe v. Begertal, a black and tan bitch, was born on March 28th 1948, bred by Herr Kurt Ehlebracht:

                         Blitz v.d. Domstadt SchH1
             Zar v. Stahlhelm
                         Citta v. Braunschweig
    Donathe v. Begertal
                         Helios v. Bassewitz
             Asta v. Teufelstal
                         Gida v. Burgberg

Donathe was also owned by the Surrey Police Dog Section, and qualified CDex., UDex., after winning the Senior 'A' and 'B' Stakes at the Working Trials held during 1951. But it was in her role as a dam that she made such an important contribution to the Breed. She was mated to W/T Ch. Ulf v. Margaretenhof on two occasions. The first litter, the 'J' litter, produced a working trials champion, W/T Ch. Mountbrowne Julie CDex. UDex. TDex. PDex, and according to the Dobermann Pinscher Club's booklet issued in 1952, the entire 'J' litter had qualified UDex. by the time they were twenty months of age! Not content with this, Donathe v. Begertal was the dam of yet another working trials champion, W/T Ch. Mountbrowne Karen UDex. TDex. PDex., through a mating with the German import Astor v. Morgensonne. So, looking back, that accounts for three of the early working trials champions, yet there was one more in those far-off days – W/T Ch. Joseph of Aycliffe CDex. UDex. TDex. PDex. He was sired by Dober v. Oldenfelde, but his dam was W/T Ch. Mountbrowne Julie (an 'Ulf' x 'Donathe' daughter). So, as you can see, Donathe v. Begertal was the dam of two working trials champions, and the grand-dam of another. She was a truly remarkable Dobermann, but sadly her life was short, just four and a half years.

It wasn't until 1961 that The Dobermann Club decided to hold its own Working Tests. The first of these took place at Bexley on July 2nd, judged by Sgt. Harry Darbyshire. The Tests proved very popular with Doberfolk; in fact, such was their success that 1986 saw the celebration of the Working Tests' Silver Jubilee! This was a truly happy event, judged by Mrs Jean Faulks (a qualifier at the very first Tests,) and Mr Jim Burrell. The two-day event was held at the home, and farm, of Mrs Jane Parker, in Hitchin, and ended with a great 'get-together' of Doberfolk from the earliest days. After the presentation of diplomas and rosettes, we all settled down to an evening of happy memories.

It may have been that this memorable occasion sowed the seeds for a Working Dobermann of the Year Competition, for by this time three clubs were holding Working Tests – The Midland Dobermann Club, The Birmingham & District Dobermann Club, and of course, The Dobermann Club. After much discussion between the three, it was decided that the first Working Dobermann of the Year Competition would be hosted by The Dobermann Club, and would be open to Dobermanns that held the highest working awards of any of the participating clubs. November 14th 1987 was the chosen date, Mrs Jane Parker's Pound Farm, Hitchin, the venue, and Mrs Jean Faulks the judge, and the weather was perfect. The winner of the first Working Dobermann of the Year Competition was Jo Magness' My Gem of Sunnygift CDex. UDex. WDex. TDex.

CHAMPION SHOW DOGS

Dobermanns were obliged to wait until 1952 before the joy of the challenge certificate was theirs, but even in 1950 there were nine Dobermanns shown at Crufts. They had two classes, Novice Dog or Bitch, and Open Dog or Bitch, and these two classes, judged by Mr H.G. Sanders, had a total of fifteen entries, seven in 'Novice', and eight in 'Open'. The winner of the Open Class, and Best of Breed, was Mr L. Hamilton Renwick's Birling Rachel (Birling Bruno v. Ehrgarten x Birling Britta v.d. Heerhof). Her litter brother, Birling Rebel, was placed second, with Mrs B. Butler's South African import, Frieda von Casa Mia of Upend (Rudolph von Arras x Brown Princess the Second) placed third, but this time judged by Mr J. W. Beynon. Winner of the Open Class and Best of Breed, once again, was Birling Rachel, with her litter brothers, Birling Rogue and Birling Rebel, taking second and third place. The Novice Class was won by Mrs Julia Curnow's Dutch import, Waldox v'h Aamsveen of Tavey (Graaf Dagobert v. Neerlands Stam x Astridona), second place went to Mrs Curnow's Worth of Tavey, with third place going to Mountbrowne Joe, a Dobermann in Police Service (litter brother to W/T Ch. Mountbrowne Julie), sired by W/T Ch. Ulf v. Margaretenhof x Donathe v. Begertal. Mountbrowne Joe qualified CDex. UDex. TDex. PDex. in working trials, winning the Police Dog Stake in 1953.

Now, one can well imagine the anticipation of competitors as Crufts 1952 loomed large on the horizon. Challenge certificates, at last! The judge on this great occasion was a man known throughout the world of dogs, and a founder member of The Dobermann Pinscher Club, Mr Leo Wilson. He awarded the Bitch CC to Elegant of Tavey (destined to become the Breed's first UK champion), and the Dog CC to Ingot of Tavey, who, in spite of winning his second challenge certificate under Mr Joe Braddon later the same year, failed to attain the third CC that would have made him a champion. Ch. Elegant of Tavey gained her 'crown' under Mrs Rita Price Jones at the Blackpool & District Canine Society, and such was her beauty, that in 1952, she won a Challenge

The first UK Champions: Ch. Wolfox Birling Rogue (Birling Bruno von Ehrgarten – Birling Britta van de Heerhof) and Ch. Elegant of Tavey (Brunno of Tavey – Prinses Anja v't Scheepjeskerk).

Certificate at eight consecutive shows. Another claim to fame for Ch. Elegant of Tavey was that both she, and Ch. Wolfox Birling Rogue were awarded CCs by Herr Philipp Gruenig in 1952, when he came to the UK to judge Dobermanns at the Croydon, Coulsdon & District Canine Society. So, as you can see, 1952 was quite a year for Dobermanns and their Doberfolk!

THE AMERICAN EXPERIENCE (**By Judy Doniere**)
Several books have been written about the first Dobermans to come from Germany to the US; most of them were quality animals, which began to make a great impression on the newcomers to this rare breed. In 1898 the first Doberman was imported to the United States by a Mr E. R. Salmann. Not until 1908 was one to be officially registered in the AKC Stud Book. He was Doberman Intelectus, a black and tan, sired by Doberman Bertel, a German import, registered in Germany as Bertel v Hohenstein. Intelectus was out of a bitch named Doberman Hertha, who became the first AKC Doberman Champion.

The Doberman of the 1920s and 1930s certainly resembled the dogs of today, but the low croups have been replaced with a more respectable tail placement, even to the extreme of being sometimes gay. The thick short necks are now elegant, arched and longer. The sagging, or roached, and often too long back, is now short and strong. The light eyes and straw-colored markings are very dark and clear. The short, blocky heads have been replaced with long, dry wedge shapes. The french fronts are now straight-legged. The straight and hocky rears have become beautifully angulated and true. The flat hare feet are now tight and catlike. The double-coats and undercoats have disappeared and we now have short, sleek, glossy coats with hardly a trace of undercoat on the neck. The sharp, one-man dogs are now family pets, living in harmony with the community.

The legends of the greats of yesterday, such as Dictator, Alcor, Delegate, Meadowmist, Jessi, Blank, Lux etc., are talked about when long-time breeders get together. But the past twenty years have their own legends. Some have passed away, some are still here. B-Brian, Demetrius, Carly,

Ch. Royal Tudor's Wild as the Wind: Top winning American bitch in the history of the breed. Owned by Susan Korp.

Mikron Photos.

Ch. Brunswig's Cryptonite: A top show dog and stud dog. Owned by George Murray.

Mikron Photos.

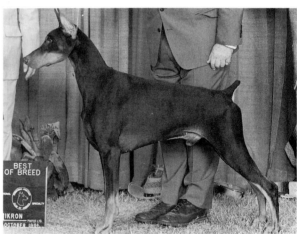

Sunhawk, Dark & Debonaire, Devel D, Windwalker, Nite Rider, Cryptonite, Dexter, Damian, Cairo and Caught Redhanded are talked about as top show and stud dogs. And among the great bitches are Missle Belle, Miranda, Impertinence, Irish Fantasy, Mary Hartman, Touch of Class and, of course, the great "Indy" Wild as the Wind, and several up and coming girls who are now making a name for themselves in the show ring and whelping box.

Not only are dogs, past and present, legends, but so are a great many notable breeders from the past who have somewhat retired from the show and breeding arena, but who occasionally still whelp a litter or two, just to keep their hand in and show the youngsters of the breed how to do it. Peggy Adamson (Damasyn) continues judging on a weekly basis and, although she rarely breeds any more due to her hectic schedule, is still Mrs Doberman to the Fancy around the world.

Another great is the incomparable Tess Hensler (Ahrtal). Tess judged bitches at the 1993 DPCA National, where she astounded the exhibitors by her youthful attitude and appearance. She announced that this was her swan song and that she would not judge again – but no-one entirely believed her! Frank Grover is still going strong, actively judging, writing, giving seminars and being chairman of the DPCA Judges Educational Committee. He still breeds on occasion and is

Misty, a member of the Dobermann drill team of Los Altos Hills, CA, leaping nine barrels – a distance of 28ft. In the USA the Dobermann has been trained to a high level in Obedience, Agility and Working Tests.

one of the mainstays of the DPCA. Marge Kilburn still keeps herself updated on the progress of the breed and the activities of the DPCA through her many friends. Jane Kay (Kay Hill), the vivacious ex-handler, all-breed judge and breeder has discontinued her duties in the whelping box, but still has her hand in guiding many protégés to a successful breeding program. Jane is the DPCA delegate to the AKC. Joanna Walker (Marks-Tey) is still breeding occasionally, but her first love now is training guide dogs for the blind. Joanna is an excellent writer, author of the well-known *The New Complete Doberman Pinscher* for Howell Book House.

The Doberman breed recently lost one of its outstanding advocates, Charles A.T. O'Neill, Past President of DPCA, Executive Vice-President of AKC, Show Chairman of the AKC Centennial Show, well-known breeder and exhibitor of Dobes, Manchesters and Whippets. Chuck will be sorely missed by the Doberman people, but carries on his tradition through his charming daughter, Mari-Beth O'Neill, who is presently on the staff at the American Kennel Club.

Schutzhund was banned as an AKC event in 1989, since the problem of Pit Bull attacks on humans was scaring many people. AKC thought any occurrence of dogs seen attacking, or doing what seemed like attack work, was not a good image for breeds such as the Doberman and Rottweiler, who were likely to be the next breed on the list of banned animals in a great many cities. This ban angered a number of Schutzhund enthusiasts and caused a split between some of them and the DPCA. They formed the United Doberman Club, which is not sanctioned by the AKC. Former DPCA President and AKC judge, Ray Carlisle, is very active in this organisation. Ray is doing some fine breeding these past few years, combining the lines of German and American breeding. He recently lost his outstanding German import and top producer, Ch. Alida v Flandrischen Lowen, who has more titles than this chapter has room to print.

Special tribute must be paid to Ch. Brunswig's Cryptonite. Called Kafka, he is alive and well and producing many, many outstanding Champions. He holds the record as the number-one working dog of all time, as well as the number-one Doberman of all time. He is owned by Mr and Mrs Samuel Lawrence of Orlando Fla. Another outstanding Doberman, still going strong, is the lovely Ch. Royal Tudor Wild as the Wind. Indy, as she is known, won Best in Show at the Westminster KC Show, was twice Best of Breed at the DPCA Nationals, was the Top Twenty winner, is a Top Obedience winner, and a great producer of Champions. Indy will long be remembered as a bitch whom everyone loved, regardless of whether they were Doberman owners or not. She is owned by Mrs Sue Korp of California.

Chapter Two

ACQUIRING A DOBERMANN

Humans and dogs have lived together in harmony for thousands of years. We have taken the dog into our homes and provided shelter, food and protection. In return the dog has given man companionship, love and loyalty. Humans have probably derived the most benefit from this relationship, since we have selectively bred dogs over the years in order to produce a wide variety of specialist breeds to perform specific tasks.

The Dobermann is no exception, being evolved specifically as a highly intelligent and athletic working dog. The early Dobermann breeders certainly achieved their objectives and, at the same time, managed to produce a dog of great style and distinction. Selective breeding over the years has refined the Dobermann to give us the ultimate aristocrat of the dog world that we know today, and probably the most rewarding breed of dog that it is possible to own.

RESPONSIBILITIES OF OWNERSHIP
Whilst the love, companionship and loyalty of a dog is one of the finest experiences that anyone can have, it must be remembered that a dog is a living animal. Ownership of a dog, of any breed, not only gives pleasure but also imposes responsibilities, and requires a commitment to care properly, to feed, to exercise and to ensure that the dog receives proper veterinary treatment when needed. You must be prepared to adapt your way of life to accommodate what will, effectively, become an additional member of the family. It will also require a financial commitment, in that purchasing, feeding and looking after a dog will cost money. This will be particularly important with a puppy, which will need more specialist and frequent feeding, more companionship, supervision and training.

If you can make the necessary changes to your way of life to accommodate a dog, there is no reason why there should be any undue problems. However, it must be accepted from the outset that dogs can be mischievous, they can cause damage to your house and garden, and they can be noisy. This is particularly true of puppies, which have been well described as 'little atom bombs of stored-up energy, full of curiosity and mischief'. If you are particularly house-proud, or even garden-proud, and can't bear the thought of a dog helping to make everything untidy, then you would be better off not having one. If you really want a dog, then you are going to have to compromise. This may involve restricting the puppy, or even adult dog, to certain parts of the house or garden, until such time as you are sure that the dog can be trusted. Alternatively, you will have to become less house-proud, as the price to be paid for the joys of owning a dog.

You should also ensure that every member of the family really wants a dog. There is nothing worse, particularly for the poor dog, than being loved by one member of the family and hated by another. Not only is this likely to be extremely confusing for the dog, but it is likely to be the cause

Roanoke Periwinkle (Twinglo The Silver Wraith of Roanoke – Roanoke Galaxy) pictured with Jimmy Richardson. The Dobermann is a loyal and faithful family dog.

Photo: East Anglian Daily Times.

of matrimonial discord. *It must also be remembered that a dog is not a toy and should never be purchased as a child's play-thing*, unless you, the parents, are prepared to accept the responsibility for looking after the animal. A dog is a real, living creature with highly specific needs, a character, feelings and a dignity of its own. These must be acknowledged and respected.

THE PERSONALITY OF THE DOBERMANN

Having decided that you are going to acquire a dog, you will need to give serious consideration to which breed you want to own. Assuming that you are one of those discerning people who are searching for the ideal, you are sure to consider the Dobermann. This suggestion should not come as a surprise to you, since this is now one of the most popular breeds of dog in the world today.

The Dobermann is instantly recognisable, being a medium-sized dog with a short, fine, smooth black coat with distinctive rust-red markings. Brown Dobermanns are fairly common but are numerically fewer, the brown being a recessive colour. Grey (normally described by the genetic term, blue) and fawn Dobermanns also occur, but only rarely. The Dobermann is a fine upstanding dog, with a stylish, elegant outline. The head is carried proudly on an arched neck, with a facial expression that clearly suggests a combination of intelligence and interest in everything that is going on. If you are not already a Dobermann fan, or are not familiar with the breed, or have been indoctrinated by the reputation of the Dobermann as a fierce guard dog, that look is one which could strike fear into you and make your blood run cold. Even so, it is sure to generate in you a feeling of respect and admiration for such a noble animal.

If all breeds of dog were tested and ranked in terms of their IQ, the Dobermann would come out very close to the top. This intelligence means that the dog will very quickly learn the routines of the home. It also makes the Dobermann a very rewarding dog to live with, often learning far more than you ever intended – and sometimes using that knowledge against you! For example, it does not take a Dobermann long to discover what you keep in the fridge, what is in every cupboard and even what food goes on a particular plate. The next stage is a very simple and obvious one – total participation in everything that you do, including sharing your meal, your cup of tea, your chair and even your bed.

The Dobermann is very loyal, faithful and loving to the family, wanting to be with you constantly, and expecting to follow you everywhere, no matter which room of the house you choose! If not let in, the Dobermann will wait outside the door and let you know quite clearly that this arrangement simply isn't acceptable. You may just as well give in gracefully and accept that your Dobermann is the nearest thing that you will have to a shadow. This intense love and affection is something which cannot be imagined by someone who has not lived with a Dobermann, and is one of the unexpected joys which awaits the first-time owner.

THE DOBERMANN AS A GUARD DOG

The Dobermann is a natural guard dog, looking upon the house, the garden, the car, even the family and their cat, as possessions which need to be protected from unwanted intruders. This guarding instinct will become apparent when a Dobermann reaches about six to nine months of age, depending on how quickly an individual dog matures. It is this natural guarding instinct which makes the Dobermann such a desirable dog to have in the home with you, and is undoubtedly one of the main reasons for the continuing popularity of the breed.

The Dobermann has a reputation for being a fierce guard dog, which is going to attack the moment any intruder enters the house. This has grown up largely due to the use of the Dobermann as a war dog, guard dog and police dog in many countries over many years. The film industry also has much to answer for in this respect, since it often uses a Dobermann when it wants to portray an aggressive guard dog defending territory against intruders, or a dog which can be used to do man-work. This reputation may be justified in some instances in some countries where the dog is expected to be sharp, and is not considered to be a true Dobermann unless prepared to defend territory or owners by force, if necessary. Generally, however, this is more myth than fact, certainly in the UK and in the USA. Most Dobermanns seem to have an uncanny knack of knowing who is allowed in the house and who is not. The ideal balance, which most owners want, is for the dog to challenge strangers who come onto the premises, but to welcome them, or at least to accept them, once they are invited in to the house. This is what most owners would define as 'good temperament'. The dog should not represent any threat to those that you allow into the house and, equally, should not fear them to any great extent. Many Dobermanns will be friendly to visitors, particularly if encouraged in this from an early age. Others can be relatively aloof towards strangers, simply tolerating them because you have approved them; but they should not run away and hide, or show fear of them, though such a trait is not going to prevent the dog being the ideal companion in other respects. It is this reputation, and the uncertainty in the minds of would-be intruders, that makes the Dobermann such a good deterrent. Only someone who is ignorant of the breed, or is extremely foolhardy, will challenge a Dobermann on the dog's own premises. It is the one deterrent for which most intruders have a healthy respect. Whether or not any individual Dobermann would actually attack an intruder if he decided to push his luck is open to question. Some undoubtedly would, particularly if the intruder chose an unorthodox means of entry, such as through a window. I suspect that there are many very gentle and soft-natured Dobermanns who would also react violently in these circumstances, and probably surprise their owners in the process. As I said, the Dobermann has an uncanny ability to know when someone should not be allowed to come in. In practice, you do not want too aggressive a dog, as you will then have a liability, and never be quite sure about reactions towards your friends, neighbours or visitors when they come to your house. What you require is a well-balanced dog that you can totally trust, but who, so far as intruders are concerned, is a threat not a weapon.

THE DOBERMANN AND CHILDREN

If you have children in the house, there is no need to fear for their safety because you have acquired a Dobermann. A Dobermann puppy will tend to accept everyone in the house without question, and will grow up treating them all as family, having been familiar with them from an early age. Introducing an adult Dobermann into a home in which there are children may not be quite so easy. A lot will depend on previous experience. If the dog is already familiar with children and the relationship was a happy one, then your children are likely to be accepted without any difficulty. If, however, there was an unhappy relationship, and the dog has already developed a mistrust or dislike for children, then you may have a problem. You may either decide that the risk is one which is not worth taking, or you will need a lot of time and patience for a bond of friendship to develop. It is very sad that so many people feel that once a baby comes into the house, the dog must go. Many lovely dogs, Dobermanns included, are needlessly thrown out of their homes in the belief that the dog will be a threat to the baby, or that it is unhygienic to have a baby and a dog in the house together. Both these concerns are unfounded. The Dobermann will simply accept the new baby as an addition to the family and consider it to be one more thing to be protected and guarded. To start with, the Dobermann may well be jealous of the new arrival, which is likely to receive a lot of attention, and will need reassurance about being still loved and still wanted, in order to reduce any feeling of rejection. Problems can arise with young children where they mistreat the dog. *You will need to remember that you must train both the dog and the children, particularly the latter.*

EXAMINING YOUR OWN CHARACTER

Having decided that you want a dog and, more specifically, that you want a Dobermann, you should stop and think about yourself; are you the right person to own one? As I have already indicated, the ownership of any dog imposes certain commitments and obligations on you, and that of a big dog, such as a Dobermann, should not be undertaken lightly until you are satisfied that you can provide the home, the care and the attention the dog needs.

The Dobermann is a large, active breed, with apparently limitless energy, therefore needing somewhere to run in order to maintain physical fitness and let off steam. This means that you should have an area of garden which can be used for exercise and also for toilet purposes. The dog will very quickly assume ownership of this garden and will frequently need to check that it is still secure and to investigate every creature, real or imaginary, that has been there since the last patrol. This is just as important as the physical exercise, since the Dobermann is a highly intelligent dog which needs constant mental stimulation.You will also need to be able to take the dog out for walks, giving the opportunity for free running, unless the garden is really large enough for this. The need for extensive walks in order to maintain the dog's physical well-being is much overstated. Nevertheless, the Dobermann does derive some good from them, but they are also of great mental benefit, as a Dobermann will always want to know what is going on anywhere near home. This is only one short step away from claiming such areas as territory. It is not always easy to find places where you can let a dog run free without being at risk of meeting other dogs, farm livestock or traffic. You will therefore need a car in order to go somewhere for exercise. You will quickly find with a Dobermann that what is a privilege today becomes a right tomorrow; and once drives to suitable exercise areas have started, you will never be allowed to stop them.

MAKING THE GARDEN SECURE

Your garden will need to be securely fenced in order to prevent your Dobermann going into neighbours' gardens, onto farmland or even onto the highway. Although not a breed that wanders by nature, a Dobermann always wants to know what is happening on the other side of the fence, which should, ideally, be six feet in height, in order to prevent escape. Even this height will not contain a Dobermann that has learnt to jump, so never teach your dog to jump in fun – that knowledge will be used to the dog's own advantage when convenient. Equally, a Dobermann is clever enough to know that it is easier to go under a fence rather than over one. Fencing should therefore be solid and substantial. If wire-netting is used, it should be sunk below the surface of the ground and if necessary concreted in. Secure fences also have a secondary benefit in that they prevent other people's dogs from getting in.

THE IMPORTANCE OF CONTROL

For your Dobermann's own safety and well-being, it is important to keep the dog securely on your own premises. A wandering Dobermann is likely to cause concern, probably more than any other breed, which is likely to result in complaints surprisingly quickly. In the UK, any Dobermann owner should always have the Dangerous Dogs Act in mind. Few people seem to realise that Section 3 of this Act applies to all breeds of dog. Section 10(3) describes a dog as being 'dangerously out of control on any occasion on which there are grounds for reasonable apprehension that the dog will injure any person, whether or not it actually does'. This means that if you do not have the facilities for a Dobermann, or cannot properly control one, then you should not possess one. Whilst any dog is likely to protect its owners, breeds such as Labradors and Poodles are not likely to 'cause apprehension' in the same way as a Dobermann. Do not allow your inability to control a Dobermann to result in the breed receiving a bad name, providing ammunition for an increasingly anti-dog media, and resulting in the breed as a whole being penalised under the Dangerous Dogs Act.

Being a very intelligent breed, the Dobermann is not a fool's dog, and is a very quick learner, who will soon find out how far you can be pushed in terms of seeking to be the dominant member of the household, which is, in effect, the pack. You must therefore be strong-willed enough to remain the boss and ensure that you have proper control. There is nothing worse than a big powerful dog in the hands of someone who cannot control it. It is a recipe for disaster. This also means that you need to be physically capable of holding and controlling a Dobermann. If you are unable to do this, then you would probably be better off with a smaller or gentler breed of dog.

You will need to consider whether you are able to control a breed of dog which is likely to be more aggressive towards other dogs than most. Whilst many Dobermanns are very soft and gentle, you should not assume that all are like that, or even that individual dogs may not reveal that aggression, possibly when you least expect it. As a breed, the Dobermann tends to have a low flashpoint and requires very little provocation to have a fight, and, once this has happened, will always be willing, and maybe even anxious, to have further fights. This not only reinforces the need for you to be able to physically control a Dobermann and to contain the dog within your own premises, but means that you must be extremely careful how and where you let a Dobermann off the lead for free-running exercise. Doing this in areas to which the public have access is always likely to be out of the question. You will gradually get to know your own dog who, with maturity, may be extremely reliable, so you may be able to relax your caution. It is not always what your dog may do that causes a problem: it may well be someone else who is free-running a dog which they cannot properly control.

FINANCIAL CONSIDERATIONS

You will need to consider carefully whether you are financially capable of paying the cost of feeding a Dobermann, and meeting any other expenses which might be involved, such as vets' fees, insurance, bedding and toys. There are also many hidden costs, such as replacing chewed-up furniture and shoes, particularly if you are rearing a puppy. Whilst a dog should never be considered to be a substitute for a human, having a dog in the house is, in many ways, similar to having another person in the house, whose individual needs and requirements must be taken into account when the household budget is considered.

HAVE YOU THE PATIENCE FOR A PUPPY?

The final, but possibly the most important, thing to ask yourself is whether you have the patience and understanding to cope with a lively, mischievous puppy. Dobermann puppies can be little angels but, more often than not, resemble a tornado on four legs. You will never, even for a moment, be able to take your eyes off the puppy, who will always be getting into trouble. Dobermann puppies only seem to have two speeds – flat out or asleep. They will quickly tire of the toys that you provide, and find their own, usually a table leg, the arms of the armchair, or a shoe or other item of clothing carelessly left within reach. They are liable to chew or nibble anything within reach, and carpets, wallpaper and even the plaster on the walls all suffer. They will rearrange the garden for you, digging up plants or simply digging holes in the lawn or the flower beds. When they come into the house, they will leap from chair to chair like little jack-in-the-boxes, and they seem to have unlimited energy.

Dobermann puppies often become very boisterous and will try to make you play with them. If you encourage them to play rough, they can become unacceptable, grabbing your hands or legs in mock battle. You should never encourage a puppy to grow up being rough. Apart from anything else, the puppy teeth are very sharp and can inflict painful nips or bites, even though the puppy is only playing.

Raising a Dobermann puppy is, effectively, a full-time occupation. You will need to ensure that you, or a member of the family, will be at home, if not the whole time, then most of the time. In any event, the puppy will need to be fed and let outside for toilet purposes and exercise. You should never leave a puppy alone in the house for lengthy periods. The puppy will get bored and so become destructive, and will be likely to bark and cry, causing neighbour problems. It will also encourage the puppy to become dirty in the house and possibly get 'neurotic' through being left for long periods.

If you are really understanding and have a deep love for your small hooligan you will be able to tolerate these little problems; otherwise you will most certainly wonder why you ever wanted to buy a Dobermann puppy. The good news is that these difficult growing-up stages generally only last for about twelve months, after which the puppy begins to settle down, seems to develop an understanding of what to do, or not to do, and generally becomes the wise, gentle, responsible and sensible Dobermann that you thought you were buying in the first place. Those who have previously had a Dobermann are often the most disbelieving when it comes to the problems of rearing a Dobermann puppy, simply because they have forgotten their old dog's puppy days and only remember the sensible adult dog. Puppy owners often find it necessary to contact the breeders of their puppies or others knowledgeable about the breed in order to seek advice. What they need is reassurance that most Dobermann puppies are like theirs, but that they usually grow out of it by the time they are twelve to fourteen months old.

If you think that you meet these requirements for being the owner of a Dobermann puppy, and have not been completely put off the whole idea by the difficulties that I have described, then it is time to start considering how to acquire one. For those who are not so sure, let me reassure you that even though raising a puppy can be a traumatic experience, you will also enjoy endless hours of fun and joy. The real pleasures will come once the puppy begins to grow up, both mentally and

Dobermann puppies are very appealing – but a young pup can be like a tornado on four legs!

physically, and these pleasures will far outweigh any little difficulties that you might experience on the way – though at times you may wonder!

LOOKING FOR A DOBERMANN

There are many ways of acquiring a Dobermann. I know of one Dobermann breeder who became involved in the breed only because he bought a house, and the Dobermann went with it. For most people, however, the preferred way is to purchase a puppy. It is also the best way for most would-be Dobermann owners, as it means that the puppy will enter into their homes at about eight to twelve weeks of age, will have no strong bonding with the breeder, no preconceived ideas about anything, and will readily accept your way of life and anything else in your home, such as children, other dogs and cats. You will also be able to teach the puppy whatever you like in whatever way you wish; you will be effectively starting from scratch, as the puppy will know almost nothing, and will also bond very quickly with new owners, which will make training that much easier. You will also have the joys of watching your cuddly little puppy grow into a handsome adult. For many people this puppy stage is one of the most enjoyable and one which they would not miss for anything.

Puppies should start to be weaned at about three weeks of age, be fully weaned by five to six weeks and settled in a regular feeding routine, be it three, four or five meals per day. The breeder has to ensure that all the puppies are eating properly, growing and thriving and are free from worms. Above all, the breeder must ensure that each puppy is sufficiently well advanced, mentally and physically, and is robust enough to leave the kennel and to start a new life in somebody's home. This cannot be done in under seven weeks, which means that no puppy should be sold by a breeder or acquired by a purchaser under this age, unless there are special, extenuating circumstances. Ideally, puppies should be eight weeks old before they leave for their new homes.

A breeder who tries to persuade you to collect your puppy younger than this is simply being ignorant, or irresponsible, or even both. It should also make you somewhat suspicious as to why they are being shifted so fast at such an early age. The 'we are going on holiday in a few days time' is an often-heard justification for this action.

Occasionally you may be able to acquire an older puppy, say between five to nine months old, which has been 'run-on' by a breeder. Such a puppy is likely to be the best one in the litter, which the breeder had hoped may make the grade as a show dog or as part of a future breeding programme, but has subsequently had a change of mind. A puppy like this is likely to have been reared properly, given some basic training and to have been given a reasonable amount of human contact, possibly including car journeys and visits to local training classes, and would be a worthwhile acquisition, being a good-quality puppy with much of the hard work of rearing, socialising and training already done. You should not expect to pay much above the normal puppy price and would be getting good value for money.

BUYING AN ADULT DOG
The alternative to buying a puppy is to acquire an adult dog. From time to time, these are offered for sale, for a variety of reasons and, more often than not, on a 'free to good home' basis or in return for a nominal sum of money, which is much less than would be the normal purchase price of a puppy. Such Dobermanns may be available because of financial, personal or family problems, and so be likely to adapt to a new home without too much trouble. Older dogs will take longer than puppies, however, as they will have been uprooted from everything and everyone that they know, and suddenly find themselves in a strange home amongst strange people. It is surprising really how quickly a Dobermann can accept such a dramatic upheaval and come to terms with it. But it can take a long time; you must be patient and not expect an older dog to feel really at home and totally integrated for at least six months.

RESCUE ORGANISATIONS
Dobermanns are often taken in by rescue organizations. These are either general, in that they rescue and rehome all dogs of whatever breed, or they are breed-specific. In the UK, Dobermann Rescue rehomes Dobermanns on a regular basis. These rescue organizations are generally very careful about how they rehome their dogs, since the well-being of the dogs is their principal concern. This is a good thing, as it does give you some protection, in that the dogs will have been screened for any known health or temperament problems, and every effort will be made to ensure that the dog is likely to be compatible with any new home and family.

'BUY FROM A BREEDER'
There is an old maxim which says 'Buy from a breeder'. At first glance, this may seem like a good publicity slogan by breeders to promote puppy sales. While this may be true of a few, it is a proposition that merits serious consideration.

Responsible breeders are generally concerned about the quality of their bloodlines and will try to maintain them by the careful selection of the bitches from which they breed and the stud dogs that they use. They are also concerned about maintaining the overall standard of the Dobermann by breeding from the best stock available. The better breeders will have a reputation, earned over many years, which they will be anxious to maintain. As a consequence, a breeder is likely to have a better knowledge of the breed, to be able to breed a litter of puppies of a more predictable and consistent type and temperament, and to charge you a fair price. With a breeder you should be able to see a number of adult dogs which are closely related to the litter of puppies, which will give you a very good idea as to what the puppies will be like when they grow up. Visiting a number of kennels will also enable you to see different bloodlines and strains and to make a judgement as to the strain from which you would like to acquire your puppy.

But it must be pointed out that the majority of Dobermann puppies, certainly in the UK, are not bred by longtime breeders but by people who may own only one or two Dobermanns. Some of these people can be just as knowledgeable and concerned about the well-being of the breed and what they themselves produce, and probably qualify to be considered as breeders. Many will also be show exhibitors, so will have an extensive knowledge of the current Dobermanns. They may have bred their own bitches, or acquired them from highly reputable kennels or bloodlines, and mated them to top-quality stud dogs. As a result, they are able to breed puppies of as high a standard as any kennel. You should have no fears about purchasing a puppy from such a breeder.

Many 'one bitch owners', however, do not aspire to such levels of concern for their puppies, or the breed in general. They may have a bitch of dubious ancestry, have used a stud dog simply because he is a winning dog or because he lives just around the corner. With such litters, you will have less of a guarantee or certainty as to the type or temperament of the offspring, since there is more likely to be a wide variation between individual dogs within any litter.

Inevitably, the categorization of breeders can never be as clear-cut as maybe I have implied. This means that you should exercise caution before rushing out and buying the first puppy that you are offered. Seek advice about potential breeders or litters from the Kennel Club, the Dobermann breed clubs or from the long-established top kennels in the breed.

There is one further category of breeder that you may be unfortunate enough to encounter and that is the puppy farm, or puppy mill as it is known in the USA. They are establishments which generally breed a wide variety of different breeds, with little or no interest in the quality of their product or its eventual destination. The principal objective of the operation is to make money. Puppies may be sold from the premises, but are more likely to be sold in bulk to dealers, who provide retail outlets. Puppies produced by puppy farms may well be of uncertain conformation and temperament, have been poorly reared, carry various diseases, been shipped to dealers at too young an age and been mixed with puppies from other litters, thereby increasing the likelihood of infection.

FINDING AVAILABLE LITTERS

Having decided to purchase a Dobermann puppy, you will need to find out where litters are currently available. Puppies are sometimes advertised in one of the specialist canine publications or in the local newspapers. The Dobermann breed clubs usually have details of litters bred by their club members. The Kennel Club is often approached by those looking for puppies but they tend to give details of breeders rather than individual litters. Contacting breeders is an alternative approach. Although they may not actually have any puppies available, they may well know the whereabouts of litters, possibly sired by their stud dogs. It must be realized that when a breeder or a breed club tells you about a litter, they are not able to give you any guarantee as to the quality of the puppies. They may not have seen them or know anything about them, other than the fact that they exist. It will be up to you to see the puppies and make your own decision.

This approach may not always be possible, however, as the demand for Dobermann puppies frequently exceeds the supply. As a consequence, you may have a limited selection of puppies from which to choose, or indeed you may be reduced to booking a puppy from a prospective litter, or even having your name put on a breeder's waiting list, and hoping that they may eventually be able to provide you with a puppy. This latter approach is particularly appropriate if you want a particular bloodline or strain, and does not commit you to anything; it merely ensures that you will be offered a puppy, which you can then either accept or reject.

If you reserve a puppy from a litter you may be asked to pay a deposit at the time you make the reservation, with the balance of the cost to be paid on collection. The amount of the deposit depends on circumstances but is generally about 10% of the agreed purchase price. Deposits can be the source of problems and have been known to become the subject of litigation. If the breeder is unable to supply the puppy for some reason, such as its death or injury, then clearly the purchaser is entitled to a refund. Equally, if there is a change of mind by the purchaser, who decides not to take the puppy, then it is normally accepted that the deposit is forfeited. The problems arise where the breeder no longer wants to sell to the purchaser, or where the purchaser considers that the puppy is not up to the required standard. Should such problems arise, then professional advice should be sought.

Having been offered a puppy, you should make an appointment to visit the litter and to see the puppy for yourself. You should also ask to see the dam (the mother) of the puppies and any other close relatives. If necessary, visit several litters before making your final decision. If you have any doubts about a puppy, you would be well-advised not to go ahead. As said previously, do not buy the first puppy that is available. You should be quite sure in your own mind about the right puppy for you.

DOG OR BITCH?

One of the first decisions that you have to make before going out and buying your Dobermann puppy is whether to have a dog or a bitch. For some people, this choice is easy as they already have a clear preference, whereas for others, it may be a difficult decision to have to make.

While dogs and bitches have obvious physical differences, they are otherwise similar in appearance, personality and temperament. This is not surprising, since these characteristics are determined genetically and all the puppies in a litter, whether dogs or bitches, will be genetically similar. Very few of the genes acquired from the sire or the dam are sex-linked. But these inherited characteristics are modified, to some extent, by the sex of the individual puppies, mainly because dogs and bitches produce different hormones. The variations are relatively minor in puppies but become more obvious as the puppies grow up and mature into adult dogs. This means that you will need to consider the different characteristics of the two sexes as adults, rather than simply choosing your eight-week-old puppy on the basis of which one takes your eye when you visit the litter.

Bitches tend to be slightly smaller than dogs both in height and weight. This means that they may be easier to hold and control when on a lead, which may be an important consideration if you are not physically strong. With proper training, however, even the strongest dog can be properly controlled. Unfortunately, this does not always happen. I know of one lady who owns a powerful male Dobermann and the outward leg of the evening walk consists of her being dragged along the street, only regaining control at certain points where she can grab hold of a fencing post, lamp post or some other convenient fixture. The journey home is no problem as the dog trots at her side, under total control. In this case, either she should have had a bitch rather than a dog, or she should have trained her dog better, if only to ensure that the dog accepted her as the pack leader who gave the commands rather than the dog knowing that he could dominate her with impunity. In all probability, she would have been better off with a smaller or a gentler breed of dog.

The bitch also tends to be less aggressive than the dog. Male Dobermanns can be very dominant and aggressive towards other males of any breed. Often a male Dobermann will not actively look for a fight but will react very quickly to anything that he considers to be a sign of aggression by another dog. This does not mean that bitches will never fight or be aggressive; some of them are just as bad, if not worse, than the dogs, just as some of the dogs have a gentle, non-aggressive reaction to other dogs. This is yet another area in which environment and upbringing play an important part. Dogs which are exposed to aggression at an early age are more likely to become aggressive. Bitches are often considered to be more loving and affectionate towards their humans. I am not convinced that this is entirely true, as I have had many dogs which have been wonderfully affectionate towards me. Even so, I do accept that it is the bitches that tend to want to be loved and cuddled more than the dogs. If you want to cuddle your Dobermann a lot, then again you would be better with a bitch. I have experienced a number of male Dobermanns that do not like being over-cuddled or having their heads smothered. They seem to become embarrassed and can react by growling. If you do have a young male and he reacts in this way, simply accept that he does not appreciate it, and respect his dignity. As he gets older, he is likely to object less, particularly if he is in a loving and stable home environment.

Both sexes will protect, guard and defend their property and their humans, but in this respect, the dog probably has the edge over the bitch due to his extra size and greater territorial instincts. Both sexes can also be equally self-willed and obstinate. As a breed, Dobermanns usually know what they want to do or where they want to go. They have a wonderful way of trying to convince you that their ideas are the ones that should be implemented, whatever you may think. This apparent obstinacy is, to some extent, a consequence of the breed's high level of intelligence. Dobermanns learn very quickly to associate your individual actions with your intentions. It is not uncommon for Dobermanns to watch you put the kettle on and then to poke the cup to tell you that they also want a cup of tea. Yes, all Dobermanns seem to love tea. They will then tell you that they would also like a biscuit, by poking the biscuit tin and shouting at you. Yes, they love biscuits too.

Dobermanns are brilliant at Obedience, learning what is required to be done very quickly. However, they very quickly become bored with the repetition and will simply switch off. For example, a Dobermann that can do a perfect retrieve will often play around, refusing to retrieve the article. This is often interpreted as the Dobermann being self-willed and obstinate, but to the Dobermann it is pure repetition of a boring exercise which has no worthwhile end-result. To me, this indicates a high level of intelligence rather than any lack of it.

Bitches come into season at about nine months of age and at six month intervals thereafter. These seasons usually have a duration of about twenty-one days, which is the period of time during which there will be a visible discharge of blood, which may lead to drops of blood being left on bedding and on floors, which can be a nuisance. The degree to which this is a problem can vary considerably from bitch to bitch, both in terms of the amount of the discharge and the extent to which they will keep themselves clean. Bitches in season need to be kept safely away from any male dogs, particularly from about the seventh day onwards. This means that you will not be able to take your bitch for walks where there is a risk of male dogs getting to her. It must always be remembered that a bitch in season is just as anxious to be mated by a dog as a dog is to mate the bitch. This problem can normally be overcome without too much difficulty by adjusting the daily routine. Spaying the bitch will prevent her coming into season.

There are a number of drugs available to suppress a season once it has started, or to prevent the bitch from coming into season. I know of many bitches which have had unfortunate side-effects from these drugs, so I am not a supporter of their use. These side-effects, which manifest themselves once the drugs are discontinued, include disturbance to the normal cycle of seasons,

The male is bigger and has stronger territorial instincts than the female. Ch. Othertons Statesman (Ch. Merrist Reluctant Knight – Airborne of Otherton). Bred and owned by Mr and Mrs P. Rock. Winner of 4 CCs and 3 Reserve CCs, Junior Warrant – believed to be the youngest Brown and Tan Champion, made up at 21 months.

Photo: Foyle.

resulting in erratic seasons, extended duration of the seasons, and difficulty in producing litters from treated bitches. However, like so many aspects of the world of veterinary medicine, drugs and treatments are constantly being improved, and it may well be that the time will come when these side-effects no longer occur. However, as a general rule, it is always wise to avoid hormone treatments unless they are really necessary, as they do tend to affect the natural hormone balance in the dog. False pregnancies, if they are going to happen, usually follow some two months after the season and can cause emotional problems as well as some physical changes. These are usually temporary phenomena which do not cause undue difficulty. While considering the question of the bitch's seasons, it should not be forgotten that the male Dobermann is always in season. This fact is rarely a problem, but a dog that becomes aware of a bitch in season in the vicinity of his home may well stop eating, lose weight, bark or howl and generally lose interest in other things. This is more likely to happen to a dog which has previously mated a bitch, *so is a good reason for not using a pet dog as a stud dog*. It is also likely to be more of a problem if you have both a dog and a bitch in your home, as you will need to keep them apart during the bitch's seasons.

Breeders have a role to play in helping would-be purchasers to decide whether to have a dog or a bitch. For instance, they should ensure that anyone asking for a male puppy does not already have another male dog, of any breed, in the house. Breeders should also try to assess whether they would be better with a dog or a bitch. Sometimes they need to go further and assess whether the would-be purchaser is a suitable person to have a Dobermann of either sex. This can be a difficult and embarrassing exercise, since doubts may only appear in the breeder's mind after meeting the prospective purchaser. However, it never seems so difficult when it is remembered that it is the well-being of the puppy that is at stake. This assessment may be based on the sort of criteria already discussed or on the apparent health of the person. I well remember being somewhat shocked, when meeting a lady wanting a male puppy, to find that she was elderly, troubled with arthritis and could only walk with the aid of a stick. The only way that I could persuade her that she would probably not be able to handle a lively young male Dobermann was to put an adult male Dobermann on a collar and lead and invite her to take him for a short walk around the garden.

If you choose a bitch, you must cope with the seasonal cycle. Ch. Pompie Aint Miss Behaving (Ch. Dimrost Freedom Fighter – Gaby Okdorp of Pompie (Dutch import)). Bred and owned by Hilary Partridge. Winner of 3 CCs, 1 Reserve CC, Junior Warrant, Best Puppy in Show Dobermann Club Ch. Show 1991.

Photo: Gascoine.

Needless to say, she was startled by his power and strength and readily conceded that she would never be able to handle any Dobermann, and we parted on amicable terms. As I suggested at the outset, the decision whether to buy a dog or a bitch is really a matter of personal preference. I was once told by a very experienced Dobermann breeder that men always prefer to own bitches and women always prefer to own dogs. I have subsequently spent many years wondering whether this is actually true, and if so, whether it should be considered to be surprising.

WHAT TO LOOK FOR IN A PUPPY

The first thing to check is the physical condition of the puppy, which should give the appearance of being full of health and vigour. The eyes should be bright and shining and the skin should be clean, with no rash or spots. Do not be too concerned about scratches or tooth marks, particularly on the head and neck, as these will probably be no more than rough play between the puppies. The damage is only superficial and can generally be cleared up within a few days by rubbing some healing ointment or hand-cream onto the affected areas. It is not unusual for the puppies to have the occasional toothmark on their head, courtesy of the mother. This will appear as a dry, white scab or scar and, again, will soon disappear. The mother needs to teach her puppies the basic rules of life and the puppies sometimes have to learn the hard way. One does sometimes come across a litter where the puppies go beyond the stage of playing and can really fight amongst themselves, even as young as eight weeks. Such puppies may be severely lacerated around the head and neck and on the legs. Again, with treatment, these injuries soon disappear. Interestingly enough, such puppies do not always grow up to be abnormally aggressive dogs.

It is also worth checking that the puppy is not deaf. This may sound silly, but a puppy may not be identified as being deaf when with littermates, as the pup will react to everything that they do. A deaf puppy should definitely be rejected, as deafness can lead to real problems with an adult Dobermann. Fortunately, deafness in Dobermanns appears to be uncommon, which is probably why it is not something that is checked as a matter of routine, as is the case in certain other breeds.

Check the dentition of the puppy, who should have a mouthful of sharp needle-like teeth (unbelievably, there are only twenty-eight of them). Make sure that the puppy has a correct bite, with the inner surface of the upper incisors (the front teeth) tightly overlapping the outer surface of the corresponding lower incisors when the mouth closes. Although a correct puppy bite does not always guarantee that the adult bite will be correct, a puppy with a faulty bite is most unlikely to be correct as an adult. A Dobermann having a bad bite is not prevented from being a perfectly adequate pet, but should never be considered for exhibiting or breeding. The only problem that such a dog is likely to have is the early wearing of the teeth, though this rarely seems to worry them. The puppy should look well fed – well-covered to the point of almost appearing too fat. We are all influenced to some extent by the surroundings in which the puppies have been reared and tend to consider, even if only subconsciously, that puppies living in a dirty or untidy environment must be inferior. This may not necessarily be the case and care should be taken before making too hasty a judgement. Provided that the puppies are sound and you like them, there is no reason why they should not grow into entirely satisfactory Dobermanns. Even puppies which have been poorly reared can soon catch up with proper care and attention. If the puppies themselves appear to be sick, nervous or otherwise adversely affected by their poor environment, then caution should be exercised. There is no reason why you should take on the liability of a sick or defective puppy. Leave the breeder to sort out his own problems.

Which puppy to choose is always a problem. This has to be left to the purchaser, though the breeder can give advice and guidance. Assuming that any show potential is not the overriding consideration, it may be the puppy that comes to you, the one that wants to pull out your shoe-laces, the one that sits a few inches away from you and waves a paw at you, or it may be the one that wants to go off and scrag the other puppies. Any puppy that does not run away and hide, and is willing to be picked up and held, is probably a reasonably safe bet. If a puppy shows real signs of being nervous, it may well be better to reject that one in favour of one which is bolder. Assessing puppy temperament is always difficult. A puppy may only be acting shy because of being dominated by other puppies and, once taken away from them, will be able to develop its own personality and probably quickly cease to be shy. The puppies in any litter will tend to establish a hierarchy of dominance and submissiveness, as this is instinctive behaviour. It is all relative, however, as a submissive puppy in one litter may well be more dominant than a dominant puppy in another litter.

A nervous puppy is always likely to be nervous. Such puppies frequently turn out to be loving and loyal to their owners but rarely socialise with other people and may also be too shy and lacking in sufficient self-confidence to train properly. Such a puppy may fit happily into your home if you simply want to lead a quiet life with your dog, but would be likely to be a misfit if you lead an extrovert lifestyle. Conversely, a particularly dominant puppy may well turn out to be a strong-willed, personality-plus Dobermann. Such a dog is a joy to own, but can also be a challenge. The safest bet would be one of the puppies with an average amount of dominance, who will be an easier Dobermann to train and will not be sufficiently dominant to want to challenge you for the position of pack leader. Predicting the eventual temperament of individual puppies is never easy and there is no guarantee that a friendly puppy will turn out to be a friendly adult. This depends principally on inherited genes and the rearing environment – an important factor in determining the temperament of a puppy. Puppies must be adequately handled and loved before they reach six weeks of age, in order to make them loving and friendly towards humans. Puppies which have had little or no human contact by six weeks old frequently have difficulty in bonding at a later date. You have no way of checking a puppy's genotype to ascertain future potential temperament. However, you can get a reasonable idea of what it will be by looking at the mother and other close relatives. It is always a good idea to ask to see the mother, not only as a check on potential temperament but also on the general type and appearance. Whilst the mother should be in reasonably good condition by the time the puppies are eight weeks old, having a litter can really take it out of some bitches. The bitch ought to be willing to be handled in the presence of the owner. If she is unduly nervous, aggressive or unwilling to be handled, then you would be entitled to be concerned for the eventual temperament of the puppies. Nervousness is one of those natural instincts in dogs which tends to surface from time to time, and the chances of a puppy being nervous are much greater if the parents are nervous. If possible, look at the sire or at any other close relatives of either the sire or the dam, as these will also give you some idea of the temperament that the puppies will inherit. Alternatively, you can look at the pedigree, but this is likely to be of little help unless you know something about the dogs on the pedigree. Someone looking for a pet Dobermann is probably not going to learn anything from the pedigree.

When you do go to visit the puppies, do not take hordes of screaming, excitable children with you, as this is guaranteed to upset the puppies. It may well also upset any adult dogs that are on the premises. You should be very quiet and unobtrusive, so as not to unsettle the puppies and to enable yourself to see them as they really are.

Before you pick up any of the puppies, do make sure that the owner is agreeable. You should also ensure that you know how to do it correctly. One hand should support the hindquarters, whilst the other hand should be placed under the forechest and brisket, between the front legs. Never pick up a puppy by the middle; this could cause serious internal damage.

Do not be surprised if the breeder is not willing to allow you to handle all the puppies. Breeders are always fearful of their puppies becoming ill because of cross infection. They do not know where else you have been and what other puppies or dogs you may have handled. If a breeder does take this approach, do not automatically assume that there is something to hide. If you genuinely want to purchase a puppy, you should certainly be allowed to handle those from which you can make your selection, even if you cannot handle the whole litter.

THE SHOW PUPPY

If you are contemplating a show career or hope to work your dog, then you will need to look for a puppy which seems likely to offer you the best prospects. You will want to ensure that your puppy has reasonably sound conformation, no obvious faults and a reasonably steady and outgoing temperament. Whilst this may seem easy, it most certainly is not. There are breeders with a lifetime of experience who still pick the wrong puppy. Even so, your best chance of obtaining a potential show dog is probably to approach someone who is recognised as a breeder of good show stock and whose dogs actually win in the show ring. This will not guarantee you success, but it will increase your chances. You may have to pay a slightly higher price for your puppy. You can obtain advice about likely breeders of show-quality puppies from the Kennel Club, from Dobermann breed clubs or even from other breeders.

Alternatively, you can always ask someone who has experience of assessing the show potential of puppies to help you. This may be particularly appropriate where the litter in which you are interested has not been bred by an established breeder. You will probably find that most breeders are somewhat reluctant to pass judgement on the puppies produced by a fellow breeder. If the litter has been bred by a breeder or a show exhibitor, then it is more than likely that they will already have assessed the show potential of the puppies and will be willing to advise you. Most breeders are only too pleased to ensure that the puppies with real show potential go to homes where they are likely to be shown, as any success that you achieve will also reflect credit on them.

The term 'show-dog' is often used in such a way as to suggest that there is a wide gulf between the show dog and the pet dog. This is a totally artificial distinction. A show dog is only a dog which is, or has been, shown. Most show dogs are really family pets which merely happen to be shown because their owners enjoy it. Many of the best quality dogs never get shown – and many of those that are shown would be better left purely as pet dogs.

ASSESSING CONFORMATION

You will need to stack the puppies up individually on a table, or on some other flat surface, in order to study their conformation. You should also watch them running around so that you can check on their temperament and personality. A self-confident, out-going puppy is always more likely to be an easier dog to show. Picking the 'best' puppy in a litter is never easy; how often one hears the owner of a champion say that it was not the pick of the litter, but the one that nobody wanted! It must always be remembered that the 'best' puppy in the litter may still not be good enough to be a successful show dog. If you only plan to compete at the lower levels of dog showing, then your selection may not be as critical. Even so, this should not be an excuse to lower your standards, as exhibitors who begin by winning at the smaller shows frequently wish to go on to greater things. The dividing line between a successful show dog and an also-ran can be a very fine one. At between about eight weeks and twelve weeks old a puppy is a miniature of what the adult dog will look like. After that a puppy will change in all sorts of strange ways and become much more difficult to assess. Usually, but sadly not always, the balance and soundness of that beautiful little puppy returns, to some extent, when the puppy reaches about six to eight months old, but you have to wait until the dog is fully mature – often not until two years old – before you can see the finished article. Having selected a puppy at eight weeks, you have to have faith in your judgement and hope that your faith is justified. Start by stacking the puppies up on a table-top or on some other flat surface. Ensure that the table is firm and that a non-slip material such as a blanket is placed on it. A rocky table, or a slippery surface, will quickly make the puppies lose what little self-confidence they started with. This stacking-up routine is valuable as it enables you to assess the individual puppies. It also enables you to distinguish one puppy from another, which may not be easy if you have a large and very even litter. It is also essential training for the show ring, as puppies submit very quickly to being stacked-up. The objective is to assess the puppies against the Breed Standard and against each other. While they may protest initially, their resistance is likely to be short-lived. You may need to be fairly firm with them but you should not frighten them. If this stacking up is done for a few minutes each day, they will accept it without question after a few days. Inevitably, you will always get one puppy who flatly refuses to cooperate, but even this one will cooperate with experience. Having got your puppy stacked up, you can begin to make your assessment. The better you know and understand the basic requirements of the Breed Standard, the more meaningful will be your assessment. The first impression that the puppy creates is always important, just as it is when one looks at an adult dog for the first time. The general outline, balance and flow should be pleasing to the eye. The puppy should have good strong bone, straight front legs and tight feet. There is no need to worry about the knobbly knees, as these will gradually go as the puppy grows. The chest should be down to the elbows with the elbows held close to the chest. If you place one hand on the withers and rock the puppy gently from side to side, the elbows will tend to spring outwards if they are too loose. If possible, avoid shallow chests and loose elbows. It is often said that a shallow chest will drop as the puppy grows. I think that this is a fallacy and that it is more of a hope than a realistic expectation. If it is shallow at eight weeks it will always be shallow. If the feet turn out, it may be that there is inadequate width to the chest, or it may be due to a shallow chest. This fault is often associated with loose elbows. If you are satisfied that the chest and elbows are reasonably good, then the turning-out feet may correct themselves as the dog grows, though not completely until two years old.

*A puppy with show
potential. This seven-
week-old Dobermann
became Ch. Jowendys
Tokjo Joe at Damarills.
Bred by Wendy Burge,
owned by Karen Brown.*

You should see a good layback of shoulder, giving an angle between the shoulder and the upper arm as near the ideal 90 degrees as possible. The top of the shoulder should not be too prominent, giving the appearance of a hump on the withers; there should be a clean, unbroken flow down the neck, across the withers and into the topline. The neck itself should be reasonably long, but since the neck tends to pull out as the dog grows, one should merely try to avoid a neck which is obviously too short. The topline should be level, with no humps or dips, and the tail should be high, in that the upper side of the tail should, so far as possible, be a continuation of the topline. Avoid puppies which have a croup which falls away from the topline at an angle and tails which are low-set, as these faults will always detract from the dog's elegance.

There should be a good sweep of stifle, with the thighs being of adequate thickness, and the hocks should be parallel. I once kept a promising bitch puppy though her hocks were slightly cowhocked. The bigger she grew, the more obvious her cowhocks became; they never did come right. The puppy should appear to be more or less square, in that length should be about equal to height. This proportion will change during the puppy's development, but if it is right at eight weeks, it will probably be right when the dog is fully grown. Heads present more of a problem, as they tend to pull out as they grow. Even so, particularly coarse heads, or faulty head planes, can be spotted. As already indicated, avoid any puppy with a faulty bite; unfortunately, a correct puppy mouth does not guarantee a correct bite when the second teeth come through. Eye colour cannot be checked too emphatically, since it tends to be bluish in young puppies. Even so, if the eye looks an unusually light blue, it may signify that the eyes will be too light. Ears usually look too big, but the correct balance between ears and head will come about in due course. Check to see if dog puppies are entire. This may not be easy, but it should be possible to confirm by eight to twelve weeks. In my experience, if the testicles are not descended by twelve weeks, they never will be, though sometimes one or both may be 'floating', i.e. they have descended but have not dropped.

Having stacked up each puppy in turn, it is necessary to balance the faults and virtues of any one

Ch. Albadobe Shalimar (Ch. Holtzburg Mayhem – Cool N' Kinky at Holtzburg and Sigismund) pictured at six weeks. Bred by Alan and Barbara Waterhouse, owned by Sharon Bardsley-Hodgkiess.

Photo: A. Waterhouse.

Ch. Albadobe Shalimar pictured as an adult. Winner of 20 CCs, 7 Reserve CCs, 14 Ch. Best of Breeds, 2 Group wins, Top Puppy 1991, Top Bitch 1992, Top Dobermann 1993.

Photo: A. Waterhouse.

puppy against those of the other puppies, in order to come to a first choice. The puppies may be readily identifiable, or it may be necessary to mark them in some way, either as ones to be sold, or ones to be kept, as the case may be. I have always found an aerosol spray an invaluable aid, as one quick squirt puts a nice purple spot on the puppy's tummy. It is quite harmless, but will wear off after about two days. Coloured 'neck-collars' can be used, but care must be taken that the puppies do not become caught up by the collars or that the collars do not get chewed off their necks.

If you want to work your dog, either in Obedience or Working Trials, then it would pay you to seek advice from those who have already gone down that path. There is considerable merit in

Ch. Halsband's The Joker (Bronco von der Konigundenhohe, German import – Halsband's The Sonnet). Bred and owned by Roger James and June Lewis. Roger is an expert falconer, and his dogs are used to guard his birds.

seeking a puppy bred from working stock, since there is a strong probability that the willingness or ability to work will be greater from successful working dogs than from a puppy acquired from a random litter. This may simply be that they will inherit the right temperament and aptitude for working, rather than that they have superior intelligence, but nevertheless, you are more likely to obtain a suitable puppy for working purposes. It is always worth casting the net fairly wide if you want a puppy for working, as breeders sometimes have puppies which they sense will make good working dogs, due to their outgoing nature, their quickness to learn and their willingness to please. Even at eight weeks of age, these characteristics can sometimes be evident. I am not aware of any difference in working ability between dogs and bitches, but for serious Working Trials, dogs may be better owing to their greater size and strength. The bitches can certainly work, however, as evidenced by the fact that the two most recent Working Trial Champion Dobermanns in the UK are both bitches.

DOCUMENTS
You will be expected to pay for the puppy when you collect it, unless you have made other arrangements. In return, you should receive a full set of documents from the breeder including a signed pedigree, a Kennel Club registration certificate with the transfer of ownership form signed by the breeder, a diet sheet, a temporary insurance cover and a receipt for your money.

This receipt is important as it represents the legal transfer of ownership. It may also be useful if you are able to claim tax relief on your guard dog; there are many Dobermann owners who can claim this, but do not realize it. Do not be too concerned if the registration papers are not available when you collect your puppy. They can be posted on to you by the breeder once they have been issued by the Kennel Club. If you have any reason to doubt that you will get them, ensure that 'Registration papers will be supplied when available', or similar wording, is written on the receipt as a condition of sale. This could make it easier if you have any problems later. The diet sheet should give you basic information on how the puppy is being fed, what food is being used, how it is being prepared and what quantity is being given. It may also contain a wider range of information, such as whether the puppy has been wormed. You should also receive a vaccination certificate, if any vaccination has been given, with details of the vaccine, the date it was given and the signature of the person giving it.

Chapter Three

OWNING A DOBERMANN

So, you have made the decision and you have bought your Dobermann puppy. You realise, of course, that life will never be quite the same again. If you are replacing a lost Dobermann, or acquiring an additional one, then you will have some idea of what to expect, though one can so quickly forget the trials and tribulations of having a puppy. But if this is your first time, then it will be a combination of culture shock and joyful experience.

Arrange to collect the puppy at a mutually convenient time for you and the breeder – preferably early in the day so the puppy will have time to settle into your home before being expected to go to sleep for the night. Make sure that you will be at home for the following few days and do not let the puppy's arrival coincide with any special events, such as Christmas or birthday parties, which will only create additional excitement. The puppy needs to come to a quiet, stable environment, with just members of the family.

Everything will be unfamiliar to the puppy, who will be missing both mother and litter-mates. The move to a new home is probably the most stressful part of a puppy's whole life. This stress may be shown by the puppy hiding away, or crying when handled, appearing shy or suffering internal disorders which result in diarrhoea. Your first objective must be to reassure the puppy. Encourage the puppy to wander round, to come to you for petting, and to relax. Do not over-crowd the little thing with too much handling. Ensure that the puppy is not frightened through being picked up awkwardly, or too often, by any children in the family. Make all introductions carefully. Puppies and children, if trained together in the right way, sense that they are kindred spirits and a strong bond soon develops between them.

A puppy who has been bred and reared in a house may already have learned to accept the normal sounds of a household. This will not apply to a puppy born in a kennel, who will experience a whole range of noises that are new, strange and confusing. Remember that a dog's hearing is sixteen times more sensitive than that of humans, so ensure that televisions and stereos are not too loud, and that children are not making too much noise. If the puppy seems concerned by any particular sound, such as that made by a washing-machine, give lots of reassurance.

TRAVELLING IN CARS
Cars and puppies do not generally get along with each other. You should therefore anticipate this problem when you set out to collect your puppy. Take a proper travelling crate, in which to place the puppy for the journey home. Or let the puppy sit on the lap of a passenger. If you, as the driver, are the only person in the car, then you must use a travelling crate. *Do not* just put the puppy on the back seat.

You should anticipate that the puppy will either be sick, or at the very least, drool, during the

Remesca Dream Lady and Remesca's Dream of Darkness (Ch. Jowendy's Kilowatt – Ch. Remesca Firelight) pictured at five months of age. Bred and owned by Allison Moss. Puppies should be introduced to the car from an early stage, and then they will quickly consider it to be an extension of their own property.

journey, and will probably do both. Take an old blanket or towel for the puppy to sit on, a roll of kitchen paper for mopping up, and a pile of newspaper to spread around to receive the vomit.

Although puppies are almost always car-sick to begin with, they soon grow out of it, particularly if taken, with an empty stomach, as often as possible, on short journeys, preferably to somewhere nice, like exercise in the country, or training classes. The puppy will then associate the car with having an enjoyable time, and will begin to take an interest in everything that is going on.

Continue to take a supply of newspapers and kitchen roll with you until the need for these diminishes. How badly a puppy will be affected, or for how long, depends on the individual. I have know ones that have never been sick and, equally, ones who have never grown out of it and are always unhappy in cars. I will never forget going to a training class one evening: on arrival I found my two puppies had not only been sick and drooled over each other but, in their apprehension, had also had diarrhoea. They looked so wet, dirty and miserable that I went straight back home again and gave them a bath. However, both eventually became normal Dobermann travellers.

Only use travel-sickness pills as a last resort, for they treat the symptoms rather than the cause. Try giving the puppy a toy, for occupation during the journey. Sometimes it is a car with soft springing that is causing the problem.

It is a wise precaution to tether your Dobermann in the car, if you are not using a crate. This will prevent the dog from roaming around and from distracting you. It is not unheard of for dogs to suddenly leap onto the front seats if something exciting happens outside the car. There is also the risk of injury to an untethered dog in the event of an accident. It is possible to get dog harnesses for cars, rather as seat belts can be fitted for children. However never use a choke chain, or too long a lead, which can either permit the dog to climb out of an open window, or to be strangled. I well remember one very distressed Dobermann owner phoning me to tell me that she had just lost her beautiful dog. It appeared that she was driving around Hyde Park Corner in London when her Dobermann, who was tethered in the rear part of her estate car, jumped over the back seat and strangled himself. By the time she could stop to attend to him, he had died.

Training your Dobermann to be a good passenger, and not to jump around or bark at everything, is as important as any other training. Once the dog enjoys travelling, the car will become as much of a possession as the house, and will be guarded accordingly. And no-one is likely to break into a car which has a Dobermann sitting in it. Be careful, as Dobermann puppies are sometimes stolen from parked cars. Teach your dog, from an early age, not to jump around the car and bark. One effective cure for bad behaviour in the car is the use of water; an old washing-up liquid bottle filled with water makes an excellent water pistol, and one well-aimed squirt can have a dramatic and subduing effect.

You should also train your dog not to jump out of the car the moment you open the door. Puppies, and even young dogs should be lifted out, as jumping out can lead to damaged shoulders or pasterns. And do remember, in hot weather, to have ventilation and drinks of water available while travelling and never to leave your dog in a stationary car – even with the windows open. The temperature inside can rise to very high levels and every year there are reports of dogs literally being cooked alive in the backs of cars. This is unforgivable carelessness and, believe it or not, even happens in the car parks of some major dog shows.

ACCOMMODATION INDOORS

You have to decide whether you want a house dog, or one living outside. In my view Dobermanns should always be house dogs, because they are very much oriented towards humans, and like physical contact with them. They spend half their life working out what the human is going to do next – and the other half trying to persuade the human to do what they want them to. Such a dog is not going to be happy in isolation, and you will never derive the full pleasure and joy that you should have from a Dobermann, if you leave the dog outside.

Also bear in mind that having a Dobermann inside is probably the ultimate deterrent for would-be intruders. I have known of houses being raided where the Dobermanns were kept outside in kennels. This would not have happened if the dogs had been in the house. But, apart from the security aspect, I am not in favour of a Dobermann being put outside during the day while everyone is working, or being with the humans during the day and put outside for the night while the family is sleeping. You must remember that your house will become your dog's house, you will become your dog's humans, so the Dobermann who is going to be a house pet, and a fully integrated member of the family, should live in the house with the family the whole time.

This means that you must supply a proper bed, in a suitable place. This should be a draught-free box, or basket, with sides which give a warm cosy sanctuary to which the puppy can retreat whenever the need arises, but still be in a position to watch the world go by. It should be close to where everyone is going to be, but out of the main pedestrian routes. The box should be slightly bigger than the puppy, but small enough to give a sense of enclosure and security, warm but out of the direct rays of the sun, and lined with a woolly blanket or a similar soft material. As the puppy grows, so the box can be replaced with a more permanent, adult bed, but one still offering the same amenities. Beware of wicker baskets, which look good but are likely to get chewed around the edges. Plastic beds are good, but can be cold unless lined properly. There are excellent bean-bags and quilts made for dogs, but these are susceptible to being chewed and to being scratched up by a Dobermann trying to make things even more comfortable before settling down to sleep. And I know of one Dobermann who owns a beanbag and carries it around the house to deposit it wherever he has decided to settle down.

You will also have to decide at a fairly early stage whether you are going to allow your Dobermann on to the furniture You cannot allow a puppy to use the furniture and then try to stop this habit once the dog has grown. My own view is that the Dobermann who is to be a truly integrated member of the family should be allowed to sit on the furniture like the rest of the family. You can compromise by putting covers on the chairs, or allocating one special chair for the dog – but usually the dog will want to be near you, or sitting on you, when you are sitting down!

Crates, or large wire cages, are sometimes used to provide beds for dogs inside the house. These are probably a good idea if you need to confine a puppy for a while, or to provide a convenient, temporary and highly mobile bed. But the use of such cages to confine an adult dog for long periods of time is frowned upon, certainly in the UK. If you really need to use one for any length of time, you should ask yourself why you have a Dobermann in the first place.

As you will have gathered, Dobermanns always want to find the most comfortable place in which to rest. It will, therefore, only be a matter of time before your bed is discovered and, because that is where you sleep at night, that will also be the place where your dog wants to sleep. This is normal pack instinct. Dogs always sleep as close to one another as possible. Since you and your Dobermann are now of the same pack, what could be more natural than for you to share the same bed? Whether or not you see things in quite the same way is for you to decide. But you have to make up your mind, from day one, what you want, and then stick to it. If you put your puppy in another room, you might be disturbed by crying for a few nights but, if you don't want a dog on your bed, you have to persevere. You will need to harden your heart, ignore the puppy's misery and state your intentions firmly. It sometimes helps, during these first few days, to place a ticking clock somewhere near the puppy's bed. This is an age-old remedy which really seems to work.

A compromise is to provide an old armchair in your bedroom. But Dobermans are extremely adept at finding a space on the communal bed without disturbing the human occupants. Many new owners vow that their Dobermann will never sleep on their bed, but a high percentage relent in due course. It has been estimated that sixty per cent of British dog owners sleep with their dogs for all or part of the night – so you can at least console yourself that you are part of the majority when all your good resolutions come to naught.

OUTDOOR ACCOMMODATION

If you propose to keep your Dobermanns in a kennel, then a wholly different set of conditions apply. The major requirement is that, whatever building materials are used, the kennel should be substantial, be wind and water-tight, and be warm. It can be fitted with a top-hung trap-door, to enable the dogs to enter and leave at will, without the need for the door to be left open all the time.

You must provide a bed for each dog. Even if they tend to share one bed, there must be the option of sleeping alone. The beds should be solidly constructed, ideally of wood, and should be as enclosed as possible. A Dobermann box should be about three foot six inches wide, two foot six inches deep and three foot six inches high. These dimensions allow the dog to stand up and turn round as well as to stretch out full length. For the front of the box I use a sliding board, about eight inches in height, which creates the feeling of enclosure and also holds the bedding in the box. If you are housing puppies in the kennel, it might be necessary to use a lower board at first, but once they reach about sixteen weeks of age, they will have become very agile and have no problem negotiating the board.

There are a number of options regarding bedding. Blankets can be used but they are liable to be torn up, or used as toys and dragged around the kennel. Bits of old carpet are also suitable, but difficult to keep clean if the dogs go into an outside run when it is wet underfoot. My own preference is for straw. This needs to be fresh, dry and clean. It is easy to obtain, relatively cheap, and easy to dispose of. It can be renewed as necessary. It makes a very warm and comfortable bed. Another alternative is shredded paper, but in my experience this tends to get everywhere, and ends up being blown around the dog run and the whole garden. Puppies, of course, are only too delighted to spread it!

The outdoor kennel will have to be heated. Dobermanns have a single coat and tend to feel the cold. In my experience the simplest and safest method is to use electric infra-red strip heaters,

This group of ten Dobermanns, with owner Barbara Scarlett (Bronsilk), shows the importance of breeding for good temperament as well as good conformation.

linked to a thermostat, so the heating comes on automatically when required. The temperature setting should be in the region of five to eight degrees Centigrade, but can be varied to meet individual circumstances. To avoid the heater being a fire risk, it should be mounted on the kennel wall well above the dogs' reach, and backed with some form of insulating material. Great care should be taken if paraffin or calor gas heaters are used, for these absorb the oxygen in the air and give off poisonous fumes, not to mention the risk of them being knocked over.

If the dogs have permanent access to an outside run, they will probably keep their kennel floor clean, but if they are locked in for the night they are likely to foul it, so you will need some form of floor covering. You could just clear and wash the kennel floor each day but this is time-consuming and creates an unhealthy, damp environment. The best method is to put sawdust on the floor, which can be changed whenever necessary.

The kennels should be cleaned out thoroughly at regular intervals. The ideal method is to remove all beds and bedding and use a pressure pump. The washing water should contain detergent, washing soda and some disinfectant. This thorough cleaning should, preferably, be done in periods of warm weather, when everything dries quickly

RELATIONSHIPS

You have taken on a major commitment. It is up to you to make your Dobermann puppy a fully integrated member of your family and you must provide as much human companionship as possible, thus allowing the puppy to develop mentally and physically and to learn acceptable behaviour, both at home and outside. Do not let your chosen breed down. It only takes one bad dog to give the breed a bad name.

A puppy is very responsive to training when aged between seven and twelve weeks of age, and experiences during this period are likely to influence the dog's attitude for life. The puppy will start off being somewhat indifferent to you, while being dependent on you and your companionship. You should spend as much time with, and show as much love to, the puppy as you can, to foster the puppy's love for you and forge the bond of affection and loyalty between the two of you. Be gentle and let the puppy come to you. After about three days the puppy will have gained self-confidence.

From the outset you must talk to your dog, as this is the basis of communication between you.

Am. Ch. Julmar's Jeronimo: The Dobermann must be trained to become a fully integrated member of the family, accepting, without question, a subservient role.

Photo: Rush.

Your tone will be important, as this can convey approval and love, and disapproval, when warranted. You should always be firm, friendly and fair. Encourage your dog to come to you, using your open hands, which should always signify love and friendship. By four months the puppy will have learned the meaning of a number of words and will have sized up the household, knowing which members can be relied on for a cuddle, for a game, for dinner and for protection.

DOMINANT BEHAVIOUR

There are many ways in which your puppy is going to get into mischief. But you must remember that this is not deliberate, merely the result of having to investigate everything – which includes chewing it or carrying it about. This is, in a sense, the puppy learning how to learn. Be careful that you do not correct any behaviour too forcefully as the puppy is too young to associate punishment with any crime, and will only become confused and lose the faith and trust in you which you are trying to build up.

Introduce your puppy to people outside the immediate household, and to other animals, as early as you can, so that the puppy learns to accept that they are part of everyday life. A Dobermann who is introduced to cats at an early age is always likely to accept them, forming a close relationship with the household cat but able to distinguish between that one and any outsiders.

Remember that dogs are pack animals and, after about twelve weeks, the puppy will begin to try to establish dominance over you. A puppy who is given the free run of the house and never controlled or disciplined may well decide to adopt the mantle of pack leader. Once this happens, the dog is going to be difficult to handle and train. It is therefore very important for you to establish that you are the dominant member of the pack and that the puppy must be submissive to you from an early age.

If your Dobermann tries to exert dominance over you, it is necessary to check this immediately. In the pack environment, the dominant dog would grab the puppy round the neck in a threatening way, thus bringing about quick submission. Using the same principle is often very effective – shake the puppy by the scruff of the neck and say No. This will exert a strong psychological dominance and make the puppy submissive. If the puppy shows any unwillingness about allowing visitors into the house you should say No with a firm tone of voice. Dobermanns are sometimes awkward about accepting visitors because they are perceived as a threat to the bond between the dog and the owner. Early exposure to visitors helps the dog to understand that this is not the case. In some instances, anti-social tendencies may be due to the dog's breeding rather than the home environment.

SOCIAL BEHAVIOUR

Puppies have bursts of activity, then go off to bed and have a sleep. You should encourage this and make sure the puppy is not on the go the whole time. Do not let children play with a puppy who should be resting. Try and establish a routine for everything you do. Dogs are much happier when they are working to a known schedule.

Apart from encouraging your Dobermann to accept people who come into the house, you should also encourage the dog's acceptance of meeting people and of being handled by them away from the home environment. This socialisation is very important, particularly if you lead a sociable life or if you want to show your dog.

One habit which must be curbed is that of jumping up, which is at best annoying and can be hazardous for children or elderly or infirm people. This is a habit which is best checked early, and is relatively easy to cure.

You need to get your puppy used to traffic, but do this gently. If there is any sign of fright, stop, and give reassurance. Go into a shopping area, even though today's hygiene regulations mean that you will not be allowed into many of the shops. Take the puppy around the park and watch the children playing. In fact, go wherever your puppy will benefit from absorbing the atmosphere of daily life. Obviously keep the puppy on the lead, particularly if you are near any farm animals, as it is not unknown for some farmers to shoot dogs on sight which are running loose in the vicinity of livestock.

GUARD DUTIES

You will want your puppy to learn to guard the house. To a considerable extent, this is an instinct which exists naturally in every Dobermann. All you need to do is encourage your puppy to bark when anyone comes to the door, or when anyone is prowling around the outside of the house. You can help by saying "Who's there?" in an apprehensive tone of voice and encouraging the puppy to look out of the window to check whether anyone is outside.

It will not be long before the puppy realises that keeping uninvited guests out of the house is a duty. This needs to be carefully balanced with encouraging the puppy to welcome and accept people once you have invited them in. It is surprising how quickly the puppy's guarding instincts will develop and the dog does not have to be aggressive – in fact it is better not to be so: you want a deterrent, not a weapon. A Dobermann that really would attack someone would be more of a liability than an asset.

Your Dobermann should learn to bark when people come to the house, as this alerts you and also warns off a would-be intruder. But you must be careful that this is not overdone. It is very easy for a dog to develop a habit of barking at everything and so become extremely unpopular with your neighbours. The dog must be taught to stop barking on your command.

If you have a road or pavement outside your property, you must discourage the dog from running up and down along a fence barking at people. This is an annoying habit which will quickly lead to complaints. You should separate your front and back garden, so that the dog does not have unrestricted access to the gate. You owe the right of free passage from your gate to your front door to all legitimate callers. You should have a side gate, giving access to the back, on which a notice should be fixed saying "Caution, dogs loose" or something similar. Avoid the words "beware of the dog", as this has been construed in a court case as an admission that the owners knew they had a dangerous dog.

LEARNING TO BE ALONE
You should teach your Dobermann to accept being left alone. This is very important as you do not want a dog who howls and barks all the time you are out. This is bad for the dog, who will become neurotic and will think that barking is acceptable behaviour, and bad for the neighbours, who would be justified in complaining. A dog which is left alone is also likely to get bored and become destructive.

Training should begin at an early age, ideally before twelve weeks old. Put the puppy into bed, with some toys or a chew, and give the firm command to 'Stay'. At first leave the puppy alone for about ten to fifteen minutes, after which you return and give the puppy lots of praise. If the puppy barks before you are ready to end the exercise, return and firmly repeat the command 'Stay'. Then leave the puppy again for about five minutes or so. Once the rules of the exercise have been learned, you can leave the puppy for longer periods of time. This is an extension of the 'learning to sleep alone' routine that you will have gone through when the puppy first arrived. The main thing is that the puppy needs to learn that every time you go away, you will return. A puppy who realises that will usually settle down.

It is generally accepted that you should not leave any dog alone for long periods of time. While this is certainly true of a puppy which needs constant care and attention, it need not be true for an adult dog. I have known of instances where circumstances have changed, and all the family have to go out to work all day. The Dobermanns have invariably accepted this new routine without any problem – and make up for lost time once the family return. This is not an ideal arrangement, but it is usually better for both the dog and the family than having to give the dog away. However, every case should be considered on its merits.

When you do return home after leaving your Dobermann for any length of time, you will get the traditional welcome, with the tail wagging so hard that it is moving most of the body as well, and the Dobermann smile, which ranges from a slight raising of the upper lips to show the tips of the canine teeth, through to a full toothy grin. Some Dobermanns smile extensively, particularly if you encourage this by laughing back at them. Most Dobermanns will bring you a present – a cushion or a piece of paper – which you are expected to accept with profuse thanks, after they have spent some time rushing round to show it off to you. Some will also take your hand or arm in their mouths. You may need to teach the meaning of the word 'gently' if the dog gets too carried away, but the objective is to hold you, and shower you with affection, not to bite you.

TEETHING
Puppy teeth are as sharp as the proverbial needles, but these are shed between four to six months of age, to be replaced by the second teeth. This process will cause the dog a certain amount of

discomfort, and there will be a tendency to chew everything in sight. To save your furniture you should provide chewy toys which will give comfort but cause no harm. Avoid anything which is small enough to be swallowed or which can be chewed into small pieces.

You will need to be very tidy and put items such as clothing and slippers out of reach. You will have to accept that a Dobermann puppy is more than likely to cause some damage to your home, but this can be minimised by vigilance and proper management. This destructiveness usually diminishes as the dog matures.

TOYS

Even as an adult, your Dobermann will still require toys. Again, these should be too big to be swallowed, and sufficiently robust to withstand the dog's powerful jaws. Some Dobermanns are more destructive than others and a rubber ring which will last one dog for years will be shredded by another in a few hours. Try to discourage your dog from being destructive, but you will learn by trial and error which are the most suitable toys. I have found heavy-duty rubber toys, nylon bones and knotted ropes are the most acceptable. Squeaky toys, soft rubber toys, and anything made of cloth, are generally best avoided, as they are likely to have a short life.

It is often the simple things that provide the most pleasure. Paper always seem to attract Dobermanns, as it can be torn up easily and the pieces carried around for hours. Logs, sticks and fallen branches are irresistible, but care should be taken if two dogs are playing together with these, as a stick could poke one of them in the eye.

Most Dobermanns like fruit, so apples can be used as toys, though I know of many totally trustworthy dogs who have developed a taste for them and cannot resist stealing apples from the table, or even off the tree, if the opportunity arises. Another favourite is coconuts.

Bones are frequently given to dogs to keep them occupied in the belief that they are good for them. In fact you should not give bones to your Dobermann. While they might keep a puppy occupied for a while, they are extremely dangerous for adults, whose very powerful jaws can chew pieces off them. These then get swallowed and become impacted in the intestines, or perforate them, and both conditions can be fatal. Baked knuckle bones are a safer alternative than fresh, raw bones. Always avoid chicken or rabbit bones.

Do not make the mistake of giving old clothes as playthings. Your puppy will be unable to distinguish between them and your new clothes and shoes. Be very careful of stones which seem to hold a fascination for puppies and which, again, can be swallowed. If your puppy suddenly becomes ill but does not seem to have an infection, stops eating, loses weight and appears not to be passing motions, arrange for an X-ray immediately – though not everything will show up on this. I once knew a Dobermann who swallowed a nylon pot-scraper, which was only discovered when the vet decided to do an exploratory operation. The moral is very simple; not only do you need to keep an eye on your puppy all the time, but you must learn to be tidy!

ROUGH PLAY

Dobermann puppies sometimes get over-excited and indulge in what can best be described as play nipping. They are using you as a substitute for their litter-mates and do not intend to hurt you. However, you must discourage this by walking away if the puppy starts to do it, and signifying that the game is over. Be careful not to correct too harshly: you will only upset the puppy, who will not associate punishment with the game. It is tempting to tap the puppy on the nose and say 'No', but this will only be interpreted as an extension of the play. So, walk away and give the puppy something else to play with. A variation of this is the puppy grabbing your coat or trouser-legs. This must also be discouraged, but these habits do tend to fade away once the puppy reaches about six months of age. Never get down on the floor and play rough-and-tumble games. While this may be great fun for you both, you will end up with a rough dog who will cause you many problems in later life. A full-grown male Dobermann who always wants to play rough with you, with children or with visitors, is a disaster. You must never encourage your puppy to attack or bite anyone, whether in fun or not. Once your Dobermann gets the idea that this is acceptable behaviour, you have a problem which you may not be able to control. Probably your main difficulty will be training your children not to play rough games with the puppy – although a few nips from the puppy teeth may prove to be an effective deterrent.

PUNISHMENT

The question of controlling, checking, correcting or punishing puppies needs to be considered. As already suggested, no form of punishment is appropriate for puppies, because they cannot associate the punishment with the crime, certainly not until about the age of six months. This means that the punishment is ineffective and will merely create mistrust and fear of you in the puppy's mind, which will negate the bond of love and trust that you are trying to establish.

Another aspect to consider is that a puppy is a very delicate and fragile creature, whose boisterous actions and sheer vitality sometimes lead one to forget this. A puppy is easily hurt physically, as well as mentally, if hit with any object, be it a shoe, a stick or even a dog-lead.

In my view, hitting a dog is an admission of failure on your part, and should never be done. The best way to correct a puppy, or even an adult Dobermann, is by means of the tone of voice. If you really have to correct your Dobermann firmly, then a smack with a rolled-up newspaper can be very effective. This creates a lot of noise, but no pain. You will hurt the dog's dignity, but not the dog's body. Even this action should rarely be necessary, but may be the simplest and quickest way of checking two young puppies who have lost their tempers with each other over something, such as the possession of a toy. Once the quarrel has been broken up, both puppies should be praised and given affection, to show them they are still loved and that there is no weakening of the bond between you and them.

TEMPERAMENT

Your puppy, having settled in and gained some self-confidence, will be relatively extrovert towards everything and everyone. This can be misleading, as it lulls you into a false sense of security, believing that your Dobermann has the ideal temperament. Even though the environment and training you provide will have some effect on temperament, the puppy's true nature will not begin to show until somewhere between eight and twelve months of age.

A Dobermann reaching this age often goes through what can best be described as a teenage hooligan stage. This is more noticeable in males than females, tending to make them rougher, more boisterous, self-assertive and generally full of their own self-importance. This is the time, as I have mentioned earlier, when you will need to reinforce the fact that you are the pack leader and are not going to be displaced. You will also need to anticipate how your Dobermann is likely to react to any given situation and to take the necessary action. It could mean that you will need to be more circumspect about places where there are likely to be other dogs. Bear in mind that male Dobermanns are always likely to fight with males of any breed, particularly if the other dog shows aggressive tendencies, even if this is just shown in body language. You will need to ensure that your Dobermann only runs free when you are quite sure that it is safe and when you know that your obedience training has reached the stage where you can really control your dog.

Dobermanns can also begin to show nervous tendencies as they reach this adolescent stage of their development and begin to shy away from things that previously they ignored. They will seem

Frankskirby Jubilee Blulad of Roanoke (Phileens American Express – Frankskirby Red Christel) pictured at five months of age. As your Dobermann matures, an increasing self-confidence will be evident.

Photo: David Prop.

to lose self-confidence for no apparent reason and may begin to back away from people. This can be quite disturbing, particularly if you have begun to show your Dobermann. This may be your dog's true temperament showing, or it may just be a phase. Do not isolate the dog from people, as this will only tend to reinforce the problem; but do allow the dog to come to terms with life in the dog's own good time.

HOUSE TRAINING
This begins as soon as your puppy arrives home. At eight weeks there is only limited control of bladder and bowels and the puppy will be eating several meals a day, so will need to toilet frequently. It is a natural instinct of all dogs to keep their beds clean. Your puppy will soon exhibit this trait, which will make housetraining that much easier.

The first objective is to teach the puppy that the appropriate place for toileting is outside, not inside. Puppies reared in a kennel, having had regular access to an outside run, will probably already have learned to keep their kennel clean. Puppies reared in a house may not have learned to go outside, so may take a little longer to train.

The key is to anticipate when your puppy needs to go out. This means that you put the pup out immediately after wakening up, after eating a meal and whenever the puppy starts circling round looking for somewhere to squat. It is surprising how quickly the puppy will develop the necessary association of ideas, often within a week of training. This does not mean that you will never have the odd accident. These are inevitable, but you must not punish the puppy for them. Blame yourself, for not anticipating the puppy's needs quickly enough. Keep a mop handy, for cleaning-up purposes. Newspaper is useful as it acts like blotting paper and will absorb those little puddles.

For the first few days there is much merit in adopting a damage limitation policy. Keep your puppy confined to one or two rooms of your house, so that any accidents which occur will at least be confined to a smallish area. Limit the puppy's intake of fluids late at night. Allow a drink with, or soon after, the evening dinner, then take the water away until the morning. Go outside with your puppy to encourage the puppy to perform. Some people use a particular word and their dogs very quickly develop an association between the word and the action. This can be useful if you are away from home and your young bitch will not perform away from her own garden. Male puppies rarely have such inhibitions. Remember to praise the puppy afterwards.

House training is obviously easier in warm or dry weather, since the door can be left open and your puppy can go outside as and when necessary. In cold or wet weather it is always more difficult – even adult Dobermanns hate the rain. If your puppy does get wet, give a good rub with a dry towel to avoid any risk of a chill developing. Some people advocate the use of newspaper inside the house near the door to start toilet training. But I think that this is counter-productive in that you are teaching the puppy to mess inside the house, which is the opposite of what you are trying to achieve. It is far better to train puppies to go outside right from the start.

Being dirty in the house is a problem that does occur occasionally, even with Dobermanns. This may be because it is wet outside, or the dog has been left in the house alone for too long, or is slightly off-colour. Bitches in season or in whelp need to urinate more frequently and this is often a time when accidents do happen. But all these cases are infrequent and are not deliberate actions by the dog.

What is more difficult to overcome is where a Dobermann seems to be dirty in the house on a more regular basis. Then you have to try to ascertain the underlying reason. Dogs who are fed in the morning are sometimes dirty at night because it is only then that their meal has been fully digested. The cure is simple – feed the dog in the evening. Spayed bitches can be partially incontinent and allowance must be made for them. Sometimes cystitis can be the cause. But if all these reasons have been eliminated it may be that the Dobermann has just got into bad habits. Try putting the dog out last thing at night and a little bit sooner in the morning. But if all else fails, an old-fashioned but well-tried remedy is to chain the dog to the bed. The chain should be long enough to allow the dog to turn around in the bed but short enough to ensure that the dog cannot go far enough away from it and to foul the floor. This remedy works on the basis that no dog likes to foul its bed.

Occasionally dogs may eat their own or other dogs' faeces. This is normal behaviour for them but extremely distasteful for their owners. It is not really known why dogs will do this, and opinions differ as to whether it is harmful. But it should be strongly discouraged. Faeces should be removed regularly, the dog told of your displeasure and, in the final resort, a substance sprinkled on the food which will give the resulting waste matter a really unpleasant taste. This is worth trying if you have a persistent problem.

FEEDING

Whole books have been written about the art and science of feeding dogs. These can be summed up very simply – feed your Dobermann adequate quantities of a good-quality, well-balanced, nutritional and palatable food. However, a little knowledge of the science of feeding will help to give you a better understanding.

The nutritional requirements of a growing puppy can be as much as two or three times that of an adult dog of the same weight, which means that puppies need to be fed on more concentrated foods which give them a higher energy intake, and they require feeding three or four times a day. As the puppy gets older, so the energy requirements gradually decrease and requires a smaller volume of food. Puppies have this higher relative food requirement because they have a large surface area in relation to body weight, which means that they need extra food to compensate for the relatively great heat loss through the skin, and they are growing rapidly, so need the extra food to support this growth. It is important to remember that an incorrectly fed puppy may develop poor conformation, whatever the puppy's breeding and genetic inheritance may be, and that good feeding will not change bad inheritance. Also, greater care needs to be taken in feeding puppies of the bigger breeds, such as the Dobermann, than of smaller breeds. This is because the bigger dogs grow much more, and at a faster rate, during their relatively short growth period than the smaller breeds. This makes them more vulnerable to nutritionally induced abnormalities, because their developing bones are being asked to carry relatively more weight.

It is therefore very important not to overfeed Dobermann puppies, particularly by giving excessive amounts of vitamins, minerals and protein, since this merely exacerbates a problem for which the puppy already has an underlying inherited predisposition. Whether you are feeding a puppy or an adult Dobermann makes little difference. The general procedure is similar, with only the amounts and the frequency varying. The transition from puppy feeding to adult feeding is a very gradual one and there is no clearly defined point at which one switches from one to the other.

Your puppy, when brought home, will probably be eating three or four meals per day, depending on the preferred procedure used by the breeder. By the time a puppy reaches eight weeks old I think three meals per day is sufficient. There should be a main meal in the morning and in the evening, and a light, nutritional, milky meal in the middle of the day. A helpful breeder will supply you with a small quantity of the food that the puppy has been receiving, so that you can continue with this during the settling-in period. If you then want to change the food, this can be done gradually, by changing first one of the daily meals and, if there are no adverse reactions, then changing the others.

It is very difficult to suggest the correct quantity of food that you should be giving your puppy, because this depends very much on the individual. The best way to find out what is required is by trial and error. If the puppy does not eat everything, then you are probably giving too much. If the puppy asks for more, then you are not giving enough. Leave the dinner down for a reasonable length of time, possibly for up to two hours. Puppies love to eat a bit, then have a game, and then come back and eat some more.

I feed three meals a day until the puppy is about five months old, when the midday milk pudding meal can be dropped. I continue with two meals a day until the puppy is about ten months old, when the morning meal can be discontinued. This one meal a day regime can then be continued for the remainder of the dog's life. This is a guide, which must be varied where circumstances dictate. If, for example, your ten-month puppy looks light and lacks the amount of body you think proper, then continue with the morning meal for as long as necessary. I have had hyperactive young Dobermanns who have continued receiving a second meal for as long as a further year. Very often, it is the dog that tells you whether you should continue with a certain feeding regime or change it.

Remember to balance feeding with exercise. Just as it is important to give adequate amounts of food, so it is necessary to control the amount of exercise. A dog who is allowed to run unrestricted all day will never keep an adequate amount of body substance.

There are many different ways of feeding your Dobermann and it would be impossible to state that any one method was the correct one. As long as the dog is fit and healthy, then one must conclude that the diet is suitable. Be prepared to try different foods, particularly if they are well recommended, but if you are happy with what you are using and your Dobermann is thriving, why change just for the sake of changing?

The traditional method of feeding dogs is with meat and biscuit, which is the way everyone fed their dogs before the introduction of complete dog foods. It is still perfectly acceptable; but it is now more difficult to obtain suitable raw meat, it is very time-consuming, and it requires greater care to ensure that the dog is receiving a properly balanced diet. If you do want to use this method you will need to give your adult Dobermann about one pound of meat per day. This may be either cooked or raw, but most dogs prefer the meat to be slightly cooked, which also produces gravy which can be used to soak out the biscuit meal. *Meat on its own is not an adequate food and must always be used as part of the diet.* An ideal balance is about one third meat to two thirds biscuit. Meat is almost devoid of calcium and some of the important vitamins, such as Vitamin A. It is therefore necessary to supplement this diet unless you are satisfied that there is an adequate range of vitamins in the biscuit. I believe that any dog will thrive better on a good-quality, complete food. The manufacture of complete foods is now a multi-million pound industry and there is a wide variety of excellent brands available, containing the ideal balance between protein, carbohydrate and fats, plus all the necessary vitamins and minerals in the correct proportions and in a way in which the dog can absorb them.

Most complete foods can be fed either dry or soaked. My own preference is to soak the food before use, as I feel that it is easier for the dog to digest and ensures that the dog consumes adequate water. It also reduces the risk of the dog suffering from bloat or gastric torsion, which can be caused by eating dry food which then swells in the stomach when the dog has a drink. While I am sure that this is taken into account by manufacturers, and the Dobermann is probably not a high-risk breed for this, it is always a fear in my mind, whether justified or not.

If you are going to use a complete food, try one or two, see how your Dobermann reacts, and then stick to the one that seems most suitable. Alternatively, use one food, soaked satisfactorily, for the main evening meal and another one, dry, for the morning meal. When soaking dry foods add hot, but not boiling, water. The food should have a crumbly consistency, with all the water absorbed. Never give wet and sloppy food. There are 'mixers' available which are designed to be added to tinned dog meat. Complete foods are, by definition, complete, and it is both wrong and unnecessary to add meat to them. However, there is no harm in adding a small amount of meat, tinned meat or gravy, in order to make the food more appetising if your Dobermann is a bit finicky, or you are feeding a pregnant bitch. Many dogs enjoy eating fish. Make sure, if you are giving this, that it is cooked and all bones are removed. Eggs are good, but only in moderation, and always cooked as the white of the egg, the albumen, inhibits the absorption of biotin. Milk should be given sparingly, and is probably best avoided, although it is a natural food. Table scraps and tidbits are legitimate, in small quantities, but should never be regarded as a constituent part of the dog's diet. Dobermanns will eat virtually anything that comes off a human's plate. This is part of the pack animal's instinct and reinforces the bond between you. But do exercise common sense and avoid any rich food. Tea is a special favourite, and many Dobermann owners have to make cups of tea for their dogs in order to get a little peace in which to drink their own.

Your Dobermann must always have access to fresh, clean drinking water and the only time I would suggest removing this is when, as I have said, the puppy is being house-trained. The best container is a metal bucket, which should be chained to a fence or a post. Dogs also like routine, so this must apply to their feeding. It does not matter too much what type of feeding dish you use, though my preference is for stainless steel bowls, which cannot be chipped or chewed. They must always be cleansed thoroughly after each meal.

Never tease, or allow your children to tease, a dog who is eating a meal. Once you have provided the food, it then belongs to the dog, and the meal-time must be respected.

WORMING
Your puppy should have been wormed before being collected by you, and you should check that this has been done. It should have removed all the roundworms from the puppy's gut system,

which would have been passed on from the mother via the placenta and the umbilical cord, as well as through the milk supply. However, do not assume that your puppy will be free from worms. It is always worth worming again at about twelve to fourteen weeks, when your puppy is being vaccinated. Your vet will advise you on how to do this, the dosage and the frequency. There is an important public health aspect associated with worms, so you must ensure that your dog is worm free. Your dog should be wormed regularly at about six-monthly intervals.

VACCINATION

Puppies acquire some protective antibodies from their mother, through the colostrum, but this declines quite quickly, so that by the age of twelve weeks, most puppies have lost their protection, particularly from distemper. The amount of protection the puppy acquires, and, hence, the speed with which it loses it, depends on whether the mother has been given regular or recent vccinations herself. Where the bitch has not been recently vaccinated, some vets and breeders advocate giving puppies a distemper vaccination at six to eight weeks of age as an added precaution. This is even more important if the puppies have not received any colostrum due to difficulties at birth.

The normal age for receiving the primary vaccination is twelve weeks. From then on boosters will be required and your vet will advise you about when these should be administered.

Vaccination against parvovirus can be a particular problem, as this is a disease to which Dobermanns are prone. If a mother's immune system is high, then the puppies will also acquire a high level of protection, so they may not need a vaccination until as late as twenty weeks. You will, again, need veterinary advice. Some breeders resort to blood sampling to detect the level of antibody protection.

Always keep your puppy away from areas frequented by other dogs until the primary vaccination has been given, and, preferably, isolated for about another two weeks, until you are certain that the necessary level of immunity has developed.

EXERCISE

Up to the age of about sixteen weeks, your Dobermann will have no real need for exercise beyond running around the house and the garden. After fourteen weeks your puppy will have been vaccinated, and will be used to a collar and lead, so can be taken out of the house for very small, exploratory walks to get used to the sight and sounds of the wider world.

From about the age of four months the puppy will be ready for limited exercise, but remember that the bones have not yet properly formed and damage could be caused to the front legs and the pasterns if this is overdone. Free exercise in the garden is fine, but restrict walking on the lead. After the age of eight months it is safe to increase the amount of exercise. The puppies that have to be watched very carefully are those that are very heavy-boned and carry a considerable amount of substance. These puppies, more often than not males, may benefit from having even their uncontrolled exercise regulated.

There is a widely held public belief that a big dog like a Dobermann requires walking for miles and miles every day in order to keep fit and healthy. This belief is also shared by a number of dog owners. It is, however, a fallacy. While your Dobermann is capable of walking long distances each day, and would certainly enjoy it, it is not necessary. A Dobermann will keep perfectly fit with relatively little exercise, provided it is balanced, in that it includes some on-the-lead, controlled exercise and some free running, supplemented by free running in your garden whenever the dog feels like it. This will maintain a lovely, hard condition and ensure that the dog is well-muscled, particularly on the hindquarters. The main benefit of going out for walks is that your Dobermann will have the opportunity to explore beyond home territory, and ensure that everything is as it

Ch. Chancepixies Friend Or Foe (Findjans Giovanni of Mascol – Vincedobe Eternity of Chancepixies): Bred by Dave Anderson and Jean Frost, owned by Marc Harvey. Winner of 8 CCs, 8 Reserve CCs, Top Dobermann Bitch 1989. A Dobermann will learn to fit in with your lifestyle and does not require an enormous amount of exercise, provided it is balanced between lead-walking and free-running exercise.

Photo: Pearce.

should be. It is therefore as much a mental and psychological need as a physical one. It is somewhat ironic that too much exercise with a young puppy can result in soft, bending pasterns, yet plenty of steady roadwork will help to overcome this problem with dogs of eight months or older. However, if the problem is genetic, then no amount of exercise will overcome it, though it might improve it. Steady roadwork will also help to develop and harden the dog's muscles, strengthen the body and produce that hard, strong, muscular appearance with is so important for a Dobermann.

As previously indicated, you also need to balance exercise with feeding. Too much exercise will result in the dog being too thin, lacking body and substance as well as bone. And it is no good regulating the exercise if you do not provide enough food. If your Dobermann is too thin, try a combination of reduced exercise and increased food, possibly to two meals a day.

Dobermanns do not like cold, wet or windy weather. To some extent this is due to their thin coat, which means they feel the cold more than many of the longer-haired breeds. You will find that your Dobermann will protest greatly at being pushed out into the garden in the rain. Do not allow your Dobermann to get wet or remain in the cold unnecessarily. The key to good health is to keep the dog warm, dry and well-fed. Obviously the dog will get wet from time to time, and must be dried off thoroughly when back in the house. You can use towels, but crumpled newspaper is the quickest and easiest method, for it acts like blotting paper and will remove most of the moisture. Then finish off with a towel. A bit of printer's ink may come off the newspaper, but this is not a problem – except on a white dog.

Keep a watchful eye on the dog's general health and condition and check feet and pads regularly. If there is a serious problem, the dog will limp. You need to look for stones or grass-seeds between the toes, cracked or damaged pads, or for items such as tar or chewing-gum stuck to them. In the autumn check for harvest mites which can cause intense irritation. They look like small orange-coloured pin-heads and can be removed very simply by being swabbed with surgical spirit.

When you take your Dobermann out for a walk, always use a collar and lead. In some areas there are laws requiring dogs to be kept on the lead. You must also put an identity disc on the collar giving details of your address and telephone number. Make sure this cannot be broken or become detached. You should also give serious consideration to using more permanent identification, such as an ear tattoo or a microchip. Both methods give the dog a unique identification number which can be checked against a central register.

You must also ensure that your Dobermann does not roam. You owe it to your dog and everyone living in your area to ensure that your Dobermann is always confined to your garden. A wandering Dobermann would cause great concern to your neighbours and would not be in the best interests of the dog. You should also ensure that your Dobermann is not allowed to toilet in public places or on other people's private property. Again there are probably bye-laws regarding dog fouling. It has now become the widely accepted practice to clean-up after your dog, and appropriate doggie-bins are provided in many areas. While the risk of toxicariosis is probably very small, dog mess is not pleasant and can cause great distress if walked in or handled by children. You must therefore adopt a socially responsible approach and not allow your Dobermann to exercise and foul in areas where children play, or on sports grounds. It only takes a few uncaring owners to give all dog owners a bad name.

GROOMING

Your Dobermann, if well fed, fit and healthy, should have a smooth, glossy coat and give the appearance of being super-fit and in good condition. Grooming cannot create this impression, but it can help, and the grooming needs, for the short-coated Dobermann, are minimal. Use a soft hand-brush and brush the coat gently along the line of the flow of the hair. This stimulates the skin and helps to remove the dead hair from the coat. If there is an excessive amount of dead hair, gently rub through the coat with the palm of your hand covered in baby oil. Then massage it in with your fingers to loosen the hair, which will then come away more easily when the coat is brushed. Finally wipe the coat carefully to remove any surface oil. This dead coat problem may be more noticeable with a brown Dobermann, where the old, dead coat will appear as a lighter, more gingery brown.

Although the grooming needs are minimal, you should try to groom at least once every week. Surface dressings on the coat are not really needed, though it is conventional to use a coat spray immediately prior to taking a dog into the show ring. Grooming also provides the ideal opportunity to ensure that your Dobermann is not harbouring any undesirable visitors, such as ticks, flees or lice. This may show up as an irritation on the skin or a slightly bare patch, usually found behind the ears or on the shoulders due to the dog's scratching. Excessive nibbling around the tail is also a tell-tale sign that fleas may be present. As part of your equipment you should have a fine-toothed metal comb, which will soon remove any fleas. Have a bowl of water with some detergent in it close to hand, then comb the dog and immediately plunge the comb in the water, which kills the fleas. Use an aerosol flea-spray when necessary, or a flea collar. These need to be treated with care, as they do contain a rather dangerous chemical. Nevertheless I have never had any difficulties with them, but you must ensure that your Dobermann does not show any skin reaction, partcularly when wearing a flea collar.

*The short-coated
Dobermann is easy
to care for. Use a
soft hand-brush to
remove loose hair,
brushing along the
line of the hair.*

Photo: Steve Nash.

BATHING

Do not even consider bathing your Dobermann puppy. However, an adult will benefit from this
treatment from time to time. I would suggest that once every year is perfectly adequate, with the
spring or early summer being the best time. However there are occasions when a bath is essential,
particularly if your Dobermann has found something – to him – nice to roll in!

Excessive bathing will do more harm than good, by removing the natural oil from the coat and
leaving the skin and coat rather dry, lacking gloss and shine. Use your own bath or a specially
reserved dog bath, but do make sure that the first bath your dog has is fun. This will make life
easier for both of you on subsequent occasions.

The bath water should be warm, not hot, and should be about twelve inches in depth. Keep a
collar on the dog, as this gives you something to hold on to, otherwise you could find you have
lost your dog in mid-bath! Stand the dog beside the bath, then swing the back legs in, followed by
the front legs. This is far easier than trying to lift the dog in bodily. Use a good-quality dog
shampoo, not one designed for humans. Dilute it in a jug, pour it over the dog and massage it in
gently, not forgetting legs and underside. Then pour water over the dog to remove the shampoo.
Take great care not to get soap into the dog's eyes or ears. The head should be wiped down with a
damp cloth separately. Remember to dry the dog off thoroughly – and to give lots of praise for
being so co-operative.

EYES

It is normal for your Dobermann to have a greyish discharge of mucus in the corner of the eye,
particularly in the morning. This should be gently removed with a small swab of cotton-wool or a

piece of soft tissue, which must be wiped away from the eye, not across it. If the discharge is a thick, yellowy colour, then an infection is indicated, and your vet should be consulted.

EARS

These should be checked regularly. It is quite normal for a blackish waxy secretion to build up, which should be cleaned out as often as necessary, but with care, as the ears are very sensitive. If you lack the confidence to do this, get your vet to show you how. I always use a pair of artery forceps with a swab of cotton wool, dipped in methylated spirits, clamped in them. Squeeze the surplus spirits out with your fingers, leaving the swab damp, then work this gently around the folds of the ear, removing the wax. Replace the swabs as often as necessary. Methylated spirits is ideal, as it disolves the wax, kills any mites and evaporates dry. Avoid leaving water or oily substances in the ear, as these can cause problems

If the insides of the ears are red, sore or otherwise infected, they should be cleaned carefully, so as not to hurt them, and treated with drops or an ear ointment, obtained from your vet. One probable cause of this irritation will be ear mites, which look like small, sandy granules when removed by your ear swabs. Ear mites cause intense irritation which leads to scratching of the ears. Fortunately Dobermanns tend not to suffer from ear problems in the way that some long-coated, heavy-eared breeds do.

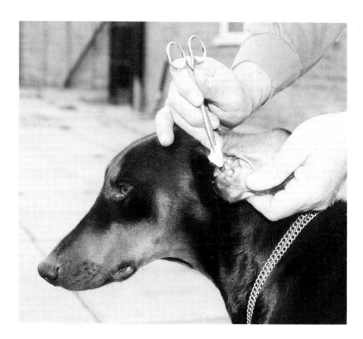

The ears should be cleaned regularly to remove any waxy discharge.

Photo: Steve Nash.

TEETH

Little needs to be done to puppy teeth, which are shed relatively quickly. The adult teeth should be checked regularly and cleaned as often as necessary, so that tartar does not build up. It is a good idea to get your dog used to this experience as early as possible. Any yellow discoloration can be removed using a solution of sodium bicarbonate and a cotton-wool swab. Put some of the powder in an egg cup with a small amount of water added to make a paste. Rub this on the teeth.

Scale, which is a heavy, chalky deposit due to the secretions from the salivary glands, will

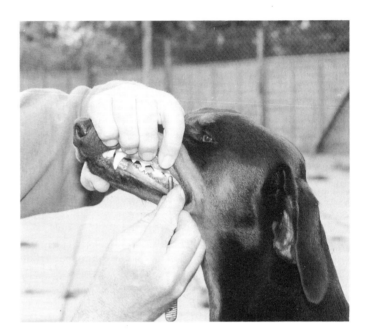

A dental scaler should be used to remove tartar that can accumulate on the teeth.

Photo: Steve Nash.

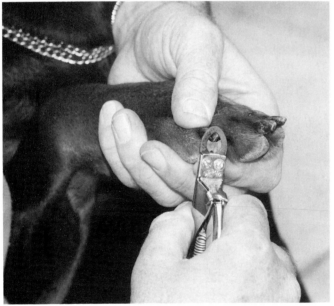

Nails should be trimmed regularly, making sure you avoid the quick.

Photo: Steve Nash.

normally build up on the teeth, particularly the molars. This should be removed on a regular basis with a dental scaler, but great care must be taken. Always work away from the gums, to avoid damaging them. Once you have mastered the technique it becomes relatively simple. The difficulty is in holding the dog!

From time to time some of the teeth will shows signs of damage, particularly as your Dobermann gets older. Always seek your vet's advice if you think canine dentistry is required.

TOENAILS

These must be trimmed regularly, unless your Dobermann has the sort of foot conformation that renders this unnecessary. Use either a pair of nail clippers or a guillotine-type nail cutter. If you use clippers, nick the nail on each side, at the point where you wish to cut it, then cut through the nail. This will avoid the risk of splitting the nail. I find guillotine cutters are easier and safer. The main thing to avoid is cutting too far back and thus cutting the quick, which will make the nail bleed. If you are unfortunate enough to do this, the bleeding can be staunched very quickly by the application of some crystals of potassium permanganate. Always err on the side of caution, leaving too much on rather than too little.

OLD AGE

A Dobermann at the age of seven years is officially considered to be a veteran. This landmark does not necessarily indicate the beginning of any decline in health, but it should alert you to the fact that you should be a little more careful about your dog. The life span of a Dobermann should be between eight and twelve years, with ten as a realistic average.

I have found that males and females tend to age differently and, indeed, die from quite different problems. The males seem to remain in peak condition, then suddenly collapse with heart problems. This can be either quite sudden, with the dog simply dropping dead at your feet, or more gradual, when the heart valves pack up. In this case you will find him, possibly in the morning, unable to get up, with a deep chesty cough and congested lungs because the heart cannot circulate the blood properly. Such dogs are inevitably doomed, usually very quickly.

Bitches tend to grow old more gracefully. They put on weight and slow down, taking only what exercise they need, and in their own time. They tend to develop mammary tumours and other lumps and frequently die as a result of cancer-related problems. Most of the lumps develop relatively slowly and are benign. I have always found it better to leave these alone. They can grow to quite frightening sizes, but rarely seem to bother the bitch. Even when removed they often come back again.

You have to start thinking for a dog who has passed the seven year milestone. With the males, control the exercise more carefully, and help them to pace themselves. Do not let any dog get too fat, particularly the bitches, who may need encouragement to take a little more exercise. Or control the food intake more carefully. However, some bitches will put on excessive weight quite naturally and this you should accept, and not try to reduce the weight artificially.

Older dogs may have difficulty digesting all their food if they are fed one meal each day. This problem may reveal itself if the dog cannot finish its dinner, or appears uncomfortable after eating, or vomits up the food later, or appears to have bloat. If there are any of these problems, then divide the meal into two smaller ones, one for the morning and one for the evening.

Watch the water consumption. Excessive drinking can be a symptom of kidney problems or diabetes, or can lead to problems such as bloat. This raises the question about whether to allow the dog to drink normally or to control the water supply. A vet's advice is needed.

Loss of bladder or bowel control is another problem encountered with older dogs. It is usually progressive and causes distress to both dogs and owners. There is little that can be done to relieve it, apart from allowing the dog to go out more frequently. This may sometimes be associated with the progressive loss of co-ordination, and eventually the hind legs will cease to function. This starts with unsteadiness on the hind legs and the weakness will become progressively worse. Your dog may suffer a deterioration in sight. If this happens, make sure that you do not move furniture around, or leave things, such as wheelbarrows, on paths. The dog will appear to have no particular problem in getting around, but will be doing it from memory and the senses of hearing and

Ch. Song and Dance Man (Ch. Crossridge The Jazzman – Bomper is Black Pearl). Bred by Mr and Mrs Stewart, owned by Sue and Dave Johnson. Winner of 3 CCs, 4 Reserve CCs, five times Best in Show at Breed Club Ch. Shows. He continued his winning ways as a veteran, taking a Reserve CC at Crufts at eight years of age.

smelling. Cynics will say that most Dobermanns are partially deaf all the time – they can hear the biscuit tin being opened from one end of the garden to the other, but seem deaf to your calls for them to come in at other times! If your Dobermann does appear to hear less well than in previous years, avoid doing anything which will startle the dog. Particularly make sure that the dog can see anyone who is approaching, even yourself.

Older dogs feel the cold more than younger ones, so should be kept warm, and they will need more sleep. Many old dogs only surface a few times during the day in order to answer the calls of nature and to offer their help at meal times.

DEATH

Whenever you acquire a dog you must accept at the outset that the day will come when the dog will die. This seems hard to imagine as you watch your lively young Dobermann bounding around with limitless energy and vitality. It is always possible that your Dobermann may die young, from illness or accident. If this does happen you will, indeed, be unfortunate. We always hope that our Dobermanns will live a full life-span. Dobermanns who die suddenly or unexpectedly leave you with nothing to do but to mourn their passing. The real problems come with those that get old and become ill or infirm, eventually reaching the stage where you are not able to do anything to relieve their problems. The situation then arises as to whether they should be allowed to continue living or whether you should intervene and end their lives to prevent any further suffering. There is no simple answer to this problem, and every case has to be judged on its merits. I believe the main consideration is quality of life. Some owners are over-sentimental and cannot let their dogs go until long after they should. Others betray their dogs by acting with unseemly haste, purely because they look old, tatty and senile. You must stand by your dog who is nearing the end of the road and show you still care. And you will surely know when the time has come to end the burden. When the dog cannot eat, or has lost interest in life, or is in pain, be kind. You will never be able to replace your dog, but you can acquire another Dobermann to fill the void that is left.

Chapter Four

OBEDIENCE TRAINING

By ALAN RIDOUT

The Dobermann is a superb athlete, strong in body and mind, intelligent, and quick to learn, thus possessing all the attributes for an excellent obedience dog. Unfortunately, in the UK, the Dobermann's working ability is not taken very seriously. That is because the vast majority of people who keep Dobermanns have them purely as pets. They do make excellent pets, but they are basically working dogs who need plenty of exercise daily. They need to be occupied. Left to their own devices they soon become boisterous and mischievous. All Dobermanns need some form of obedience training and, when they are obedient, they are a pleasure to own. But an unruly Dobermann is a pain and a liability.

IDENTIFYING PROBLEMS

When I was part of the Dobermann Club Training Team we had various people coming along with all sorts of problems. By far the biggest was the young male who had taken over as head of the household. This was usually a dog of twelve to eighteen months, who had pitted his wits and physical strength against those of his owner, and come out on top. This is perfectly natural behaviour. As a very young puppy, he will play-fight his litter brothers and sisters to attain his pecking order within the pack. When you remove him from his pack and take him home, you and your family become his new pack and so he starts all over again and, if left uncorrected, will take over. Remember, he is strong-minded, so will try to dominate as soon as he is physically able. This behaviour is easily controlled while the puppy is very young. Not so easy once he has established himself. The second biggest problem we encountered were dogs not coming back when called, or dogs that ran off when let off the lead. This, again, is natural behaviour, as the Dobermann has a strong natural hunting instinct and is a superb athlete who has never had enough – even if you have. Unfortunately this behaviour contravenes the Dangerous Dog Act, here in the UK. It is described as "keeping a dog not under proper control" (even if the dog is doing no harm).

So you see, training is a very important part of a Dobermann's life. I am a firm believer that you only get out of a dog what you put in. I look at dog training as an investment.

TRAINING DISCIPLINES

Let us look at some of the disciplines Dobermanns are trained for. First, Working Trials – for the Dobermann is an excellent nose work dog. Second, agility – the Dobermann is agile and athletic. Third, Flyball. This is becoming very popular in the UK. The Dobermann is a good choice for this discipline. Fourth, obedience. This is the hardest discipline for a Dobermann, for competition obedience requires one hundred per cent concentration and accuracy from both handler and dog throughout all the exercises. The Dobermann, being smooth-coated, cannot hide minor errors, but is well up to the job and cannot, because of being highly intelligent, be brain-washed, as are some of the more popular breeds in the discipline. Fifth, gundog. Dobermanns make good gun dogs once you have taught them to retrieve, and not to eat, the quarry. The sire to my own dog Wilkie was a gun dog.

All these disciplines are sports and pastimes to do with your Dobermann. But, on a more serious note, some Dobermanns are used in the USA as pilot dogs, or guide dogs as they are called in the UK. They are also used as police dogs in various parts of the world.

As you can see, a Dobermann can be trained to do almost anything. It all depends on the time you are prepared to invest in it. I, personally, have only been in the breed for eight years, acquiring my first Dobermann in 1987. I have had German Shepherd Dogs since 1959. At present I have two male German Shepherd Dogs, Saxon, who is nine, and Kye, who is eight. I also have two male Dobermanns, Wilkie (Hartsman Laird), aged seven years, and Strauss (Tanbowtra's Front Runner) who is fourteen months. I found the Dobermanns completely different to train. Being quick learners, they are easier, but they are equally quick at switching off through boredom. They need to be doing something new all the time.

HAVING THE RIGHT ATTITUDE

You have to approach your training with this is mind. Think about it. To teach your Dobermann an exercise takes a very short period of time. Most will pick it up on the first or second time of being shown it, but they won't do it perfectly first time. That comes with practice, which is something completely different. You must not practise an exercise which you have just shown. Once the dogs have got the gist of it, move on to something else, or you may bore them. If you persist, you run the risk of putting them off that exercise for a long time.

It can be very frustrating spending ages showing your Dobermann an exercise, only to have the dog looking at you in bewilderment. If this happens, leave it. You are at fault, not the dog. You are not communicating, you are not using the right key to unlock the brain. Play with your dog and, while doing so, think about a different approach, a different angle. For example if, when teaching scent discrimination, the dog keeps bringing back the wrong cloth or clothes, fix all the neutrals and decoy cloths to the floor. The dog soon learns the only cloth that can be retrieved is the one with the target scent on it, and eventually will go out and search for it. Problem solved. Think before you act, think of all the implications of what you are about to do. Remember, the dog is a quick learner and so will pick up errors just as fast as correct behaviour. If you are not careful, training a Dobermann can be one step forward and three steps back.

I remember teaching my dog Sendaway all in play as it was new to him, but he got the gist of it, and was doing it, after a fashion. I thought that would do for that day, so I praised him, played with him and put him back in the car while I laid out a scent test. I then got him out of the car, set him up, gave him my scent and commanded him to 'Find'. He flew out like a gazelle and did a perfect Sendaway to the markers I had forgotten to pick up. Luckily I had my wits about me, and gave the command 'Down' as he hit the Sendaway, followed by 'Good Boy'. I then approached the Sendaway, turned right, called him and continued heelwork away from the scent pattern. He did a super recall and heelwork. I played with him and put him back in the car, then gathered up both the scent clothes and the Sendaway markers before I got him out again.

I could have paid dearly for my stupidity and confused him in both exercises. Not only had I forgotten to pick up the markers, I had also set him up for Scent in the same place I had set him up for Sendaway. That day he taught me more than I taught him – as he has done many times since!

Training your Dobermann should be enjoyment for both you and your dog. If you find it a chore, or boring, you are not doing it right, and your dog will hate it. Done correctly it is all fun. I only have to say "Are we going to do some work?" and both my Dobermanns go mad with excitement. Each wants to do the other's Sendaway or Retrieve. Even when I am doing Heelwork with Wilkie, Strauss, my puppy, follows us around, watching intensely. He can't wait for his turn to be worked.

EARNING RESPECT

Before you do anything with your Dobermann you will have to earn the dog's respect. This is done through the three "Fs": Firmness, Fairness and Fun. Let's take these one at a time.

Firmness. All dogs like discipline in their lives, it makes them feel secure. Like all pack animals, dogs like a dominant male at the head of the pack. While he is there, keeping order, the pack functions normally. Remove him and it disorientates the pack. Infighting will result, until a new leader has established himself at the head. Then the pack will settle down gradually, as each member learns to respect the new dominant male. Whatever your gender, you have to take the place of that dominant male. What you say goes. Say what you mean, and mean what you say – ALWAYS.

Fairness. If you let your dog jump up when greeting you, then, when you put on your best clothes to go out and the dog comes running in from the garden, wet and muddy, and jumps up you, you can't tell the dog off. If you do, that's not fair. The rules and standards that apply today must apply every day. If your dog is allowed on your furniture, it is your fault if the dog gets up there while muddy. The rules must not change with your mood swings. If you give tidbits from the table while you are dining, don't tell your dog off if you have guests round for dinner and the dog starts scrounging from them, and don't shut the dog out of the dining-room. That's not fair. It is far better to keep the dog out of the dining-room at all times while you are eating. If you change the rules the dog will be confused, will not understand the reason why, and will be upset.

Fun. This is self-explanatory. Everything you do with your Dobermann should be fun. Even after correcting your dog you should make up straightaway. Let the dog feel your love. Remember, we don't have them for very long.

BUILDING A RAPPORT

Once you have earned the dog's respect, you will have the dog's trust. You will then build a rapport as your confidence in one another grows. No matter how much you love your dog, or dogs, there is no comparison between dogs that work and dogs that don't. The feedback from working a dog is tremendous. Of course, everyone who has worked a dog has had bitter disappointments. I have travelled two hundred miles to a venue, only to have one dog break Stays and the other miss Sendaways and fail Scent. Then I have a two hundred mile journey home. But I am convinced that I always take home the two best trophies from every show – Wilkie and Strauss!

USING YOUR VOICE FOR TRAINING

Obedience training should begin as soon as your puppy has settled into your home. The most important aid to training a dog of any age is voice modulation. In other words, it is not what you say to your dog, it's the way you say it. It is pointless praising, scolding and commanding your dog in the same tone of voice. You might just as well read the telephone directory to the dog. Keep your voice light for commands and praise, and higher when you break off and play. Beware – a high-pitched voice will make your Dobermann leap up in the air. Keep your head back, unless you want to be head-butted under the chin. Dobermanns specialise in the playful assault. Use a deep voice for correction and for not paying attention. Lighten up again as soon as your Dobermann starts to respond.

TRAINING USING FOOD

You can start training a very young puppy with the use of food. You have to feed young puppies four or five times a day. So you can teach them their name and the command Come at the same time. Once the puppy has come, use the command Sit and, at the same time, hold the dish of food above the puppy's head. The puppy will soon learn to look up and, in doing so, will sit naturally, because it is uncomfortable to do anything else when the head is pointing upwards. If your Dobermann is already around your feet while you are preparing the food, then move away and call the puppy to you, using the puppy's name and the command Come. Raise the dish above the puppy's head, give the command Sit and then the praise. Then give the puppy the food, accompanied by more praise. As the weeks go by, your puppy will start to get bigger and attack the dish before it reaches the floor. So you then teach the Wait. After you have got the puppy in the Sit, and given praise, show your raised index finger with the command Wait. If the puppy moves, pull the dish out of reach. Get the puppy back in the Sit, and repeat. Once the puppy waits for the dish to reach the floor, give lots of praise and let the puppy eat the food at once. You might have to hold the puppy in the Wait once or twice. Again, as the weeks go by, you can extend the Wait, so when the dish is on the floor, the puppy has to wait for you to give the signal before being allowed to eat. Once again, don't forget the praise.

   Now look what you will already have taught your dog in three to four weeks – name, Come, Sit and Wait. It really is very easy. But remember this must be done every meal-time. You can't think "I have not got time for messing around with this today." Remember you can't change the rules and standard. It's every time, or not at all.

BASIC OUTDOOR TRAINING

Now your Dobermann is ready for basic training in your garden or a securely-fenced field. A tennis court is ideal. Get your Dobermann used to a lead. Just walk around with the lead attached to the collar. If your Dobermann accepts the lead, you can start training straightaway. If your Dobermann fights the lead, i.e. pulls backwards, or does a lot of head-throwing from side to side, you will have to spend a little time getting the dog used to it. Use gentle tugs on the lead, try to keep the dog moving, keep giving lots of praise. Do not do too much of this training at one time. Training sessions for puppies should be short and often, with lots of play.

GIVING REWARDS

Up to this point all the puppy's training will have been with food, but you won't always have food with you. You can, if you wish, tidbit your dog as an incentive, or as a reward. But be careful. Dobermanns are so food-orientated, all else goes from their mind apart from the food you have in your hand. Personally, I never use tidbits. For my dogs their reward is my pleasure which I share with them after each exercise. So many times I have heard people say "My Dobermann works in training but won't work in the Ring." These are the people who train with food. Remember the dog is very intelligent and soon learns that there is no possibility of being fed in the show ring. So, therefore, the dog has lost any incentive to work. It is far better if the dog works to please you. Anyway, let's go back to fairness. You have changed the rules. The dog always gets a tidbit for doing something right, but then discovers this does not apply inside the ropes. Is that fair? Even if you are pet training with tidbits, never make out you have got food if you haven't. I have seen, many times, a dog that is reluctant to do something, so the handler makes out that there is food in the offing, bribes the dog into doing whatever is required and then – no reward. It's the quickest way to lose your Dobermann's trust.

USING A MOTIVATOR

Most people in competition obedience use a motivator, either a ball, a toy, or, as I do, the dog's lead. You do go through two or three leads a year. But it is something you always have with you, it is cheaper than tidbits and much more effective.

How does the motivator work? Well, I start with the Recall. I have already taught the Sit and Wait. So, command the dog to Sit and Wait, then walk to the end of the lead, turn round and face the dog, crouch down or even sit on the floor. I call the dog by name, give the command Come and, at the same time, give a gentle tug on the lead. As soon as the dog starts moving towards me, I gather the slack on the lead and start to use the loop handle of the lead as an enticement. If the dog comes in and grabs the lead, all the better. I command the dog to Sit, at the same time I gently pull the end of the lead, which is in the dog's mouth, upwards, to lift the dog's head up. As I said before, a dog will sit naturally this way. I keep the dog in this position for a few seconds while I gently praise and stroke my Dobermann. Because I want the dog to remember this position, called The Present, this is where I give the praise.

After a few seconds of praise and stroking, I lift my voice higher and tug on the lead to try to get the dog to play Tug with me, to start creating interest in the motivator. Once the dog starts coming to me quite happily over the next two or three days, I try the same exercise off-lead. I set up as before, but walk a little further away before I turn and face the dog, crouch down and call. At the same time I open my arms in a welcoming gesture. I have the lead/motivator in my mouth, hanging down as the dog comes in to grab it. I lift my head to make the dog do the same. I give the command Sit. If the dog tries to jump up for the lead, I have both hands free to help with the Sit. As soon as the dog sits, I release the lead. Ninety-nine Dobermanns out of a hundred will then shake the lead violently. Again I tug for a few minutes, praising all the time. Things don't always go to plan. Sometimes the dog won't wait. If this happens, go back and gently help the dog into the Sit, give the command Wait and slowly walk away backwards, commanding all the time. If the dog still won't wait, you will have to go back and stand with the dog, thus enforcing the Wait. Keep praising all the time.

Once you get the dog coming to you happily, the next stage is to set the dog as before, but this time, instead of moving away and then crouching down, go about ten to twelve feet away and sit on a chair, facing the puppy with your legs outstretched in front of you, slightly apart. Again it is the same format as before – lead in your mouth, hand gestures to call the puppy. As soon as the puppy Presents, get the command Sit in. Don't let the dog jump up for the lead – and help with the Sit if you have to. As soon as this is accomplished, release the lead. By now the dog should be ready to catch it as it drops.

Don't worry at this stage about accuracy. The most important thing is that the dog comes when called quite happily and Presents and is interested in the motivator. That's as far as I go with the Recall at this stage. I might do a few Recalls standing up; it depends how confident the puppy is.

HEELWORK

The next thing I teach is Heelwork. I just clip the lead to the dog's collar and simply start walking round in a lefthand circle, with the puppy on my lefthand side. In a light voice I keep saying the command Close, using the dog's name and giving praise. If the dog steps away from my left leg, I step into the dog and again say Close. If the dog keeps moving off my leg, I still keep stepping in. It does not matter if we end up going round in a lefthand circle as small as a dustbin lid. Eventually the dog will learn not to move off my left leg and realise that is the place to be. I then start making the circle bigger; eventually I start walking in a straight line. If the dog still keeps position I start walking in a righthand circle, again giving lots of praise all the time. If the dog loses position at any time, I go back to the lefthand circle. If the dog, at any time, jumps up after the lead or just in devilment, allow this play for a short while. Then take control once more by simply pulling the head up with the lead and telling the dog to sit. Give lots of praise – and start again.

Each time you halt, pull the lead upwards to lift the head, at the same time as giving the command Sit. It may be necessary for you to help the dog into the Sit; if this is the case, make sure the lead is in your right hand from the start, so you have the left hand free to push the dog's backside down.

EARLY LEARNING OF THE RETRIEVE

It is very important that you keep your back straight when working your puppy. Never bend over the puppy, as this will be intimidating. Once you have got your puppy sitting nicely by your side, gently unclip the lead, telling the puppy to wait. Slowly tie the lead into a bow and throw it away, at the same time say Get It, in an inciting tone. If the puppy runs out and picks it up, drop down on your knees quickly and call the puppy in the way I explained in the Recall. If the puppy brings the lead in, play tug, then take it. Throw it again with even more incitement. If this works, you have cracked the Retrieve. If it doesn't, you have lost nothing.

If the puppy picks the lead up, then spits it out, have a little play, make out you are going to get it. If the pup is still not interested, pick it up and wave it about until the puppy grabs it, then play tug, keep praising and then take it away. Throw it again and incite the puppy to Get It – but if it doesn't work this time, leave it. It will come. If the puppy picks it up and shakes it like mad, quickly move up from behind, on your knees, and take it from the puppy's mouth, saying "thank you, you clever thing". If you are quick enough and clever enough, you can make the puppy think it was all the puppy's own work – and eventually it will be. Do not chase the pup: once you start that, you will never get a Retrieve.

SOCIALISATION

This is the most important part of your puppy's training and it is where Dog Training Clubs are very handy. Where else would you get lots of dogs and people in close proximity? The right kind of socialisation, early on, will shape the puppy's personality for life. There are three basic things to remember while you are at a Dog Club.

First: beware who you mix with when you first enrol. In fact, if you are the last to join, this does not make you an idiot. Everyone who is seriously into dogs and training takes their young puppies to Dog Clubs to socialise them. But some of the people there may be with adolescent or adult dogs. The chances are these dogs are badly behaved and the handlers have no control, so someone has advised them to take the dog to a training club to straighten them out. The last thing you want is one of these dogs going for your puppy. Think about it: why else would an adult dog be in a puppy class? It's because the dog is not advanced enough in its training to go up a class, or, indeed, because the dog has had no training at all. So, check on the other members of the class.

Second: your puppy Dobermann will not be the same at a training club as at home, where there are no distractions, just you and the motivator. At the club there are noises, smells and too much going on for a puppy to concentrate. The puppy will get used to the excitement and will work eventually, but it might take two or three weeks.

Third: once you have joined a training club, it is not only your puppy who will socialise. You will meet people and make friends. Do not get carried away with this and ignore your Dobermann. As an instructor, I have witnessed this many times, with handlers sitting down talking to someone all evening, with the dog at the end of a lead, bored stiff. When it's their turn to work, they jump up and try to excite the dog into the mood. I can guarantee that if you ignore your Dobermann while you are waiting to work, your Dobermann will ignore you when the time for work comes.

One last thing to remember: you can't train a dog by going to a Dog Training Club once a week, any more than you can lose weight by going to a slimming club once a week. You only go to either to be shown the correct way to do things. Then the onus is on you. The more committed you are, the quicker and better your progress will be. It's not fair on your dog, your instructor, or yourself, if you only train your dog once a week at a club.

POSITIVE AND NEGATIVE TRAINING

All the training I have covered so far has been positive. Let me explain. There are both negative and positive ways of training dogs. Negative training involves letting your dog make errors and then correcting them. There's a bit more to it than that, but basically, that's it. This should only be practised by the experienced handler, as some dogs cannot take it. Others can, but you could solve one problem and create another if you don't know what you are doing. With positive training, we give the dog no option but to do as instructed by us, followed by praise from us. If the dog goes wrong, there is no correction or scolding, the dog is just put back in the original position held before the error occurred, and the exercise is tried again. If the dog still goes wrong, then we go back to basics again.

In the next stage which I am going to cover you might, indeed most of you will, have to use negative training. We have already taught the Recall. But that was at home and at the training club, from the Sit and Wait. What if we let the dog off the lead over in the park? The dog then runs off chasing rabbits, or other dogs, or children and won't relate to the command Come because the format is not the same. Anyway, why should a dog who is having a good time respond?

You must always have your dog under your complete control, so let's go back to the tennis court. Put your Dobermann on a long, light line. Put your lead/motivator in your pocket. We don't want the dog coming back through *any* enticement. We want the dog to come back because you have commanded it. Let your Dobermann sniff around the edge of the court, get interested in the other doggy smells there and, when the dog is fully involved in these investigations, call your Dobermann, just as you did in the Recall, but without the lead. If the dog moves towards you straightaway, don't use the line. If the dog hesitates, give a tug as you call again. As soon as the dog comes in to you, instigate a little play and give lots of praise. Don't let the dog Present, as this is not a formal recall. Then send the dog away again. Repeat this two or three times.

Then try it off-lead. This time have a pocket full of check chains. As before, let the dog get interested and then call. If the dog hesitates, call again, at the same time throwing a check chain at the dog, who must not be looking at you when you do this. There are two reasons for this: one is that we don't want to hit the dog in the face, the other is that we don't want the dog to see us throwing it. If you are on a tarmac court, so much the better. The sound of the chain hitting the tarmac will be enough to startle the dog. We don't want to actually hit or hurt the dog. We just want to dog to think "How did you do that?" The dog will immediately look at you. Again, call in the same tone of voice and use the same hand gestures. When the dog starts to come, give praise, just as before and when the dog arrives, have a little play. Then send the dog away again. You will probably only have to repeat this once or twice. All this does is let the dog think you are still in control, even when you are out of reach. Remember, never scold when your Dobermann comes back to you, whatever the reason. When the dog comes, you must give praise. If you find it necessary to give a reprimand, you must go to the dog, don't call the dog to you. Please remember, no-one has ever taught a Dobermann anything by being spiteful.

Once your dog is returning to you quite quickly, you can try your luck over your local park, or field. Pick a time when the place will not be busy. Let your dog off to run and play. If the dog runs off, let the dog go for a while. When it looks like the dog is paying attention to you, call. If the dog comes, have a little play, then send the dog off again with a playful slap on the rear end. Do this now and again while you are walking. When you want to go home, call the dog and have a little play before attaching the lead again.

If your dog doesn't come back when called, don't panic. Call again in a calm, firm voice. At the same time rattle one of the spare check chains taken from your pocket. If the dog does not respond at once, throw the chain as before. Don't do this if there is any chance of hitting someone or their dog. Go and get your dog, attach the lead and go back to the basics of the Recall. If the dog does come back, don't make a grab but play with the dog. Once your Dobermann returns on command and is fully socialised, the pair of you can go anywhere together with pride.

COMPETITION OBEDIENCE

As with pet Obedience, competition Obedience should be trained for with fun. The old-fashioned method of putting a dog under a strict regime simply is not productive enough for today's very high standards in the sport. Not only must handler and dog be one hundred per cent accurate in all the exercises, but the dog must work in a happy, natural manner. No dog who has been browbeaten or forced to work will do this. Your dog has to want to work. And the only way to achieve this is to make all training fun. You must teach the exercises in the correct order to avoid confusing your dog. For example, it is pointless trying to teach Scent if your dog does not Retrieve properly, or Sendaway if your dog will not do Distance Control. If you manage to get your dog to the Sendaway area, how are you going to then get the dog to lie down? Distance control can be taught very early, because this is one exercise that does not interfere with anything else. The order should be Stay exercises, both Sit and Down, Recall and Heelwork, Retrieve, and the Sendaway, Scent and ASSDs (Advanced Stand-Sit-Down) last.

DISTANCE CONTROL

Get your dog in the Sit. You stand facing your dog on the dog's right side. Put your right foot in front of the dog's front paws, to prevent any forward movement. Now give the command Stand or Back. At the same time touch the dog's stifle joint, with a slight pressure both backwards and upwards. The dog will feel a slight discomfort and stand. As the dog stands, give praise. Now give the command Down and, at the same time, put your right hand on the dog's forechest. The left hand should be on the dog's croup. The right hand should push the forechest backward as the left hand pushes the croup down. As the dog goes into the Down, again give tons of praise. It is important that the dog goes backwards in the Down, for two reasons. One is that if the dog goes through the Sit to the Down you will lose marks. The other is that the dog will also move forward and, again, you will lose marks.

Now command the dog to Sit, at the same time lift your right arm upwards. Again, lots of praise as the dog sits. Go through the positions quickly, playing and praising all the time. Change the order, but not too many at one time. After each little session, bring out the lead/motivator and throw it accompanied by the command Get It. As the dog starts to do the exercises unaided you can then move in front and, each time you give the dog a position, step forwards to make the dog go back. Also, each time you give a position, look as though you are going to throw the motivator and sometimes do this, throwing it over the dog's head. Make this throwing a random thing so the dog will never know when it is going to be thrown. The dog will then watch you like a hawk, giving you complete attention. Over the weeks, as the dog improves, you keep increasing the distance between you. This is an easy exercise to teach.

RECALL

We have already covered the basics of the Recall earlier in this chapter, using the motivator. Now we have got to get the dog to Present straight. If the dog, when coming in to you, is on one side, you have to compensate with your feet to get the dog in straight. You must never grab or pull your dog, if there is an error, as this will only put the dog off coming to you. Imagine you are standing in the centre of a large clock face. The ideal position for the dog to come and Present is at 12 o'clock. But if the dog comes in at 10 o'clock you keep standing up straight and keeping your shoulders square. Also keep facing 12 o'clock. Move your right foot back and transfer your weight on to it; that will leave your left leg sticking out and your dog will have to come round it to Present, hopefully, at 12 o'clock. If the dog over-compensates and is then Presenting at 1 o'clock, move your left leg back. Make sure the dog is Presenting correctly before sitting. So, whatever side the dog comes in from, move the leg which is farthest away from the dog back. As soon as the dog's rear end is on the floor in the correct Present, throw the motivator and command Get It. Never lean forward, or twist your shoulders.

THE FINISH

Once you have your dog doing a reasonable Recall and Present you can start teaching the Finish. You can do this in two different ways. From the Present you can send the dog to your right, round your legs to Heel position, or anti-clockwise to your left. Both methods are taught on lead. Let's deal with the round-the-back method first. Get your dog sitting in the Present. Make sure the lead is attached to the collar under the centre of the head. Take the lead in the right hand. On command Heel, tug the lead and pass it behind your legs. Change the lead to your left hand and continue leading the dog round to Heel position and get the dog to sit. Don't drag the dog round. Again, treat it as a game.

For the other method, get your dog sitting in the Present. Make sure the lead is attached to the collar at the back of the neck. Hold the lead up in the air with your right hand. Grasp the lead about six inches away from the collar with your left hand. Now imagine the lead is a large wooden spoon and you are going to stir a large pot with it. On the command Heel or Close, stir the pot in an anti-clockwise direction, at the same time step back with your left foot, bringing the dog with you. As you bring the dog's head around to your leg, step forward with your left foot. That should bring the dog nicely into the Heel position. Then command the dog to Sit. The Recall and Finish is one exercise, but in training it is important not to practise both parts of this exercise together. Your Dobermann will stop Presenting and go straight round to Heel, having realised that the one action always follows the other. So the Recall and Finish should only be strung together now and then. Don't forget to throw the motivator as soon as the exercise is finished.

HEELWORK

Just as in pet training, clip the lead to the collar and simply start walking round in a left-hand circle. Give light jerks upward to keep your dog's attention. Make sure the correct Heel position is kept with the dog's shoulder tight on your left leg. If the dog steps away from you, give a light jerk on the lead, accompanied by the command Close, in a deep voice; the second the dog is back in position say, in a light voice "That's clever". Once the proper position is being maintained, start walking in a straight line. If your dog still holds position, try an about turn to your right. Before you turn, give a light tug on the lead and the command Close. It is most important that you walk at a pace that will stretch your dog. We don't want the dog to pace round the ring, a sure way for the dog to lose interest. If you power round the ring you will keep the dog's attention.

It is also very important that the handler maintains the correct deportment. Shoulders back, back straight. For the right turn, take your last full step with your right foot, bring your left foot up and place it in front of the right foot at ninety degrees, as if you were crossing a capital letter T. At the same time spin on the ball of your right foot. Now move off on your right foot.

The about turn is the same as the right turn, but when you have crossed the letter T with your left foot, and spun on your right foot, turn the right foot to the direction you are going to move off. Now move off with your left foot. For the left turn, take your last full step with your right foot, bring your left foot up and place it in front of the right foot at ninety degrees, as if you were making an upside-down capital L. At the same time, spin on your right foot. Now move off on your right foot.

Left-about turn is the same as left turn, but instead of moving off on your right foot, make another upside-down capital L with it, then move off on your left foot. As you can see, you must turn at ninety degrees, which must be done in one step, and one hundred and eighty degrees, which must be accomplished in two steps and you must be on the same line when you about-turn as the one you have just travelled. In other words, you must turn on the spot.

It is most important that the handler practises heelwork without a dog until, whatever command you hear from the steward in the show ring, you flow into that manoeuvre without thinking, changing pace, or hesitating. This is so that, when you do it with a dog, you don't break the dog's gait when you change direction. It is also very important that you do not twist your body. When you turn, your hips should not beat your shoulders round, or vice versa. When your foot lands on the floor in the direction you are going to travel, your whole body should be facing in that same direction. When you turn left, your Dobermann will automatically cut off the corner – in other words, the dog won't turn as sharply as when turning right. When you turn right, your dog will have to come around your legs. We need the dog to turn left just as sharply as when turning right. To do this put an obstacle in the way, so the dog has to turn left around it.

I do heelwork round the kitchen table, giving just enough room for the dog's shoulders to get past the legs of the table. Then I turn left so the dog's rear end has to swing round. I teach this all in play. I also give the dog a playful slap when I turn left or left-about turn and say, in a playful voice "Get that backside in".

Nine times out of ten, crooked Sits in heelwork are the fault of the handler, not the dog. If, when you halt, you keep your feet still but twist your hips round to face your dog and give the command Sit or, worse still, bend over your dog to give your command, I will bet the dog will sit wide, backside sticking out. If when you halt you just drop your left shoulder back so you can see where the dog is sitting, I bet it will be fairly close, with the backside in the correct position. Guide your dog into a straight Sit. Don't pull your dog around when in the Sit. If the position is incorrect, step forward on your left foot and call the dog in close. Once the dog is sitting fairly straight every time you halt, your confidence will grow and the dog will sit even straighter, because you will stop looking down all the time and you won't be giving the wrong body signals.

Play is very important in Heelwork. A dog who never knows when you are going to break into play will watch you like a hawk. And that is what we want.

RETRIEVE

This exercise needs to be broken into four parts: the Wait, the Outrun and Pick-up, the Return and Present, and the Finish. This is another very easy exercise to teach. We have already taught the Wait, the Present and the Finish. And if you have been playing with the motivator, you have already got the dog retrieving. It is just a question of polishing it all up and stringing it together. Just one thing: if your dog runs out, picks up the article and won't bring it back, run away. Don't run towards the dog, or the game will be "I've got it, you come and get it."

SENDAWAY

Set up a Sendaway box. Set your dog up to Wait, walk out to the Sendaway and let the dog see you drop the motivator into the box. Walk back, guide your dog's head towards the Sendaway box with the instruction to Look Straight. Then incite the dog and give the command Away. As soon as the dog runs out and picks up the motivator, drop the dog with the command Down. Run out to the box to keep the dog in the Down and give lots of praise. Do this three or four times each session. After a while, only put the motivator in the box every now and then. Do not forget to run out and praise the dog every time. Soon the Sendaway will be done without any motivator at all. Then you can start teaching the Recall from the box. Just walk away from the box while calling your dog. At the same time pull the motivator out of your pocket. As soon as the dog catches you up, do a few steps of Heelwork, then throw the motivator. Again, very easy to teach.

SCENT

To start Scent, get four or five heavy articles, e.g. a car jack, a big spanner, a house brick. These articles must not be yours or kept in your house. They must not have any of your scent on them. You now need a scent cloth rubbed up in your hands, so it has your hot scent on it. Let the dog sniff it but not touch it. Get someone to put it out amongst the other articles. Make sure they don't contaminate the cloth with their scent. Now set your dog up in the Sit, and give the dog your scent by placing your hand over the dog's nose and give the instruction Find. When the dog picks up the scent cloth, give lots of praise and call the dog back.

The articles can eventually be replaced by scent boards. These are squares of 22mm blockboard about ten inches square with a scent cloth pinned on each one. They are arranged in a straight line. One board has a loose cloth with the handler's scent on it. This is the only cloth the dog can retrieve. You will be surprised how quickly your Dobermann will learn to do Scent.

ASSDs

Once your dog is confident and doing good Heelwork at all three paces, you then have to teach the Advanced Sit, Stand and Down. These positions are given during normal pace Heelwork. The dog must obey the commands instantly as the handler continues the Heelwork until instructed by the ring steward in the competition to "Pick up your dog". The dog must be picked up in a smooth, natural manner. This is very easily taught. Simply command the dog and immediately walk round the dog in a tight left-hand circle before continuing your Heelwork. When you about-turn to go back past the dog, give plenty of praise and make sure the dog does not move. When you come back again to pick up the dog, give more praise. This can also be taught in play.

Stays are a confidence thing. It is hard to advise on Stays as each dog is very different. But you must build up your dog's confidence. Don't leave a dog that is not ready to be left. It is very handy if the dog has an older kennel brother or sister to be left with, at first.

Remember, the more you enjoy your training the more fun it will be for your Dobermann. There is only one way to work a Dobermann. Head up and shoulders back. Remember, you are working the ultimate.

Chapter Five

THE BREED STANDARDS

BRITISH BREED STANDARD

GENERAL APPEARANCE
Medium size, muscular and elegant, with well set body. Of proud carriage, compact and tough. Capable of great speed.

CHARACTERISTICS
Intelligent and firm of character, loyal and obedient.

TEMPERAMENT
Bold and alert. Shyness or viciousness very highly undesirable.

HEAD AND SKULL
In proportion to body. Long, well filled out under eyes and clean cut, with good depth of muzzle. Seen from above and side, resembles an elongated blunt wedge. Upper part of head flat and free from wrinkle. Top of skull flat, slight stop; muzzle line extending parallel to top line of skull. Cheeks flat, lips tight. Nose solid black in black dogs, solid dark brown in brown dogs, solid dark grey in blue dogs and light brown in fawn dogs. Head out of balance in proportion to body, dish-faced, snipy or cheeky very highly undesirable.

EYES
Almond-shaped, not round, moderately deep set, not prominent, with lively, alert expression. Iris of uniform colour, ranging from medium to darkest brown in black dogs, the darker shade being more desirable. In browns, blues, or fawns, colour of iris blends with that of markings, but not of lighter hue than markings; light eyes in black dogs highly undesirable.

EARS
Small, neat, set high on head, Normally dropped, but may be erect.

MOUTH
Well developed, solid and strong with complete dentition and a perfect, regular and complete scissor bite, i.e. upper teeth closely overlapping lower teeth and set square to the jaws. Evenly placed teeth. Undershot, overshot or badly arranged teeth highly undesirable.

NECK
Fairly long and lean, carried with considerable nobility; slightly convex and in proportion to shape of dog. Region of nape very muscular. Dewlap and loose skin undesirable.

FOREQUARTERS
Shoulder blade and upper arm meet at an angle of 90 degrees. Shoulder blade and upper arm approximately equal in length. Short upper arm relative to shoulder blade highly undesirable. Legs seen from front and side, perfectly straight and parallel to each other from elbow to pastern; muscled and sinewy, with round bone in proportion to body structure. Standing or gaiting, elbow lies close to brisket.

BODY
Square, height measured vertically from ground to highest point at withers equal to length from forechest to rear projection of upper thigh. Forechest well developed. Back short and firm, with strong, straight topline sloping slightly from withers to croup; bitches may be slightly longer to loin. Ribs deep and well sprung, reaching to elbow. Belly fairly well tucked up. Long, weak, or roach backs highly undesirable.

HINDQUARTERS
Legs parallel to each other and moderately wide apart. Pelvis falling away from spinal column at an angle of about 30 degrees. Croup well filled out. Hindquarters well developed and muscular; long, well bent stifle; hocks turning neither in nor out. When standing, hock to heel perpendicular to the ground.

FEET
Well arched, compact, and cat-like, turning neither in nor out. All dewclaws removed. Long, flat deviating feet and/or weak pasterns highly undesirable.

TAIL
Customarily docked at first or second joint; appears to be a continuation of spine without material drop.

GAIT/MOVEMENT
Elastic, free balanced and vigorous, with good reach in forequarters and driving power in hindquarters. When trotting, should have strong rear drive, with apparent rotary motion of hindquarters. Rear and front legs thrown neither in nor out. Back remains strong and firm.

COAT
Smooth, short, hard, thick and close-lying. Imperceptible undercoat on neck permissible. Hair forming a ridge on back of neck and/or along spine highly undesirable.

COLOUR
Definite black, brown, blue or fawn (Isabella) only, with rust red markings. Markings to be sharply defined, appearing above each eye, on muzzle, throat and forechest, on all legs and feet and below tail. White markings of any kind highly undesirable.

SIZE
Ideal height at withers: dogs: 69cms (27 inches); bitches: 65cms (25 1/2 inches). Considerable deviation from this ideal undesirable.

FAULTS
Any departure from the foregoing points should be considered a fault and the seriousness with which the fault should be regarded should be in exact proportion to its degree.

NOTE
Male animals should have two apparently normal testicles fully descended into the scrotum.

Reproduced by kind permission of the English Kennel Club.
The Kennel Club March 1994

AMERICAN BREED STANDARD

GENERAL APPEARANCE
The appearance is that of a dog of medium size, with a body that is square. Compactly built, muscular and powerful, for great endurance and speed. Elegant in appearance, of proud carriage, reflecting great nobility and temperament. Energetic, watchful, determined, alert, fearless, loyal and obedient.

SIZE, PROPORTION, SUBSTANCE
Height at the withers: dogs 26 to 28 inches, ideal about 27 1/2 inches; bitches 24 to 26 inches, ideal about 25 1/2 inches. The heights, measured vertically from the ground to the highest point of the withers, equalling the length measured horizontally from the forechest to the rear projection of the upper thigh. Length of head, neck and legs in proportion to length and depth of body.

HEAD
Long and dry, resembling a blunt wedge in both frontal and profile views. When seen from the front, the head widens gradually toward the base of the ears in a practically unbroken line. Eyes almond shaped, moderately deep set, with vigorous, energetic expression. Iris, of uniform color, ranging from medium to darkest brown in black dogs; in reds, blues, and fawns the color of the iris blends with that of the markings, the darkest shade being preferable in every case. Ears normally cropped and carried erect. The upper attachment of the ear, when held erect, is on a level with the top of the skull. Top of skull flat, turning with slight stop to bridge of muzzle, with muzzle line extending parallel to top line of skull. Cheeks flat and muscular. Nose solid black on black dogs, dark brown on red ones, dark gray on blue ones, dark tan on fawns. Lips lying close to jaws. Jaws full and powerful, well filled under the eyes. Teeth strongly developed and white. Lower incisors upright and touching inside of upper incisors – a true scissors bite. 42 correctly placed teeth, 22 in the lower, 20 in the upper jaw. Distemper teeth shall not be penalized. Disqualifying faults: overshot more than 3/16 of an inch. Undershot more than 1/8 of an inch. Four or more missing teeth.

NECK, TOPLINE, BODY
Neck proudly carried, well muscled and dry. Well arched, with nape of neck widening gradually toward body. Length of neck proportioned to body and head. Withers pronounced and forming the highest point of the body. Back short, firm, of sufficient width, and

muscular at the loins, extending in a straight line from withers to the slightly rounded croup. Chest broad with forechest well defined. Ribs well sprung from the spine, but flattened in lower end to permit elbow clearance. Brisket reaching deep to the elbow. Belly well tucked up, extending in a curved line from the brisket. Loins wide and muscled. Hips broad and in proportion to body, breadth of hips being approximately equal to breadth of body at rib cage and shoulders. Tail docked at approximately second joint, appears to be a continuation of the spine, and is carried only slightly above the horizontal when the dog is alert.

FOREQUARTERS
Shoulder blade sloping forward and downward at a 45 degree angle to the ground meets the upper arm at an angle of 90 degrees. Length of shoulder blade and upper arm are equal. Height from elbow to withers approximately equals height from ground to elbow. Legs seen from front and side, perfectly straight and parallel to each other from elbow to pastern; muscled and sinewy, with heavy bone. In normal pose and when gaiting, the elbows lie close to the brisket. Pasterns firm and almost perpendicular to the ground. Dewclaws may be removed. Feet well arched, compact, and catlike, turning neither in nor out.

HINDQUARTERS
The angulation of the hindquarters balances that of the forequarters. Hip bone falls away from spinal column at an angle of about 30 degrees, producing a slightly rounded, well filled-out croup. Upper shanks at right angles to the hip bones, are long, wide, and well muscled on both sides of thigh, with clearly defined stifles. Upper and lower shanks are of equal length. While the dog is at rest, hock to heel is perpendicular to the ground. Viewed from the rear, the legs are straight, parallel to each other, and wide enough apart to fit in with a properly built body. Dewclaws, if any, are generally removed. Cat feet as on front legs, turning neither in nor out.

COAT
Smooth-haired, short, hard, thick and close lying. Invisible gray undercoat on neck permissible.

COLOR AND MARKINGS
Allowed colors: black, red, blue and fawn (Isabella). Markings: rust, sharply defined, appearing above each eye and on muzzle, throat and forechest, on all legs and feet, and below tail. White patch on chest, not exceeding 1/2 square inch, permissible. Disqualifying fault: dogs not of an allowed color.

GAIT
Free, balanced, and vigorous, with good reach in the forequarters and good driving power in the hindquarters. When trotting, there is strong rear-action drive. Each rear leg moves in line with the foreleg on the same side. Rear and front legs are thrown neither in nor out. Back remains strong and firm. When moving at a fast trot, a properly built dog will single-track.

TEMPERAMENT
Energetic, watchful, determined, alert, fearless, loyal and obedient. The judge shall dismiss from the ring any shy or vicious Doberman. Shyness: a dog shall be judged fundamentally

shy if, refusing to stand for examination, it shrinks away from the judge; if it fears an approach from the rear; if it shies at sudden and unusual noises to a marked degree. Viciousness: a dog that attacks or attempts to attack either the judge or its handler, is definitely vicious. An aggressive or belligerent attitude toward other dogs shall not be deemed viciousness.

FAULTS
The foregoing description is that of the ideal Dobermann Pinscher. Any deviation from the above described dog must be penalized to the extent of the deviation.

DISQUALIFICATIONS
Overshot more than 3/16 of an inch. Undershot more than 1/8 of an inch. Four or more missing teeth. Dogs not of an allowed color.

Reproduced by kind permission of the American Kennel Club.
Approved February 6 1982
Reformatted November 6, 1990

FCI BREED STANDARD

GENERAL APPEARANCE
The Dobermann is of medium size, strong and muscularly built. Through the elegant lines of its body, its proud stature and temperamental character and its expression of determination, it conforms to the ideal picture of a dog.

IMPORTANT PROPORTIONS
The body of the Dobermann appears to be almost square, particularly in males. The length of the body measured from the pro sternum to the ischium shall not be more than 5% longer than the height from the withers to the ground in males, and 10% in females.

BEHAVIOUR AND TEMPERAMENT
The disposition of the Dobermann is friendly and calm; very devoted to the family, it loves children. Medium temperament and medium sharpness (alertness) is desired. A medium threshold of irritation is required with a good contact to the owner. The Dobermann enjoys working, and shall have good working ability, courage and hardness. The particular values of self confidence and intrepidness are required, and also adaptability and attention to fit the social environment.

HEAD
CRANIAL REGION
Strong and in proportion to the body. Seen from the top the head is shaped in the form of a blunt wedge. Viewed from the front the crown line shall be almost level and not dropping off the ears. The muzzle line extends almost straight to the top line of the skull which falls, gently rounded, into the neck line. The eyebrow bone is well developed without protruding. The forehead furrow is still visible. The Occiput shall not be conspicuous. Seen from the

front and the top the sides of the head must not bulge. The slight bulge between the rear of the upper jawbone and the cheekbone shall be in harmony with the total length of the head. The head muscles shall be well developed.

STOP
Shall be slight but visibly developed.

FACIAL REGION
NOSE
Nostrils well developed, more broad than round, with large openings without overall protrusion. Black on black dogs; on brown and blue dogs, corresponding lighter shades.

MUZZLE
The muzzle must be in the right proportion with the upper head and must be strongly developed. The muzzle shall have depth. The mouth opening shall be wide, reaching to the molars. A good muzzle width must also be present on the upper and lower incisor area.

FLEWS
They shall be tight and lie close to the jaw which will ensure a tight closure of the mouth. The pigment of the gum to be dark; on blue and brown dogs a corresponding lighter shade.

JAW/DENTITION/TEETH
Powerful broad upper and under jaw, scissor bite, 42 teeth correctly placed and normal size.

EYES
Middle sized, oval and dark in colour. Lighter shades are permitted for brown and blue dogs. Close lying eyelids. Eyelids shall be covered with hair. Baldness around the rim of the eye is highly undesirable.

EARS
The ear, which is set high, is carried erect and cropped to a length in proportion to the head. In a country where cropping is not permitted the uncropped ear is equally recognised. (Medium size preferred and with the front edge lying close to the cheeks.)

NECK
The neck must have a good length and be in proportion to the body and the head. It is dry and muscular. Its outline rises gradually and is softly curved. Its carriage is upright and shows much nobility.

BODY
WITHERS
Shall be pronounced, in height and length, especially in males and thereby determine the slope of the topline rising from the croup to the withers.

BACK
It is short and tight. The back and the loin section are of good width and well muscled. The bitch can be slightly longer in loin because she requires space for suckling.

CROUP
It shall fall slightly, hardly perceptible from sacrum to the root of the tail, and appears well rounded, being neither straight nor noticeably sloping, of good width and well muscled.

CHEST
Length and depth of chest must be in the right proportion to the body length. The depth with slightly arched ribs should be approximately 50% the height of the dog at the withers. The chest has got a good width with especially well developed forechest.

UNDERLINE
From the bottom of the breastbone to the pelvis the underline is noticeably tucked up.

TAIL
It is high set and docked short whereby approximately two tail vertebrae remain visible. In countries where docking is legally not permitted the tail may remain natural.

TESTICLES
In males both testicles must be normally developed and be visible in the scrotum.

LIMBS
FOREQUARTERS
General: The front legs as seen from all sides are almost straight, vertical to the ground and strongly developed.

SHOULDERS
The shoulder blade lies close against the chest, and both sides of the shoulder blade edge are well muscled and reach over the top of the thoracic vertebra, slanting as much as possible and well set back. The angle to the horizontal is approximately 50 degrees.

UPPER ARM
Good length, well muscled, the angle to the shoulder blade is approximately 105 to 110 degrees.

ELBOW
Close in, not turned out.

LOWER ARM
Strong and straight. Well muscled. Length in harmony with the whole body.

CARPUS
Strong.

METACARPUS
Bones strong. Straight seen from the front. Seen from the side, only slightly sloping, maximum 10 degrees.

FRONT FOOT
The feet are short and tight. The toes are arched towards the top (cat like). Nails short and black.

HINDQUARTERS
General: Seen from the back the Dobermann looks, because of his well developed pelvic muscles in hips and croup, wide and rounded off. The muscles running from the pelvis towards the upper and lower thigh result in good width development, as well as in the upper thigh area, in the knee joint area and at the lower thigh. The strong hind legs are straight and stand parallel.

UPPER THIGH
Good length and width, well muscled. Good angulation to the hip joint. Angulation to the horizontal approximately between 80 to 85 degrees.

KNEE
The knee joint is strong and is formed by the upper and lower thigh as well as the knee cap. The knee angulation is approximately 130 degrees.

LOWER THIGH
Medium length and in harmony with the total length of the hindquarter.

HOCK JOINT
Medium strength and parallel. The lower thigh bone is joined to the metatarsal at the hock joint (angle about 140 degrees).

METATARSUS
It is short and stands vertical to the ground.

HIND FOOT
Like the front feet, the toes of the back feet are short, arched and closed. Nails are short and black.

GAIT
The gait is of special importance to both the working ability as well as the exterior appearance. The gait is elastic, elegant, agile, free and ground covering. The front legs reach out as far as possible. The hindquarter gives far reaching and necessary elastic drive. The front leg of one side and back leg of the other side move forward at the same time. There should be good stability of the back, the ligaments and the joints.

SKIN
The skin fits closely all over and is of good pigment.

COAT
HAIR
The hair is short, hard and thick. It lies tight and smooth and is equally distributed over the whole surface. Undercoat is not allowed.

COLOURS
The colour is black, dark brown or blue, with rust red clearly defined and clean markings. Markings on the muzzle, as a spot on the cheeks and the top of the eyebrow; on the throat,

two spots on the forechest, on the metacarpus, metatarsus and feet, on the inside of the back thigh, on the arms and below the tail.

SIZE AND WEIGHT
SIZE Height at the highest point of withers: Males: 68 to 72cms. Bitches: 63 to 68cms. Medium size desirable.

WEIGHT Males ca. 40 to 45 kg. Bitches ca. 32 to 35 kg.

FAULTS
GENERAL APPEARANCE: Reversal of sexual impression; little substance; too light; too heavy; too leggy; weak bones.

HEAD: Too heavy; too narrow; too short; too long; too much or too little stop; Roman nose; bad slope of the top line of the skull; weak underjaw; round or slit eyes; light eye; cheeks too heavy; loose flews; eyes too open or too deepset; ear set too high or too low; open mouth angle.

NECK: Slightly short; too short; loose skin around the throat; dewlap; too long (not in harmony); ewe neck.

BODY: Back not tight; sloping croup; sway back; roach back; insufficient or too much spring of rib; insufficient depth or width of chest; back too long overall; too little forechest; tail set too high or too low; too little or too much tuck up.

LIMBS: Too little or too much angulation in front or hindquarters; loose elbow; deviations from the standard position and length of bones and joints; feet too close together or too wide apart; cowhocks, spread hocks, close hocks; open or soft paws, crooked toes; pale nails.

COAT: Markings too light or not sharply defined; smudged markings; mask too dark; big black spot on the legs; chest markings hardly visible or too large; hair long, soft, curly or dull. Thin coat; bald patches; large tufts of hair particularly on the body; visible undercoat.

CHARACTER: Inadequate self confidence; temperament too high; sharpness/aggressiveness too high; too high or too low a threshold of irritation.

SIZE: Deviation of size up to two centimetres from the standard should result in a lowering of the quality grading.

GAIT: Wobbly; restricted or stiff gait; pacing.

DISQUALIFYING FAULTS
GENERAL: Pronounced reversal of sexual impressions.

EYES: Yellow eyes (bird of prey eye); wall eye.

DENTITION: Overshot; level bite; undershot; missing teeth.

TESTICLES: Absence of two normally developed testicles in the scrotum.

COAT: White spots; pronounced long and wavy hair; pronounced thin coat or large bald patches.

CHARACTER: Fearful; shy; nervous and overly aggressive animals.

SIZE: Dogs which deviate more than two centimetres over or under the standard.
Reproduced by kind permission of the FCI.

WHY BREED STANDARDS ARE NECESSARY

The breed Standard is a written description of what the ideal Dobermann should look like. Without this, everyone would tend to breed in isolation, and produce their own version of the Dobermann. Judges would place dogs which they liked, irrespective of how good or bad they were, since there would be no Standard against which to assess them. There would be no consideration of whether or not dogs were anatomically sound in terms of their ability to work. It would not be very long before we all had dogs that bore a passing resemblance to the Dobermann as we know it today, but there would be an ever-increasing divergence away from the ideal Dobermann, until we effectively had a number of new breeds. Without breed Standards even these new breeds would not breed true, and the outcome would be that we would have a wide range of Dobermann-like mongrels.

This state of affairs would be a disaster for anyone attempting to breed and show Dobermanns, and also for the even greater number of people who simply want to own a Dobermann as a pet. The Breed Standard offers them a considerable degree of protection, in that their dog will not only look like a Dobermann, but will also have the personality, character and intelligence of a Dobermann.

EXPLAINING THE DIFFERENT STANDARDS

There are three main breed Standards, which are used by the majority of countries. They are the Federation Cynologique Intenationale (FCI) Standard, used predominantly in Europe, the American Standard, used in the USA, and the British Standard, used in the United Kingdom and a number of other countries. There are numerous other Standards which are used in specific countries, but these tend to be just slight variations of one of the three principal Standards. For example, the German Standard is akin to the FCI Standard and the Australian Standard is like the British Standard.

The FCI, American and British Standards are very similar in terms of what they are actually asking for, but the ways in which they ask for it are completely different, as is the emphasis on specific points. The similarity is not really surprising, since Dobermanns from Europe have been imported into both Britain and the USA and have played an important role in the breeding programmes in those countries, and Dobermanns from America have played a crucial role over the years in establishing the British Dobermann as we see it today. Dogs from America have also been imported into Europe and individual dogs have played a part in some breeding programmes there. It is probably fair to say that, while Britain has always been a stronghold of dog breeding and has traditionally exported top class dogs all over the world, its export of Dobermanns has had a relatively minor effect on the Breed in both Europe and the USA. It has, however, had a major influence in many other countries.

COMPARISON AND ANALYSIS

The breed Standard is a description of the ideal Dobermann. The question which is often debated is, ideal for what? Does the Standard describe how a dog should look for the show ring, which is effectively a beauty competition, or should it describe the ideal construction for the dog, to maximise its efficiency as a working animal? This is an issue which I will consider in more detail when discussing the 'Faults' section of the Standard. However, a close analysis of the UK Standard does suggest that cosmetic faults are considered to be more serious than constructional ones. It indicates that some cosmetic faults should be penalised, even though they do not detract in any way from the dog's ability to function as a working animal. Equally, it does not specifically identify a number of basic constructional faults as being undesirable, although they will clearly affect the working ability of the dog.

It is probably fair to say that the FCI and American Standards do appear to place greater emphasis on construction than cosmetic appearance, though there are notable exceptions. The truth of the matter probably lies somewhere between the two extremes. What we require is an anatomically perfect dog, which is also pleasing to the eye. In any event a dog whose conformation is far from ideal may well still be sound enough to fulfil all the requirements of a working dog. This emphasis on appearance may also be justified by considering the pet owners, who probably constitute by far the largest category of Dobermann owners, who want a dog that looks pleasing, has a good temperament, but may not have perfect conformation.

The UK, FCI and American Standards are set out in full at the beginning of this chapter. In the following pages, the UK Standard (referred to as the Standard) is analysed in detail, to consider what it actually means, what it requires, and what should be the correct Dobermann conformation; and the three Standards are compared, mainly to identify areas where they appear to be requiring something different.

It is not necessary to be an expert on anatomy to understand the Breed Standard, but it does help. A general idea of what the skeleton looks like is very useful, as it is the framework upon which the rest of the dog hangs. A more detailed consideration of parts of the skeleton will be included in the analysis of the Standard.

GENERAL APPEARANCE
The first three sections, covering General Appearance, Characteristics and Temperament, are probably the most important sections of the Standard. They describe the whole dog and the visual picture created in the mind. The remaining sections describe individual parts of the dog. No matter how perfect these may be, if they do not combine to make a dog which meets the requirements of these first three sections, then the dog is not a good Dobermann.

The term 'soundness' does not appear in the Standard. Nevertheless, we require the dog to be sound, both physically and mentally, to carry out the work for which the dog was created. A sound dog is one which is not only physically capable of working but possesses the willingness to do it. Do not confuse the mental willingness to work with intelligence, as they are two different things.

The Standard asks for a medium-sized dog. This could mean either a medium-sized breed in relation to other breeds, or a dog which is well balanced, as between bone, body, substance and height. A dog which is too coarse and heavy will lose elegance and nobility, whereas a dog which is too light in body and bone will lack strength and power and, possibly, elegance and style as well. What is required is probably a combination of these two options.

Both the FCI and American Standards also ask for a medium-sized dog, but neither helps to clarify which of the two options suggested is the right one.

The Standard calls for elegance. This is almost the most important single requirement in the whole Standard, but, equally, the most difficult one to define. Elegance is that something which catches the eye – a combination of balance, style and general poise. It needs all the other

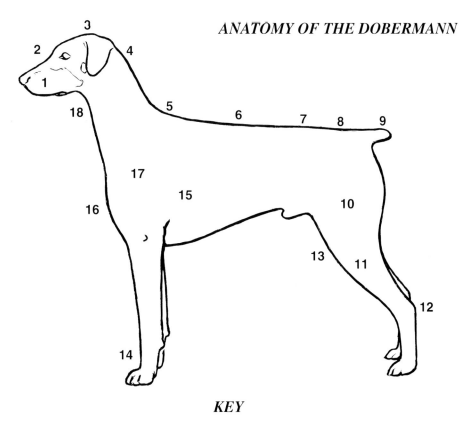

ANATOMY OF THE DOBERMANN

KEY

1. Muzzle.	*7. Loin*	*13. Stifle.*
2. Stop.	*8. Croup.*	*14. Pastern.*
3. Occiput	*9. Tail.*	*15. Chest (Rib Cage).*
4. Neck.	*10. Upper Thigh.*	*16. Forechest.*
5. Withers.	*11. Second (lower) Thigh.*	*17. Shoulder.*
6. Back.	*12. Hock*	*18. Throat*

requirements of the Breed Standard to be met, and to be combined together, so as to produce a pleasing overall picture. A dog can have individual faults yet still be elegant, but equally it can be faultless, but still lack that undefinable something which would make it elegant.

Doubtless we have all stood at the ringside at some time and looked at a dog and said "I like that one." What we are really saying is that the dog is pleasing to the eye. We must be cautious, however, since the assessment of elegance is a subjective judgement, and what is elegant to me may not be elegant to you.

The FCI Standard refers to "the elegant lines of the body"; the USA Standard uses the words "elegant in appearance". These two wordings reinforce the view that elegance is the consequence of a dog having a nice, clean outline, with good balance and flowing lines. The other requirements of this section, such as having a proud carriage, a good temperament and great mobility all help to emphasise elegance.

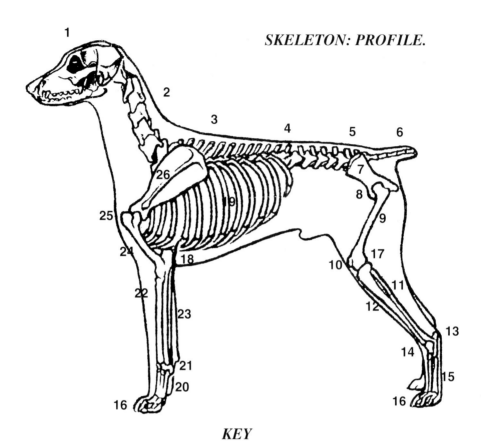

SKELETON: PROFILE.

KEY

1. Skull	*8. Hip Joint*	*18. Sternum*
	9. Femur	*19. Ribs*
Vertebrae:	*10. Patella*	*20. Metacarpal bones*
2. Cervical	*11. Fibula*	*21. Carpal bones*
3. Thoracic	*12. Tibia*	*22. Radius*
4. Lumbar	*13. Hock*	*23. Ulna*
5. Sacral	*14. Tarsal bones*	*24. Humerus*
6. Coccygeal	*15. Metatarsal bones*	*25. Prosternum*
	16. Phalanges	*26. Scapula*
7. Pelvis	*17. Stifle joint*	

The requirement for a well-set body is again not easy to define, but probably relates to the overall balance of the dog. The dog should be balanced between front and rear, height and length, depth of chest and length of leg. The outline should be symmetrical and graceful, with each part of the dog flowing smoothly into every other part, producing a smooth but clean-cut line. These relative proportions are set out in the section of the Standard relating to The Body in the UK

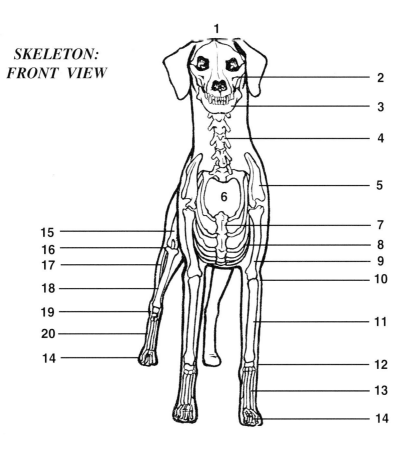

SKELETON:
FRONT VIEW

KEY

1. Skull	*8. Ribs*	*15. Femur*
2. Upper Jaw	*9. Humerus*	*16. Stifle joint*
3. Lower Jaw	*10. Elbow*	*17. Fibula*
4. Neck Vertebrae	*11. Forearm*	*18. Tibia*
5. Scapula	*12. Carpal bones*	*19. Hock*
6. Breast Cavity	*13. Pastern*	*20. Hind middle foot*
7. Breast bone (Sternum)	*14. Toes*	

Standard. In the USA Standard they are set out as part of the section dealing with general appearance, and in the FCI Standard, they have their own section, which follows General Appearance. This reinforces the view that it is these proportions which are referred to in the requirement for a well-set body.

All three Standards require the dog to have a proud carriage, and to be compact and tough. A dog having a proud carriage must not only have good conformation but must carry itself with an air of pride and nobility. This will be an assessment made in response to seeing the dog both standing and moving, and will require the dog's head to be held up high, the ears carried up high, the eyes bright, the tail up rather than tucked down, and the dog to be alert and interested in what is going on around, to be responsive to the handler, to show no fear of surrounding noises and to move with purpose, drive and style.

To be compact and tough, the dog should have a short, square body with a strong topline, and have sufficient substance, and be in sufficiently good condition, to be a working dog. It also implies that the dog should be well muscled, which is a separate requirement in the Standard. The dog should be super fit, not fat and flabby or even thin and scrawny. There should be a spring in the dog's step, and the movement should appear to be powerful and effortless. It should always be remembered that it is the general appearance of the dog, that first impression, which is so critical. It frequently determines the judge's opinion of a dog, even before he has begun to assess the individual parts that make up the whole.

The final requirement of this part of the Standard is that the dog should be capable of great speed. There is no corresponding requirement for this in either the FCI or the USA Standards. This cannot be measured in the show ring. The dog must, therefore, give the impression of possessing this virtue. A dog which meets all the remaining criteria – that is, one which is well-constructed and super fit – will be likely to do so.

The old, pre-1986 Breed Standard required a "light and elastic gait", a wonderfully descriptive phrase. This is still required, appearing in the 'Gait' section of both the UK and FCI Breed Standards.

The requirement that the dog has to be capable of great speed is an interesting one, as the Dobermann is really constructed for endurance rather than velocity. Breeds which are designed for speed rather than endurance, such as the Greyhound, are quite different in build and movement.

CHARACTERISTICS

The Standard requires the Dobermann to be intelligent and firm of character, loyal and obedient. I am sure that we all know that this exactly describes our dogs! The USA Standard is very similar. The FCI Standard, however, is more expansive, and not only describes the Breed's characteristics but indicates the type of work for which it is suited.

This section is one which cannot really be assessed in the show ring. Assumptions have to be made on the basis of what one sees. One has to assume that a dog that is alert, keen and cooperative with its handler is an intelligent dog. The eyes and the general deportment of the dog are helpful indicators. It should be remembered, though, that a dog may be intelligent and firm of character, but be a poor specimen when judged against the rest of the Breed Standard. Furthermore, a dog that refuses to show well could be the intelligent one, which means that a dog's performance in the ring should not be the criterion against which to assess intelligence.

As regards loyalty and obedience, assumptions have to be made on the basis of the way that the dog and handler work together as a team. The better the dog's temperament, the easier it is to achieve this teamwork. Good training clearly helps, as it results in responsiveness by the dog and helps in the overall presentation.

The conclusion to be drawn from this section is that it cannot really be judged in the beauty ring. We have no way of assessing the dog's mental aptitude to do the work for which the Breed was created. This part of the Standard merely defines the characteristics of the Dobermann, which make it the unique Breed that it is. However, it opens up a whole debate as to whether some form of working ability should be proved before a dog can become a champion. This is not required in the UK or the USA. In many European countries, such as Germany, however, the dog must fulfil these character requirements, by means of tests, before being able to gain the title of Full Champion. Tests are also required to be passed by both dogs and bitches before they are allowed to be used for breeding. These tests enable a dog to be assessed against the detailed temperament and working requirements as set out in the FCI Standard. They are considered elsewhere in this book.

I do not think that the vast majority of Dobermann exhibitors in the UK would want to take an active interest in the working side of the breed. They show their dogs as a competitive sport and, while they all hope to end up with a champion, they show for the pleasure that it gives them. However, if the UK adopted the European system, exhibitors need not be affected, since a dog could still win a Championship in the beauty ring, and then be referred to as a Show Champion, in much the same way as happens now with gundog breeds. To gain the title of Full Champion, the dog would need to gain the appropriate level of success in tests designed to assess temperament and working ability. Such a system might bring the added bonus of encouraging more Dobermann owners to work their dogs.

The reason such a system has not been introduced in the UK – and is unlikely to be introduced in the future – stems from the different perception of the Dobermann in the UK, and probably in the USA, compared to Europe. In countries such as Germany they want the Dobermann to be a strong breed temperamentally and to retain that ability to do manwork. In the UK, where most Dobermanns live in houses as pets with children, they have to have a very reliable temperament. It would be extremely unwise to introduce any system of testing which encouraged owners to train their dogs to show aggression. This is particularly true now, with the existence of the Dangerous Dogs Act, which contains a provision for any breed of dog to be added to the list of named breeds of dangerous dogs without any prior consultation. It would be a tragedy if a few highly publicised attacks on people by Dobermanns led to it being branded a dangerous breed and, effectively, banned from the UK. The risk is simply not worth taking. Better to keep the Breed a bit on the soft side in temperament and not to encourage training which will in any way increase its aggression. Those that wish to pursue this form of training will still be able to do so through the existing working trials framework, or in conjunction with those breed clubs that do working training and working tests. The FCI Standard also requires the Dobermann to have a reliable temperament, in that it requires the dog to be adaptable so as to fit the "social environment".

TEMPERAMENT

Correct temperament is difficult to define as it means different things to different people. Pet owners, who make up the bulk of the Dobermann owners in the UK, want a dog which is nice to live with, has a good character and personality, is trustworthy and will not bite anyone, but retains sufficient of the Dobermann aggression to be an effective guard dog. People want a deterrent rather than a weapon, as most would-be intruders will not challenge a Dobermann. An intruder really determined to enter will not be stopped, even by a trained Dobermann. It is not this category of intruder, which is very rare, fortunately, that the average pet Dobermann is being asked to keep out. As I have already said, the Dangerous Dogs Act, with its potential for quick and simple amendment, has placed the onus on all Dobermann breeders to breed for good temperament, not only for the benefit of all Dobermann owners and Dobermann Rescue, but for the good name of the Breed.

The Standard requires the Dobermann to be bold and alert and emphasises that shyness and viciousness are both, quite correctly, considered to be unacceptable faults. Such dogs are not suitable as working dogs or as guard dogs. A shy dog may run and hide, or bite in fear. A vicious dog is difficult to control and may be dangerous and unreliable. As far as the show ring is concerned, if these faults are present, it does not matter how good the conformation may be.

The terms 'shy' and 'vicious' are not defined in the Breed Standard. The USA Standard, however, does define them, in the following terms: "Shyness: A dog shall be judged fundamentally shy if, refusing to stand for examination, it shrinks away from the judge, if it fears an approach from the rear, or if it shies at sudden and unusual noises to a marked degree.
Viciousness: A dog that attacks or attempts to attack either the judge or its handler is definitely vicious. An aggressive or belligerent attitude towards other dogs shall not be deemed viciousness."

It is my view that these definitions are very clear and helpful and should be adopted when interpreting the UK breed Standard. I have noticed, however, that when American judges judge Dobermanns in the UK, they do not appreciate any aggression from one dog to another. On more than one occasion I have seen dogs sent out of the ring for showing such aggression, even though it is acceptable within the American Standard. A more tolerant attitude is taken by judges in the UK, provided the dog is not creating a totally unacceptable level of disruption. In any event, dogs which are this disruptive in the ring are no pleasure to show, and rarely show to advantage.

Although the FCI Standard does not define shyness or viciousness, the European countries will not place a nervous dog. While they do not want a vicious dog either, they do expect the Dobermann to be fearless, have good nerves, be attentive and courageous. The FCI Standard asks for a "medium temperament and medium sharpness" as well as a "medium threshold of irritation". A dog which was shy or vicious would not meet these requirements. The FCI Standard also implies that the breed should show a degree of natural aggressiveness, and a Dobermann in the ring is not penalised for showing this aggression, provided it is properly controlled. Interestingly, the FCI Standard requires a dog to be devoted to the family and to love children. These two requirements are not likely to be put to the test in the show ring or in a working test. Whether or not a Dobermann loves children often depends on whether the dog was brought up with them, and whether experiences with them have been good or bad.

Environment can play an important part in moulding a dog's temperament. Early training helps a dog to adapt to a show environment. A dog may be ill at ease, or even apprehensive, the first time in a show ring, but this may improve with experience. There is no doubt that taking puppies to show training classes is likely to help them. Judges should always make allowances for puppy shyness. They will need to assess whether a puppy is slightly apprehensive or genuinely has a bad temperament.

The temperament of the handler is also important. A nervous handler often creates a nervous dog. This is something which handlers always have to remember and try to overcome.

It is legitimate for a judge to ascertain a dog's temperament, but a judge should never deliberately try to put a dog off in the ring. Temperament quickly becomes obvious as you begin to handle the dog. Judges can help by always approaching a dog in the ring from the front, and handling with a self-confident manner.

Handling should be looked at from a balanced point of view. Expert handling can hide faults. Equally, poor handling can create faults, or, at least, make a good dog look only average. Conformation should always be judged first, and presentation second.

HEAD AND SKULL
The head is the first part of the dog that a judge sees when starting a detailed assessment. It contains many of the characteristics which help to express Breed type, such as personality, character and temperament. The Breed Standard has many specific requirements for the head, possibly more than for any other part of the dog's anatomy. However, it tends to be the overall

THE HEAD

British style: Ch. Kerajun Cousin Kate At Mytanamy. In the UK, the ears are not cropped, which gives a more gentle expression.

Photo: Carol Ann Johnson.

American style: Am. Ch. Sherluck's Castle Rock. This impressive-looking male has sired 33 Champions in a total of 30 litters.

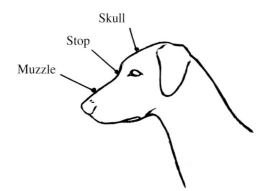 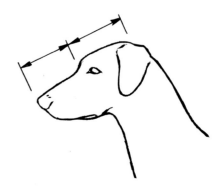

Correct head proportions.

Correct: The length of the muzzle should be equal to the length of the skull.

Incorrect: The length of muzzle is too short.

Incorrect: The length of muzzle is too great.

Incorrect: Inadequate depth to the head.

Incorrect: Loose flews.

Incorrect: Excess skin under chin and neck.

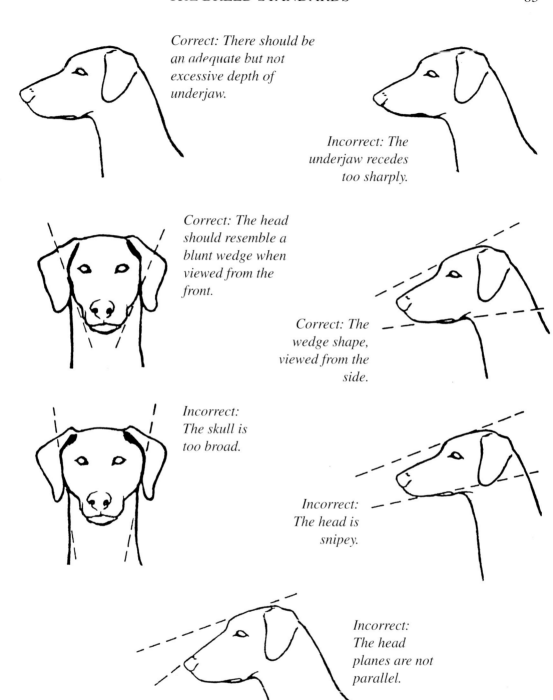

Correct: There should be an adequate but not excessive depth of underjaw.

Incorrect: The underjaw recedes too sharply.

Correct: The head should resemble a blunt wedge when viewed from the front.

Correct: The wedge shape, viewed from the side.

Incorrect: The skull is too broad.

Incorrect: The head is snipey.

Incorrect: The head planes are not parallel.

Correct: The top of the skull should be as flat as possible.

Incorrect: The occiputal bone is too pronounced

Incorrect: The ears are set too low.

Correct: The top of the skull should be flat.

Incorrect: The top of the skull is rounded.

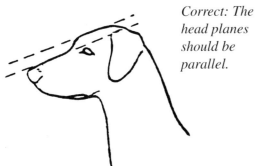

Correct: The head planes should be parallel.

Incorrect: This dog is dish-faced.

appearance of the head which is important, rather than each of the specific points required by the Standard. Although worded differently, the requirements of the UK, FCI and USA Standards are similar.

The requirement for the head to be in proportion to the body is not easy to define, being a matter of opinion rather than of fact. Like so much of the Breed Standard, it is subjective. The head should be in proportion to the remainder of the dog, both in terms of size and length. One would expect to find a heavy head on a solid male and a more effeminate head on a bitch. The head itself

Incorrect: This dog is down-faced.

Incorrect: The stop is too pronounced.

Incorrect: The stop is too narrow.

should be balanced, with the length of the muzzle being equal to or slightly longer than the length of the skull. If the muzzle is too short, the head will appear unbalanced and coarse. Too much length of foreface produces a snipey appearance. The head should be well-filled under the eyes in order to give an adequate depth to the head and thus the required proportion and balance. If not well-filled under the eyes, the dog will appear snipey, with the head not having the desired wedge shape.

The US Standard requires the head to be "clean cut" or "dry". This means that excess flesh or wrinkling on any part of the head, such as loose flews, long hanging lips or excess skin under the chin or on the neck, should be faulted. Loose flews result in too much skin around the mouth. The inside of the lips may then become visible, resulting in a hound-like appearance. In the UK it is customary for exhibitors to trim off the whiskers, in order to accentuate this "clean cut" look. I consider this to be a fallacy, since a judge rarely has time to notice whether or not the whiskers have been removed.

There should be a good depth of muzzle with a well formed chin, giving a proper depth to the lower jaw. This is necessary for the dog to have a hard, strong bite. The dog should not have the appearance of a shark's jaw, with the mouth and lower jaw receding shallowly from the nose. Beware of too much chin, however; this may lead to the front teeth of the lower jaw being pushed too far forward, resulting in the dog being undershot.

The head should resemble an elongated blunt wedge, when seen both from the front and from the side. This means that, when viewed from above, the sides of the head should form straight, but diverging lines, and when viewed from the side, the line along the skull and muzzle should diverge from the line of the under-jaw. If the skull is too broad, the lines will widen in the middle, giving a coarse head. If the head is snipey, or the head planes are not parallel, the blunt wedge is again lost. The stop should neither be too pronounced or too shallow, as this will detract from the required expression.

The top of the skull should be as flat as possible, but the occipital bone should be visible, though not too pronounced. The skin should lie flat and be free from wrinkle, as this would detract from the clean-cut line of the dog. The ears should be carried high, otherwise the top of the skull will take on a rounded appearance, and much of the expression will be lost.

The colour of the nose is required to be black in black dogs, dark brown in brown dogs, dark grey in blue dogs and light brown in fawn dogs. While the UK Standard asks for a light brown nose on fawn dogs, the USA Standard says that they should have dark tan noses. Presumably these two descriptions equate to the same colour. This nose colour requirement is largely self-explanatory and is rarely a problem. In each case, the colour is required to be solid. A loss of pigmentation on the nose, lips or the chin is an occasional problem but when it does occur, it may only be temporary.

The FCI Standard includes specific requirements for the nose other than its colour. It asks for "nostrils well-developed, more broad than round, with large openings without overall protrusion." It also requires the mouth opening to be wide, reaching to the molars, and for the pigment of the gums to be dark or correspondingly lighter on blue or brown dogs.

EYES

The eyes are, of course, always round, but should appear to be almond-shaped, because they are partly covered by the surrounding eyelids, are correctly set into the skull, and are at the correct angle to the head planes. The shape of the eye as it is seen depends, to a large extent, on the shape of the head itself. An incorrect eye shape often arises from an incorrect head. If the head planes are not parallel, it is inevitable that the eyes will be set at the wrong angle as far as one part of the head is concerned.

The set of the eye is important. If the eye is too prominent it will appear round, rather than almond-shaped. If it is set too far into the skull it will result in a small piggy eye. An eye which is set at too narrow an angle to the top of the skull will give a sinister, slit-eyed appearance. The eye should be set in the front of the brow, but should not be so close as to produce a sharp, or quizzical expression. This will not happen where the muzzle is of adequate width.

The Standard asks for a lively, alert expression. The eyes certainly contribute towards this, but they cannot create it on their own. The eyes, ears, tail set and general deportment all play a part.

The colour of the eye is particularly important, as it determines, to a considerable extent, the dog's expression. The part of the eye which is actually coloured is the iris, which surrounds the central pupil, and should be of uniform colour, and as dark as possible. While the precise shade of the eye can vary considerably, it should always blend with the base coat colour of the dog. If the eyes are not particularly noticeable, then the eye colour is probably acceptable. A light, straw-coloured eye is undesirable, as it tends to create a staring expression and to be more prominent. There is a body of opinion which considers that the eye can be too dark, in that a black (in reality a very dark brown) eye spoils the expression. I have observed over the years that dogs with excessively dark eyes tend to lose their sight in old age.

The eye colour is directly related to the presence and distribution of the pigment melanin in the iris. The greater the concentration of melanin, the darker the eye. The colour, or apparent colour, of the eye can vary considerably depending on the light conditions. In bright sunlight the pupil contracts, exposing more of the iris. Conversely, in poor light or artificial light, the pupil is

EYES

Correct: The eye should appear to be almond-shaped.

Incorrect: The eye is too round.

enlarged, so less of the iris is exposed and the darker the eye will appear. The UK Standard specifically identifies light eyes in black dogs as being highly undesirable. While this may well be reasonable, it makes no comparable reference to light eyes in brown, blue or fawn dogs. Since eye colour is genetically controlled, it is illogical to allow light eyes in brown dogs but to consider them highly undesirable in the black progeny. The FCI Standard indicates that yellow eyes are a disqualifying fault. This raises the danger that there could be disputes as to whether the eyes of an individual dog are sufficiently light as to warrant disqualification. No mention is made in the Standard of a prominent haw, but this should be discouraged, since it spoils the alert expression. The FCI Standard implies this by requiring close-lying eyelids. Its also asks for eyelids to be covered with hair, considering baldness around the rim to be highly undesirable. When it occurs, this fault is likely to be due to a dog's condition rather than to its conformation or breeding. It is probably not considered to be too serious a fault, as it is not included in the schedule of faults at the end of the Standard.

EARS
The Dobermann in Europe and America is invariably cropped, giving the characteristic erect ear appearance. This certainly gives the breed a sharper, more alert expression. The Dobermann is not cropped in the UK, the practice being effectively outlawed by the Kennel Club, which provides that dogs which are born in the UK and subsequently cropped will not be registered, nor will their progeny be eligible for registration. Kennel Club regulations also provide that cropped dogs, whether born in the UK or imported, may not be shown, including "not for competition". As a result, Dobermanns in the UK are not cropped and have a much softer, kinder expression.

The FCI Standard requires the ears to be cropped to a length in proportion to the size of the head. It provides that uncropped ears are equally acceptable in countries where cropping is not permitted. The USA Standard, however, states that the ears are "normally cropped..." – which effectively provides for optional cropping. An uncropped Dobermann would therefore not be contrary to the American Standard, but would not be in accord with the FCI Standard except in those countries where cropping is not permitted. This would, presumably, include countries where it is illegal, and those where the national Kennel Club has banned it, as in the UK.

As far as size is concerned, the ears should be in proportion to the remainder of the head and to the dog in general. Small ears are preferable to large ears, as those tend to hang down the side of the head, giving a heavy, hound-like appearance, and the dog is unable to bring them into the

EARS

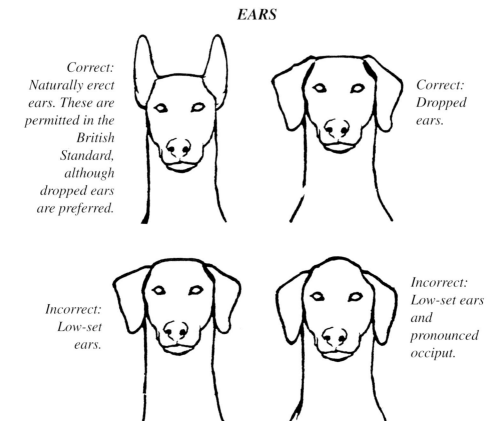

*Correct:
Naturally erect
ears. These are
permitted in the
British
Standard,
although
dropped ears
are preferred.*

*Correct:
Dropped
ears.*

*Incorrect:
Low-set
ears.*

*Incorrect:
Low-set ears
and
pronounced
occiput.*

*Jesse illustrates how
naturally-erect ears
occasionally occur
in Dobermanns.
Jesse is a rescued
dog, so her breeding
is unknown. She is
owned by Mr. R.
Albert.*

partly-erect position, which is so essential in presenting the required alert expression. If the ears are too small, however, they tend to fly, particularly when the dog is moving.

The position of the ear-set in relation to the top of the skull is important. It should be level, or very slightly above the line of the top of the skull; not be set too low, as this spoils the alert expression. Low-set ears are often associated with a domed type of head.

The UK Standard provides for the ears to be "naturally dropped, but may be erect". This wording replaces the pre-1986 Standard requirement for the ears to be "erect or dropped, but erect preferred". Naturally erect ears do sometimes occur, though they do look totally alien to the breed, possibly because they are different and not normally seen. It must be assumed that the Standard is referring to naturally erect ears and the normal dropped ears, rather than to the set of the ears, since it also asks for the ears to be set high on the head. This interpretation means that the re-wording of the Standard did, in fact, change the requirement, contrary to the Kennel Club's stated intention at the time. Whereas erect ears were preferred, dropped ears are now preferred, or at the very least, dropped ears and erect ears are equally acceptable.

MOUTH

Both the UK and US Standards require the teeth to be well-developed, solid and strong. This sounds reasonable enough, but is very difficult to determine in the show ring. A judge must assume that, if the teeth look solid and strong, then they are. It is unlikely that one will find teeth that are so obviously weak as to not meet this requirement. The FCI Standard asks for teeth to be normally sized.

Broken teeth may suggest some weakness, but this may be due to an accident. It must be borne in mind that a severe accident can damage any teeth, but weak teeth may never suffer an accident. The wearing down of the teeth is a normal ageing process and should not be construed as being due to weakness. Misaligned teeth, or a level bite, are likely to cause the early wearing down of the teeth, which is why they are such undesirable faults.

It is interesting that the USA Standard ask for the teeth to be white. It qualifies this by stating that distemper teeth should not be penalised. This concession was included in the pre-1968 UK Standard, but is not in the present Standard. The teeth invariably are white and this requirement could well be interpreted as requiring the teeth to be clean when a dog is being shown. This is the only instance in which the Standard specifies a presentation requirement, as distinct from a conformational requirement.

All three Standards require complete dentition. The FCI Standard stipulates that there should be 42 teeth which meet in a scissor bite. The USA Standard goes further, requiring 22 in the lower jaw and 20 in the upper jaw. It also defines a correct scissor bite, with the lower incisors upright and touching the inside of the upper incisors. A correct scissor bite is also described in the UK Standard.

Missing teeth are not uncommon in the Dobermann, particularly one or more of the premolars or the incisors. This fault is not really a surprising one, since prehistoric skeletons of the ancestors of the modern dog have frequently been found to have missing teeth. It must therefore be a well-established genetic factor by now in most breeds of dog.

European countries such as Germany and Holland take a very hard line on missing teeth. Having had a problem of missing teeth some years ago, the Dobermann clubs agreed that it was a fault that should be eliminated if possible. It was therefore decided that a dog with a missing tooth would not be allowed to be graded 'excellent' in the show ring, so would, effectively, be prevented from winning top awards. While this policy, allied to selective breeding, will undoubtedly reduce the incidence of this particular fault, it must be a matter of debate as to whether this over-emphasis on

MOUTH

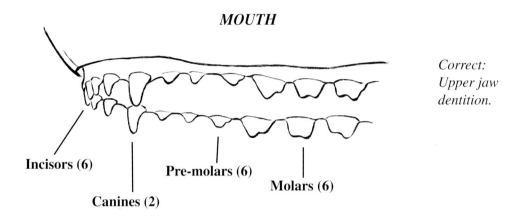

Incisors (6)

Canines (2)

Pre-molars (6)

Molars (6)

Correct:
Upper jaw
dentition.

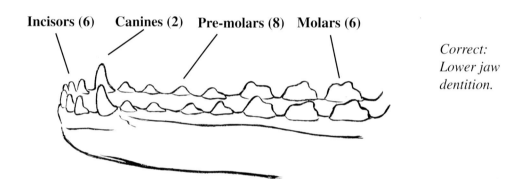

Incisors (6)   Canines (2)   Pre-molars (8)   Molars (6)

Correct:
Lower jaw
dentition.

one fault is justifiable. It could well be argued that this approach to missing teeth is in reality an example of fault judging and that a more balanced assessment of the whole dog would be of greater benefit to the well-being of the Breed as a whole. This would involve a debate as to the relative seriousness of different faults. Is one missing tooth a more serious fault than straight shoulders, a weak back or a lack of rear angulation? In my view, the more serious faults are those which reduce the ability of the dog to perform the work for which it was created.

The USA Standard takes the missing teeth debate further forward, by indicating that four or more missing teeth is a disqualifying fault. The implication of this is that, while full dentition is required, a missing tooth is a fault to be weighed in the balance with any other faults that the dog may have. The more teeth that a dog is missing, the more serious the fault becomes until you reach the point where four missing teeth is not acceptable at all. If four missing teeth is a disqualifying fault, then clearly three, or even two missing teeth must be taken seriously, since such a dog is approaching the disqualification threshold. The FCI Standard, however, stipulates that "missing teeth" are a disqualifying fault. This must therefore mean that any dog with one or more missing teeth must be disqualified.

The generally accepted view in the UK is that one missing tooth is not sufficiently serious to prevent an otherwise good dog from winning. In the absence of the tight control over judging exercised by the German Dobermann Club, UK judges will continue to be free to exercise their

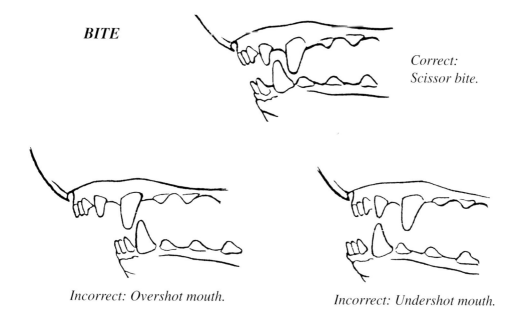

BITE

Correct:
Scissor bite.

Incorrect: Overshot mouth.

Incorrect: Undershot mouth.

Relative position of upper and lower front incisors.

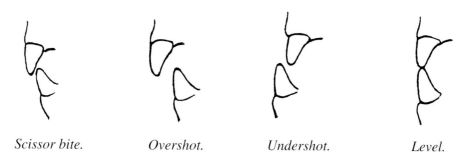

Scissor bite.   *Overshot.*   *Undershot.*   *Level.*

own judgement over how severely missing teeth should be penalised. In asking for a correct scissor bite, the Standards are simply asking for the bite to be correct. Where the upper jaw projects beyond the lower jaw, the dog is said to be overshot. Where the lower jaw projects beyond the upper jaw, the dog is said to be undershot. The dividing line between an overshot mouth and an acceptable scissor bite may be subjective in some cases. The USA Standard is of help here, in that it specifies that a mouth which is overshot by more than 3/16 of an inch or undershot by more than 1/8 of an inch constitutes a disqualifying fault. This does not mean, of course, that any deviation up to these limits is acceptable. It merely emphasises that the greater the deviation from normal, the more seriously it should be considered. The FCI Standard states that an overshot or undershot bite are both disqualifying faults.

A level bite, or pincer bite, is where the upper incisors and lower incisors meet end on. While this is not so serious a fault as an overshot or an undershot mouth, it is one which should be discouraged, as it leads to the early wear of the teeth. A tight bite on a young dog should always be viewed with a degree of suspicion, as the lower jaw tends to push outward as the dog grows older, and can eventually end up undershot. I have known of several puppies which had correct bites at five months, but by nine months the lower jaws had pushed outwards. The FCI Standard makes a level bite a disqualifying fault.

The upper and lower jaws should be of equal length, with the incisors set as square as possible to the jaw. Provided the angle of eruption of the incisor teeth is correct, i.e. as square as possible to the jaw, a level mouth is necessary if the dog is to have the required scissor bite.

The UK Standard requires the teeth to be evenly placed. There is no corresponding requirement in the FCI or USA Standards, though the FCI Standard requires them to be correctly placed.

The teeth should be evenly spaced and equidistant from each other, with no obvious gaps between them, and should be in line with each other. This is particularly important for the incisors, where it is possible for the bite to be correct, but for one or more of the teeth to be out of alignment. A dog with this fault is said to have crooked teeth. Crooked teeth should be penalised, but not so severely as an undershot or overshot mouth. A wry mouth is a similar fault, which occurs where the jaws are misaligned.

Unevenly placed teeth is a fault, but a relatively minor one, and should not be given undue weight in the overall assessment of the dog. A wider than normal gap between the teeth may indicate a missing tooth, though care is needed when checking the teeth, as a missing tooth may not result in a noticeable gap.

The UK Standard specifically states that undershot, overshot or badly arranged teeth are highly undesirable. This is additional guidance to judges regarding the relative seriousness of these faults. Undershot and overshot mouths are also highlighted as faults by the FCI and USA Standards. What, however, is meant by "badly arranged" teeth?

I think it would be reasonable to interpret "badly arranged" teeth as including crooked teeth or a wry mouth, but excluding any slight unevenness of the teeth which does not result in a defective bite or any misalignment. It is interesting to note that missing teeth are excluded from this highly undesirable category, so must be considered to be a less serious fault.

The pre-1986 Standard required decayed teeth to be penalised, but this is not included in the present Standard, which is probably a good thing, since it was never clear whether decayed teeth included broken or damaged ones. The implication is that judges will not be required to penalise damaged teeth, whether resulting from decay or injury. They will be required to penalise them if they are removed, however, since they will then be missing teeth. Equally, it is interesting to note that a misaligned tooth is "highly undesirable", but if the tooth is removed, it merely becomes a missing tooth, which is a fault, but not a "highly undesirable" one.

NECK

The UK, FCI and USA Standards are remarkably similar in their requirements for the neck. Apart from different terminology, the only difference is in the UK Standard, which does not specifically indicate that the nape of the neck should widen gradually towards the chest and the shoulders. The dimensions of the neck should be in proportion to the remainder of the dog, particularly the head and the body. To some extent, this is going to be a subjective judgement.

A reasonable length of neck is required, as this results in longer muscles which tire less easily than shorter ones, so giving better endurance. They also maximise the leverage of the dog's forward reach. The right length of neck is also important, because it will enable the dog to carry the head with the degree of nobility that the Standard seeks. With a short, stuffy neck, the dog will never be able to exhibit this, however good may be the head and expression.

To create a visually pleasing outline the neck should be carried proudly, flowing from the back

NECK

Correct: The neck should taper from the shoulders to the set-on of the head.

Incorrect: Too long and thin.

Incorrect: Ewe neck.

Incorrect: A short neck gives a stuffy appearance

Incorrect: Straight shoulders may result in a short neck and a hump over the withers.

of the head into the topline in one continuous sweep. This does, of course, depend to a considerable extent on the shoulders. The neck should be slightly convex, or arched. This is to enable it to absorb stress, and serve as the anchor for several muscles and ligaments, some of which play an important role during movement.

A straight, long, thin neck is wrong. Apart from failing the function test, it also spoils the whole outline of the dog and loses the symmetry. A concave neck is also wrong, but is a more serious fault. Not only does it spoil the outline, but it strongly suggests a straight shoulder. A short, thick neck is usually due to a forward shoulder, which gives the appearance of a girdle around the base of the neck, thereby losing the clean flow-through and giving a stuffy appearance. Straight shoulders may also cause a short neck, as well as a hump over the shoulders, which breaks the clean flow of the neckline across the withers and into the topline.

As I have already indicated, the neck muscles are very important. The Standard requires that these should be clearly visible. The neck should be free of any dewlap or loose skin, defined in the FCI and USA Standards as a "dry" neck. Dewlap and loose skin are undesirable because they look unattractive and detract from the dog's elegance.

FOREQUARTERS

A knowledge of the structure of the forequarters is essential in order to fully understand the correct conformation. The construction of the forequarters is vital, as they play a crucial role during movement. They are subject to more stresses and strains than any other part of the dog. They support the major part of the dog's weight. During movement, they check the dog's fall forward. They receive the impact, and absorb most of the shock, of landing after each step. Compare this with the hindquarters, which merely provide the power for movement. Even here, though, the forequarters provide some assistance in propelling the dog forward by giving an additional push during the final stages of each step.

The shoulder blade and upper arm should meet at an angle of about 90 degrees. This also results in a requirement for an angle of about 45 degrees between the shoulder and the horizontal. This 90-degree angulation provides the maximum ability to propel the dog forward, by enabling the front legs to rotate forwards and backwards in the longest possible arc. It therefore gives maximum efficiency with the minimum strain on the forequarters. The 90-degree angulation also maximises the horizontal (forward) movement and minimises the vertical (up-down) movement. As the angle increases, the forward movement decreases and the up-down movement increases. Conversely, as the angle decreases, the forward movement increases and the up-down movement

ANATOMY OF THE FOREQUARTERS

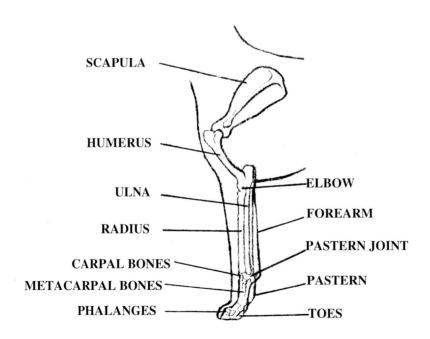

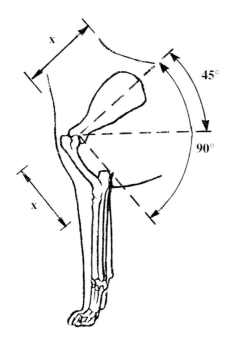

The shoulder-blade and upper arm should meet at 90 degrees; the shoulder should be set at a 45 degree angle to the horizontal. The length of the shoulder (x) should equal the length of the upper arm.

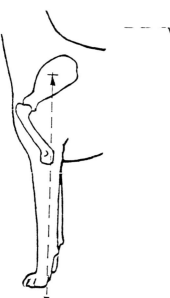

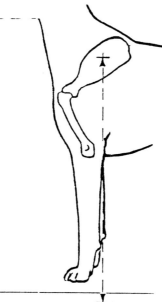

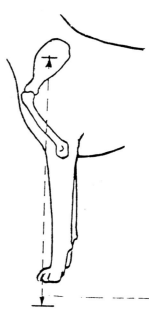

Correct: Shoulders with the centre of gravity directly over the back part of the foot.

Incorrect: Excess length of shoulder brings the centre of gravity behind the front legs.

Incorrect: Excess length of forearm brings the centre of gravity in front of the legs.

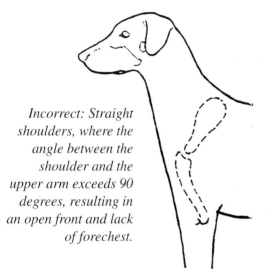

Incorrect: Straight shoulders, where the angle between the shoulder and the upper arm exceeds 90 degrees, resulting in an open front and lack of forechest.

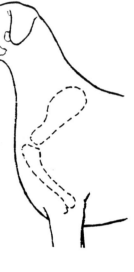

Incorrect: Forward shoulders, where the angle between the shoulder and the upper arm is 90 degrees, but the whole assembly is too far forward, resulting in a short neck, heavy shoulders, and excessive forechest.

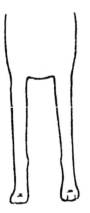

Correct: The elbows are close to the chest, the legs are straight and parallel with each other, and the feet are turning neither in nor out.

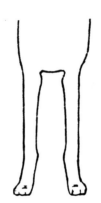

Incorrect: French front, with inadequate width of forechest, legs too close together, and feet turning outwards.

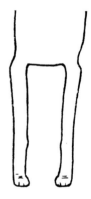

Incorrect: Bow-legged front, with loose elbows, too much width of forechest, legs too far apart, and feet turning inwards.

decreases. This concept will be considered in more detail when considering movement. Although a 90-degree angle is the ideal, the angulation normally found on the Dobermann is about 105 degrees. The FCI Standard stipulates that the angle between the upper arm and the shoulder blade should be approximately 105-110 degrees, and the angle to the horizontal approximately 50 degrees. With the correct shoulder/upper arm angulation, the centre of gravity of the dog will be

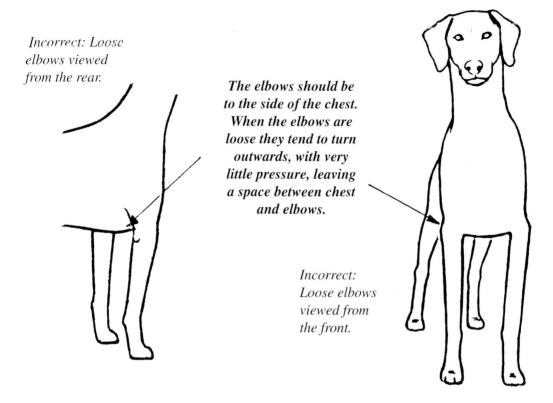

Incorrect: Loose elbows viewed from the rear.

The elbows should be to the side of the chest. When the elbows are loose they tend to turn outwards, with very little pressure, leaving a space between chest and elbows.

Incorrect: Loose elbows viewed from the front.

directly over the front legs. A vertical line dropped from the centre of the shoulder bone should be over the back pad of the foot.

Where the angle between the shoulder blade and the upper arm is too great, the dog is said to have straight shoulders, which are undesirable, as they result in a short neck, open front, lack of forechest, increased height of the front legs and reduced forward reach. This may lead to the forequarters not being balanced with the hindquarters, resulting in the front feet pounding into the ground, leading to extra shock to the forequarters.

Where the angulation is acceptably close to the required 90 degrees, but the whole shoulder assembly is pushed too far forward, the dog is said to have forward shoulders. This will result in a short neck, heavy shoulders, giving the appearance of a girdle around the base of the neck, an over-pronounced brisket, and a generally unbalanced appearance to the front of the dog. The excessive brisket may also push the front legs too far under the dog, leading to excess bending of the pasterns.

Forward shoulders will also result in the loss of the graceful flow from the neck, over the shoulders and into the topline. They will tend to give a prominent hump at the withers, a dip behind the shoulders and an apparent lengthening of the body. This may be more noticeable on the move. The FCI Standard does indicate that forward shoulders are a fault by stating that the shoulder should be well set back.

The shoulder blade and the upper arm should be approximately equal in length. They cannot be measured when judging, hence the qualification "approximately" in the UK Standard. The FCI Standard merely asks for the upper arm to be of good length. A short upper arm, relative to the shoulder, is highly undesirable. It gives the appearance of the shoulders being too steep, or straight in upper arm, and tends to pull the front legs forward, resulting in a straight front with inadequate brisket. Apart from any functional deficiency, this clearly spoils the outline of the dog.

The relative lengths of the shoulder and the upper arm are also important, as they determine the position of the elbow in relation to the rib-cage. When the upper arm is relatively short, the elbows will be positioned further forward than when the upper arm is longer. If the upper arm is shorter than the shoulder, it will also bring the front legs forward so that they are in front of the centre of gravity of the dog, rather than immediately under it.

An excess length of forearm will create the impression of a forward shoulder and will give the impression of the dog having almost too much brisket. It will also bring the centre of gravity in front of the front legs. Although undesirable, an excess length of forearm is not so structurally weak, and the excess brisket it creates is less visually unacceptable.

The front legs should be straight and parallel with each other. This is generally associated with the front feet also being straight, in that they face due forward. Where the legs incline towards each other, then turn outwards at the feet, the dog is said to be 'french fronted' or to have 'chippendale legs'. This fault may be due to one of a number of possible causes, such as loose elbows, light or weak bone, lack of width between the front legs, open fronted or inadequate spring of rib. A french front not only impairs movement, but spoils the appearance of the dog.

If the front legs bow outwards from the elbow, the feet will frequently turn inwards. The dog will thus have a bow-legged front and will be toeing-in. This fault may be due to loose elbows or a barrel-chest, causing the elbows to be pushed outwards. It may also be due to the malformation of the leg bones, possibly due to the dog's rearing or environment.

The UK Standard requires the bone to be in proportion to the body structure. While this is set out within the section on the forequarters, it does, of course, equally apply to the whole dog. The legs give the best indication of bone thickness. They should not appear spindly, nor should they appear coarse and heavy, though such bone may be appropriate for a coarse, heavy dog. To some extent, what is acceptable comes down to the subjective judgement of individual judges. On balance, it is better to err on the side of too much bone rather than too little, since the Dobermann is supposed to be a working dog.

The forequarters should be muscled and sinewy. This will only really be evident by looking at the dog as a whole, who should be hard and strong and in good condition, rather than weak and flabby.

The elbows should lie close to the chest and the brisket should extend down to the elbows. The shoulder blade (the scapula) is attached to the sides of the first five ribs and the adjacent thoracic vertebrae by means of muscles and ligaments. The dog has no collarbone, which means that these muscles and ligaments are the only attachment. Strong muscular development in this region is absolutely essential, as without it, movement will suffer, the shoulders will be loose and the back soft. Inadequate muscle or sinew will allow the shoulder blade and upper arm to turn outwards with very little pressure.

Loose elbows is a serious fault. It means that the front pillars of the dog (the upper arm and the forearm) are bent at the elbows, instead of being vertically straight. This structure is inherently weak and less efficient, as it places outward pressure on the elbow joints and the dog will tire more quickly. It can easily be detected on a standing dog. There will be daylight between the chest and the elbows, which will be particularly evident when looking at the elbows from the rear. Place a hand on the dog's withers and rock the dog slightly; if the elbows are loose, you will see them spring outwards. Loose elbows, usually due to a shallow chest, a lack of spring of rib, or a barrel-chest, are very obvious when the dog moves, as the daylight between the elbows and the chest will be even more evident than when the dog is standing. The dog may also be moving wide on the front.

Both the FCI and the USA Standards consider the pasterns as part of the forequarters. The UK Standard, however, considers them as part of the feet.

BODY

The Dobermann is a square dog: height, measured vertically from the withers to the ground, equals length from the forechest to the rear projection of the upper thigh. To put it more simply, height equals length. The depth of the dog from the withers to the brisket should equal the distance from the brisket to the ground. This latter requirement is included in the FCI Standard, though not in the USA or UK Standards. The FCI Standard also states that the length should not be greater than 5 per cent more than the height for males and 10 per cent for females.

Where the length of the dog is greater than its height, the dog is said to be 'long in body'. Such a dog may retain a strong topline but very often it results in a soft, weak back, usually referred to as

BODY

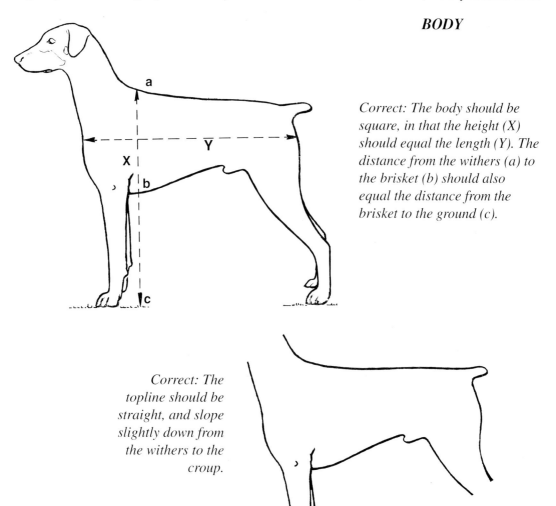

Correct: The body should be square, in that the height (X) should equal the length (Y). The distance from the withers (a) to the brisket (b) should also equal the distance from the brisket to the ground (c).

Correct: The topline should be straight, and slope slightly down from the withers to the croup.

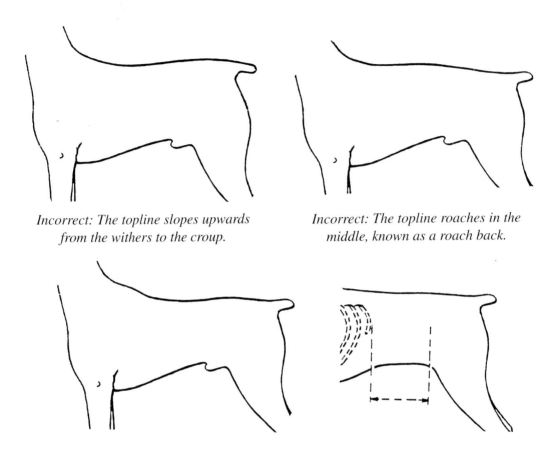

Incorrect: The topline slopes upwards from the withers to the croup.

Incorrect: The topline roaches in the middle, known as a roach back.

Incorrect: The topline dips in the middle, known as a sway back.

Incorrect: The loin is too long.

a 'sway back' or 'saddle back'. This excess length of body may be due to the dog being short in leg, long-ribbed or more usually, long in the loin. Other faults may create the illusion of a long body, such as a shallow chest or forward shoulders. Equally, a dog whose hocks are too low to the ground may appear short in height.

The forechest is that part of the chest in front of the front legs, between the neck and the brisket. It should be well developed, and be clearly visible when viewed in profile. There should be a clean, unbroken curve down the underside of the neck, round the forechest and into the underside of the brisket.

A dog lacking forechest will have an open, greyhound type of front. This is less efficient in terms of the dog's endurance, apart from spoiling the dog's outline. A lack of forechest is usually a consequence of other faults, such as straight shoulders, shallow chest or short upper arm, all of which tend to bring the front legs too far forward, so reducing the amount of forechest which is visible. A dog which lacks depth of chest may have forechest but it will not extend far enough down to the elbow. Shallow chests and open fronts often go together.

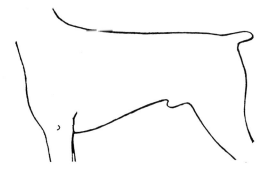

Correct: The brisket should extend down to the elbows.

Incorrect: An insufficient depth of brisket will make the dog look loose at the elbow, long in the body, and lacking in forechest.

The back should be short and firm. This is most likely to be achieved where the height and the length are correctly proportioned and where the shoulders are well laid back. The back is actually the part of the topline over the thoracic and lumbar vertebrae, which is, approximately, from the withers to the croup.

A short back is required because the gait is transmitted from the hocks, through the hindquarters via the back to the forequarters, which then take the weight of the dog on landing. If the back is too long, the correct coordination and propelling power is lost, however correct the structure of the hindquarters.

As already indicated, a soft, dipping back is undesirable, whether when the dog is standing or moving. Equally, a roach back, where the middle of the back is higher than the withers and the croup, is also undesirable. Roach backs and soft backs may be concealed on a standing dog by clever handling, but will be revealed when the dog's movement is watched in profile.

The topline from the withers to the croup should be straight. This is often incorrectly referred to as a level topline, which would, of course, be parallel to the ground, rather than sloping slightly. The topline should not slope upwards, since the hindquarters would almost certainly lack the necessary angulation. It is not unusual for puppies to grow in this manner, however, particularly between five and nine months of age. The FCI Standard asks for the withers to be pronounced in height and length, especially in males, in order to determine the slope of the topline rising from the croup to the withers. In practice, any pronouncement of the withers spoils the clean flow of the dog's outline, and is not necessary to determine the slope of the topline.

The UK Standard does not specifically refer to the croup itself, other than that it should be well filled out. The FCI and USA Standards ask for the croup to be slightly rounded. The USA Standard takes it one stage further by saying that it should not be steep, and the FCI Standard says that it should fall slightly but hardly perceptibly. What the Standards are effectively telling us is that the topline over the croup should be more or less level, and that the upper ends of the pelvic bones should not protrude above the topline. While the croup may be slightly rounded, there is no doubt that a straight topline from the withers through to the tail, with the tail appearing to be a continuation of the topline, gives the most pleasing outline for the Dobermann. Where the topline dips over the croup, the clean outline is lost, with a resultant loss of elegance.

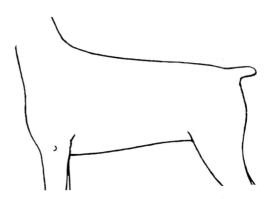

Incorrect: Insufficient tuck-up, making the underline appear almost parallel to the ground, and giving the dog a heavy appearance.

The UK Standard states that "bitches may be slightly longer to loin". This is a very interesting concession to bitches. It is also a very curious one. The pre-1986 Standard contained a similar concession, which stated "the female, needing room to carry litters, may be slightly longer in loin", and provides not only the justification for this, but clarifies that "longer to loin" actually means that it is extra length in the loin which is acceptable, rather than in the body up to the loin. The FCI Standard allows the bitch to be slightly longer in loin "because she requires space for suckling". As already indicated, the Standard allows the bitch's length to exceed its height by 10 per cent, compared with 5 per cent for males.

It is debatable whether this concession is really needed or whether advantage of it is ever taken, because it would appear to be in conflict with the requirement for a square dog, where the length equals the height. It almost implies two standards – one for males and the other for females. Breeding from bitches with this permitted feature is likely to increase the length of loin in both the male and female offspring, since, like anything else, it is genetically controlled. I am not aware of any evidence indicating that bitches need this extra length in order to facilitate their maternal duties, or, indeed, whether square bitches have any problems rearing their puppies.

The loin should be strong and muscled, since it has muscle connections with the hindquarters, so plays an important part in movement.

Just as the dog should have plenty of forechest, the brisket, which is the underside of the chest, should extend down to the elbows. When it does not do this, the dog is said to be "shallow in chest". This is an undesirable fault, as the dog will have insufficient heart and lung room, the elbows will appear loose, forechest will be lacking and the dog will appear to be long in the body.

Apart from having adequate depth, the chest should also be the correct shape. There should be a good spring of rib, showing a pronounced curvature. Ribs should broaden out from their junction with the spine, then taper downwards, almost flat to the bottom of the brisket, so giving a good width to the body. Where this is absent, the body will be too narrow, giving a slab-sided appearance. This results in the front feet being too close to each other and possibly turning outwards. It may also result in a lack of forechest, since this depends on both the depth and the width of the chest.

The chest may show too great a spring of rib, giving the dog a heavy appearance and too great a width to the brisket, so pushing the elbows out, resulting in a wide front. The upper arm/forearm structure will also be bent, giving a weak front structure.

The belly is that part of the underline under the loin. The underside of the brisket should extend level with the ground for some distance back from the front legs, then rise gently to the belly. The right amount of curvature is probably a subjective judgement to be made by the judge.

The tuck-up should not be too steep, as this results in the dog having inadequate depth to the loin, spoiling the balance of the outline. An insufficient tuck-up is probably less visually offensive, unless it is excessive. It is likely to give the dog the impression of being too heavy, or even too fat. It is certainly true that a good underline depends to a considerable extent on the physical condition of the dog. Dobermann bitches are very prone to false pregnancies; these should be viewed with tolerance, since they are only a temporary problem caused by a hormone cycle, not poor construction.

HINDQUARTERS

A knowledge of the structure of the hindquarters is essential in order to fully understand the correct conformation. They carry out two functions: supporting the weight of the dog at the rear end and providing the driving power for movement. When the dog is standing, the hind feet should be directly under the point of balance, which is the hip joint. This means that a vertical line from the buttocks to the ground should pass through the back foot.

For the dog to move properly the hindquarters should be capable of delivering great power. This depends on the length and angulation of the bones, muscles, the set of the croup and the ability of the rear pastern to straighten when pushing. For maximum efficiency the angles between the various bones should be as near the ideal as possible.

The hip bone (pelvis) should fall away from the spine at an angle of 30 degrees, which permits the maximum swing back for the hind legs when moving. The steeper the croup, the less the amount of swing-back that will be possible. This is important, since by far the largest part of the dog's power is derived from the hind legs during their backward sweep. In addition, a 30-degree angle of croup enables the muscles from the croup to the stifle (the upper thigh muscles) to be as long as possible. It is these muscles which permit the backward sweep of the hind legs, enabling them to compress like a pair of springs and to explode with the power that is so necessary in the Dobermann.

If the angle of the croup is less than 30 degrees, the femur is pulled into a more vertical position, resulting in straight stifles. If the angle is greater than 30 degrees the topline over the croup will not be level but will fall away, giving a steep croup, and a resultant low tailset.

The angle between the pelvis and the thigh bone (femur) should be 90 degrees. The angle between the thigh bone (femur) and the lower thigh bone (tibia) is normally between 110 degrees and 120 degrees for most breeds of dog. The greater this angle, the straighter will be the stifles. Most winning Dobermanns in the UK and the USA tend to be in the region of 120 degrees. The FCI Standard specifically asks for an angle of 130 degrees, which indicates that a slightly straighter stifle is preferred in Europe than in the UK or USA. This straighter stifle is considered to be better for the Dobermann when it is working.

The hind legs should be parallel to each other. This means that the two femur bones should be parallel and symmetrically attached to the pelvic girdle, and be mirror images of each other. When this is not the case, the hind legs may turn in or out, the hocks (rear pasterns) will not be parallel, or the hind feet may turn in or out. In addition, driving power will be lost, or at least less efficiently utilised, and the movement will lose balance and rhythm.

The width of the hindquarters should be about the same as the width of the spring of the ribs. If the pelvis is too small, the hindquarters will be too narrow, there will be insufficient thickness to the thighs, insufficient muscles for proper movement, and the hind legs and hind feet will be too close together. The net result of these faults would be a reduced efficiency in balancing the weight

ANATOMY OF THE
HINDQUARTERS

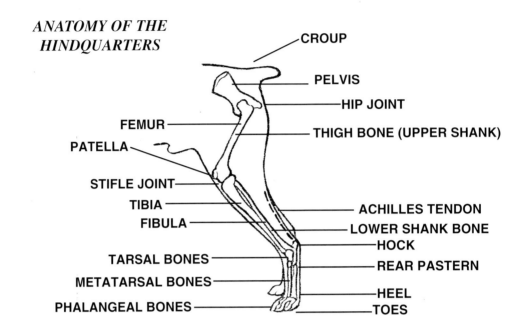

CROUP

PELVIS

HIP JOINT

THIGH BONE (UPPER SHANK)

FEMUR

PATELLA

STIFLE JOINT

TIBIA — ACHILLES TENDON

FIBULA — LOWER SHANK BONE

HOCK

TARSAL BONES — REAR PASTERN

METATARSAL BONES

HEEL

PHALANGEAL BONES — TOES

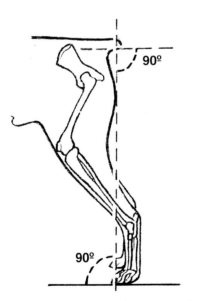

Correct: A vertical line drawn through the back of the buttocks should pass through the centre of the back foot, while the hocks are at right angles to the ground.

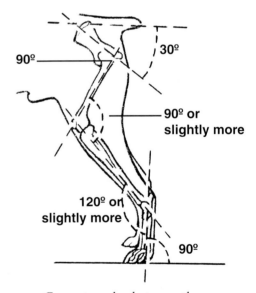

Correct angles between the bones of the hindquarters.

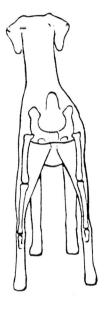

Correct: The bones of the hindquarters should be symmetrical and parallel.

of the dog, whose appearance would be spoilt by a mean, pinched-in look. It is also important that the thighs themselves should have an adequate width. Lack of this results in insufficient muscles, looking out of balance with the remainder of the dog.

The stifle, the front, curved part of the hindleg, should be long and well bent. The optimum bend is achieved when the angles already discussed are achieved, viz pelvis/femur, 90 degrees and femur/tibia, 90 degrees or slightly more. A dog with these optimum angles is said to have a 'good turn of stifle'. Where the angle between the femur and the tibia becomes too great, the bend of the stifle becomes less pronounced and the dog is said to be 'straight in stifle'. If this femur/tibia angle is not great enough, the turn of the stifle will be too great and the dog is said to be 'over-angulated'.

The amount of stifle angulation is also determined by the relative lengths of the femur and the tibia. These two bones should be about equal in length in order to allow a 90-degree angulation between them. This is specifically referred to in the USA Standard. In practice, the femur is usually slightly shorter than the tibia, giving an angle between them of more than 90 degrees, with the angle between the tibia and the rear pastern being slightly more than 120 degrees. The FCI Standard asks for an angle of about 140 degrees. This increased angle is a direct consequence of requiring a greater angle between the femur and tibia.

Straight stifles and over-angulated hindquarters are both undesirable faults. A dog straight in stifle will not be able to move correctly to achieve the long springy, easy action which is so essential for a working dog such as the Dobermann. The dog will take small, mincing steps and have inadequate thigh muscles. Conversely, where a dog is over-angulated, the hind feet will be behind the point of balance, which creates a considerable structural weakness. Movement will be less efficient, since the hind feet are too far behind the dog when driving.

It is very important that the angulation of the forequarters and the hindquarters should be balanced. This is specifically required in the USA Standard. A dog may be under-angulated or over-angulated both front and rear. The dog will be in balance, but will be faulty at both ends. Movement will also be balanced, but again, will be poor both front and rear. If the rear is more

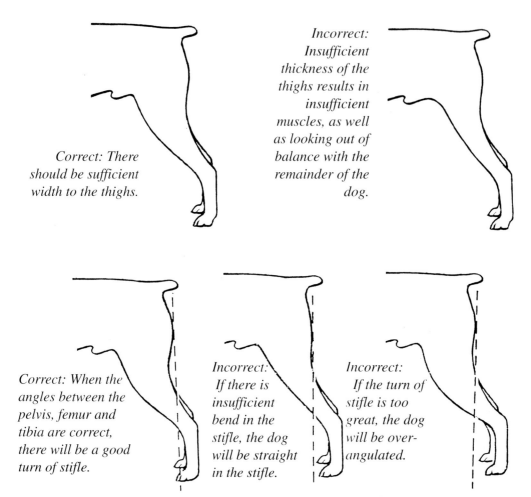

Correct: There should be sufficient width to the thighs.

Incorrect: Insufficient thickness of the thighs results in insufficient muscles, as well as looking out of balance with the remainder of the dog.

Correct: When the angles between the pelvis, femur and tibia are correct, there will be a good turn of stifle.

Incorrect: If there is insufficient bend in the stifle, the dog will be straight in the stifle.

Incorrect: If the turn of stifle is too great, the dog will be over-angulated.

angulated than the front, the rear step will be longer than the front step. If the front is more angulated than the rear, the front step will be longer than the rear step. In both these situation, movement will be unbalanced.

When the dog is standing, the rear pasterns should be perpendicular to the ground, i.e. at right angles to the ground when viewed from the side. This is the position from which the hindquarters should be assessed. The rear pasterns should be relatively short when compared with the tibia, in order to maximise endurance. Where the rear pasterns increase in length, the tibia becomes proportionately shorter, thereby reducing endurance, though increasing speed. Where the rear pasterns, often referred to incorrectly as the hocks, are too short, the dog will appear too low to the ground, giving a squat appearance. Conversely, if they are too long, the dog will appear to be too tall. In practice, the length of the rear pastern should appear to be in proportion to the remainder of the dog and should create the right visual impression. Once again, this comes down to the subjective judgement of individual judges.

The hocks should not turn inwards or outwards. In reality, it is the rear pasterns which will be seen not to be parallel. If the hocks turn inwards, the dog is said to be 'cow-hocked'. This is an

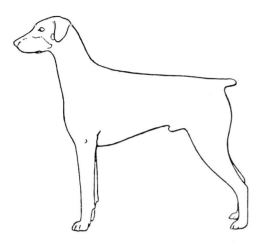

Correct angulation in the forequarters and hindquarters results in the angulation of the front being equal to the angulation of the rear.

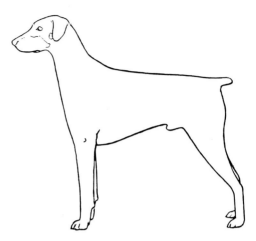

Incorrect: Under-angulated in both the forequarters and hindquarters. Although wrong at both ends, the dog is still balanced in that the angulation of the front and rear are equal, but the dog will step short at both ends.

Incorrect: Under-angulated forequarters and correct hindquarters, resulting in the dog being unbalanced, with the rear footsteps being longer than the front footsteps.

Incorrect: Correct forequarters and under-angulated hindquarters also result in the dog being unbalanced, but with the rear steps being shorter than the front steps.

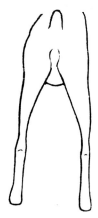

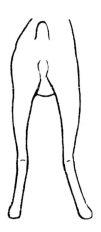

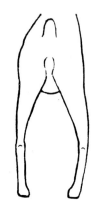

Correct: The hocks should be parallel with each other.

Incorrect: The hocks turn inwards, towards each other (cow-hocked).

Incorrect: The hocks turn outwards (bandy-legged).

Approximate areas of the main muscles of the hindquarters.

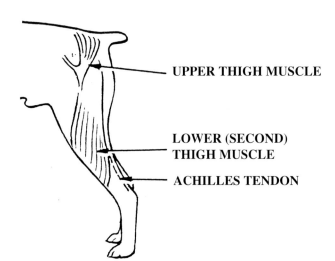

UPPER THIGH MUSCLE

LOWER (SECOND) THIGH MUSCLE

ACHILLES TENDON

undesirable fault, as it hinders the free movement of the hindquarters, resulting in poor hind movement. It is also visually unattractive. Although less frequently seen, the hocks may diverge. This again results in poor hind movement.

The UK and FCI Standards require the hindquarters to be well developed and muscular. This means that they should have adequate bone and substance as well as being well-muscled. These are essential requirements if the hindquarters are going to fulfil the functions already outlined. The muscles should be well-developed and hard, yet supple and clearly visible to the eye, and not be over-developed, as this will give the dog a cloddy, beefy appearance.

There should be three clearly defined muscles – the main thigh (upper thigh) muscles, the second thigh (lower thigh) muscles, and the inner thigh muscles. The inner thigh muscles are the areas of the upper thigh muscles located on the inside of the thigh bone. The second thigh muscles develop with exercise and are necessary to enable the dog to work all day without tiring. The achilles tendon forms an extension of the lower thigh muscle and provides anchorage for it onto the fibular tarsal bone at the point of the hock. It should be clearly defined and strong.

FEET

The feet should be round, compact and tight with well-arched toes and thick pads. Such feet are described as 'cat-like', which will give a round footprint. Where the toes are spread out and the foot lacks the required arch, the foot is described as 'flat-footed'. Flat feet are undesirable, as they are more susceptible to injury and are less efficient in absorbing the shock of impact, thereby reducing efficiency, since the dog tires more easily. A long, close-toed, narrow foot is described as a 'hare foot' and is undesirable for the same reasons. The pads should be thick in order to help cushion the impact of landing. This gives greater endurance.

The UK Standard no longer makes any specific reference to hind feet as distinct from front feet. The front feet are almost invariably bigger and broader than the respective hind feet, but in other respects they are identical. Nails should be hard and strong, shortened if necessary.

The feet should always point forward. They should not turn inwards, described as 'toeing in', nor should they turn outwards, described as 'toeing out'. Both these faults are visually unattractive, particularly as they are often associated with other faults of the forequarters.

The UK Standard is interesting in that it refers to the pasterns within the section on feet, whereas the FCI and USA Standards treat them as part of the forequarters. The front legs should drop in a straight line from the elbows to the feet, which means that the dog should have good pasterns. There should be a slight bend at the pastern joint, since it is a hinge, cushioning the shock as the feet land. It also reduces the amount of shock transmitted to the shoulders. The FCI Standard stipulates that this bend should not exceed 10 degrees.

If the pasterns have no bend, they do not provide the necessary 'give'. There is also the risk of knuckling over. If there is no 'give' at the pasterns, the shock on landing is transmitted through to the shoulders, instead of being absorbed by the pasterns. There should be just enough bend to be

FEET

Correct: The feet should be cat-like in that they should be short, deep, round, compact and tight, with well-arched toes and firm thick pads.

Incorrect: Flat feet are ugly and less efficient since the toes are not held close. The foot lacks the required arch and becomes spread out.

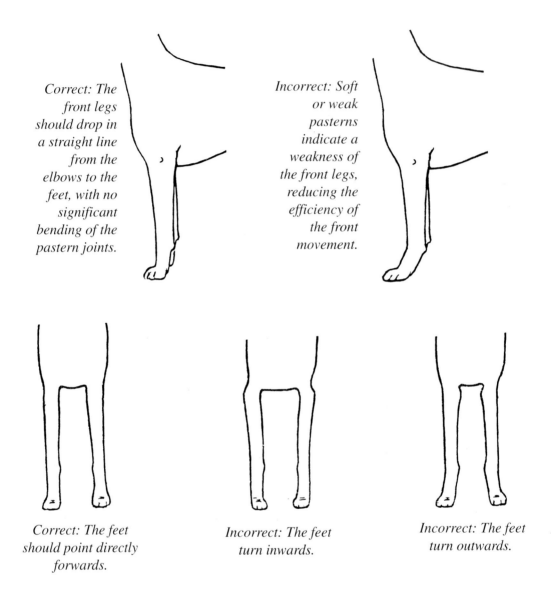

Correct: The front legs should drop in a straight line from the elbows to the feet, with no significant bending of the pastern joints.

Incorrect: Soft or weak pasterns indicate a weakness of the front legs, reducing the efficiency of the front movement.

Correct: The feet should point directly forwards.

Incorrect: The feet turn inwards.

Incorrect: The feet turn outwards.

discernible; anything greater is unacceptable. A dog which has too much bend at the stifle is referred to as having 'soft pasterns', 'weak pasterns' or being 'down on the pasterns'. Weak pasterns also usually result in the dog being flat-footed, thereby resulting not only in a structural weakness, but in legs and feet that are visually unattractive.

The FCI, USA and UK Standards all have differing requirements regarding dewclaws. Earlier FCI Standards stated that, as far as the hindquarters are concerned, dewclaws are "not permitted", but made no reference to them as regards the forequarters. However, the current FCI Standard makes no reference to them at all. The USA Standard states that for the front feet, dewclaws "may" be removed and for the rear feet, dewclaws "are generally" removed. The UK Standard simply states "all dewclaws removed". A literal interpretation of these three Standards suggests

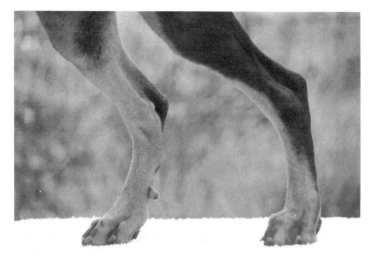

Roanoke Ember proving that rear dewclaws do sometimes occur, although they are very unusual.

Photo: Alan Waterhouse.

that the removal of dewclaws in the UK is mandatory, in the USA it is optional, and in FCI countries it is optional in that the Standard gives no specific guidance.

Dewclaws are normally removed from the front feet because they can be damaged and because they spoil the clean lines of the legs. Dewclaws do not normally occur on the back feet, but when they do, they should be removed for the same reasons.

In the UK the non-removal of front dewclaws from a dog means that the dog has a fault, because the Breed Standard requires them to be removed. If they are not removed, however, to what extent should it be penalised? Probably very little, since it is not a constructional problem nor a hereditary problem; it is a purely visual one.

TAIL

The Dobermann is one of the traditionally docked breeds. It is probably true to say that the Breed was designed to be a docked Breed, rather than a Breed which at some time in the past began to be docked. Over recent years docking has become a very emotive issue in many countries, not least in the UK.

The UK Standard was changed in 1986 by the inclusion of the phrase "customarily docked at first or second joint". This amendment was inserted into the Breed Standard unilaterally by the Kennel Club without any prior consultation with the Breed clubs. A similar amendment was made to the breed standards of all the other normally docked breeds in the UK. This phrase means optional docking. It is not open to interpretation, because it refers to the act of docking, not to the length of the dock.

The USA Standard continues to require the Dobermann to be docked. An undocked Dobermann in the USA would not, therefore, be in accord with the Breed Standard. The FCI Standard requires the tail to be docked, but allows the tail to remain undocked in countries where docking is legally not permitted.

The length of the dock plays a crucial role in determining the overall style and outline of the Dobermann. The objective when docking is to leave sufficient length of tail to give the most pleasing effect to the overall outline of the dog. The UK Standard provides for a first or second joint dock. The USA and FCI Standards are more flexible,. The USA Standard states that the dock should be at approximately the second joint, and the FCI Standard requires approximately two tail

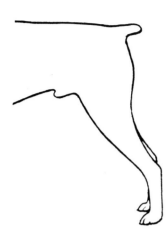

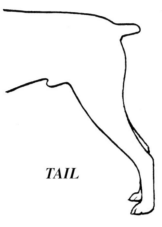

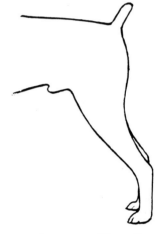

TAIL

Correct: The tail should appear to be a continuation of the spine.

Incorrect: The tail is set below the level of the topline, producing a low tail-set.

Incorrect: The tail-set is too high.

vertebrae to remain visible. This means that first or third joint docks are equally acceptable. In my view a second or third joint dock is ideal, as it gives just enough length of tail to give the dog a balanced rear end and produce the best overall outline. With a complete dock the set of the tail is hard to ascertain and tends to make the tailset look low, even when it is not.

The tail should appear to be a continuation of the topline, with no more than a minimal drop over the croup. This is an essential requirement in meeting the demand for a straight topline. Where the croup is set at an angle greater than 30 degrees, it will drop away from the topline, giving a low tailset. A low croup and a low tailset are both undesirable, as they spoil the outline of the dog, and reduce the efficiency of the rear movement by preventing the hind legs from straightening fully when moving, so cutting down the power output.

As the USA Standard indicates, the tail should not be carried much above the horizontal. It is therefore incorrect for the tail to be held vertically upwards above the level of the topline. While this may technically be a fault, it is not one to which I would attach much significance. Exhibitors in both the UK and the USA tend to elevate the tail considerably above the horizontal, and this undoubtedly adds to the pleasing overall outline of the dog.

The inclusion of optional docking in the UK Standard means that docked and undocked dogs may be exhibited together and must be judged against the same Breed Standard, as well as against each other. This raises two specific problems which are not addressed by the Breed Standard. These are the actual conformation of the tail itself, i.e. its length, thickness, length of hair, colour, kinks in the tail, etc. The other is how the tail should be carried when the dog is standing and moving. In the absence of any guidance in the Breed Standard, it would seem sensible for judges to ignore tails and their carriage when judging. The FCI Standard, similarly, gives no guidance on tails which are not docked.

It is reasonable to assume that the better the dog's topline and its associated tailset, the more likely it is that the tail will be carried high, rather than low. If the eventual consensus within the Breed is for tails to be carried low, then the Standard will need to be amended to seek this lower

Kerioak Kandle in the Wind (Taveys up Nover – Kerioaks Apache Tale Teller). Owned and bred by Christine Nichols. This is one of the few undocked Dobermanns to have been exhibited in the UK. She was won well at Open Show level, proving that an undocked Dobermann can win in the show ring if the dog is good enough to do so.

tailset. The immediate effect of such a change would be that it would alter the whole Breed type and the outline of the Dobermann as we know it today. The real problem is, however, that you cannot alter the Standard for undocked dogs only, as there would then be two Standards – one for docked dogs and one for undocked dogs.

MOVEMENT

The old maxim that correct movement indicates correct conformation is largely true. A dog is moved in the show ring in order to help the judge assess conformation. Judges must therefore watch a dog moving from the front, the rear and from the side, and be able to interpret what they see. In many ways the gait section of the Breed Standard pulls together all the individual requirements set out in the remainder of the Standard.

A dog in the show ring is normally moved at the trot. This form of movement is actually described in the FCI Standard, and is where the fore leg on one side of the dog moves simultaneously with the hind leg on the other side of the dog. The front legs should stretch out, with the front feet landing directly under the nose, as it extends forward. The rear legs should reach well forward, straighten out and transmit power through the back, then follow through with vigour.

At the trot the rear step should be the same length as the front step. The rear foot should land on the spot left by the front foot on the same side. Where the foreleg and hind leg on the same side move in the same line, the dog is said to be moving in single-track position. This is specifically asked for in the USA Standard.

A dog moving in the correct single-track position would leave two sets of parallel footprints. If this was not the case, then the dog would be moving too close or too wide at the front or the rear or both. Moving in single-track position should not be confused with single tracking.

The legs of a dog increasing speed angle inwards in order to counteract lateral displacement. The dog is said to be single tracking where all four feet touch the ground in one straight line, leaving one line of footprints. The USA Standard specifically requires the Dobermann to single track at the fast trot.

Pacing is an economical form of movement, which may be why it is so popular with Dobermanns. A dog pacing moves both legs on one side of the body simultaneously, then both

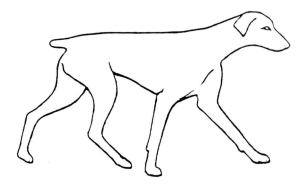

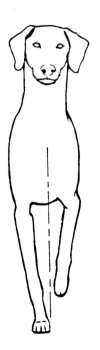

ABOVE: Correct trotting movement, with the front foot landing under the nose of the dog.

RIGHT: Incorrect: Single tracking viewed from the front.

FAR RIGHT: Incorrect: Single tracking viewed from the rear.

legs on the other side of the body. This results in a rather ungainly, cumbersome movement. It is not acceptable in the show ring because it prevents the judge from assessing the dog's ability to move properly and thus inhibits using the dog's movement to help assess conformation. However, pacing is a habit and has no constructional significance. Exhibitors who have Dobermanns which are prone to pace can easily overcome this problem with a bit of training and the necessary know-how. It is interesting, therefore, that the FCI Standard includes pacing within its schedule of faults.

Reference to the need for angulation of the forequarters to balance the angulation of the hindquarters was made when considering the hindquarters. The USA Standard specifically requires this balance, which is particularly important for a square dog such as the Dobermann. Longer-bodied breeds of dog find it much easier to accommodate any lack of balance when moving.

When a dog's angulation is balanced, the length of the front step equals the length of the rear step. As previously indicated, this must not be seen as an excuse for accepting faulty, but balanced, angulation both front and rear, such as where the dog is straight in shoulder and has under-angulated stifles. Where the rear angulation is greater than the front angulation, the hind legs are driving the dog further forward than the front legs will reach. The dog will therefore have to adjust the rear step in some way in order to compensate for the imbalance. A similar situation arises where the dog lacks front angulation, even if the rear angulation is correct. In either case the compensation may take the form of the length of step being altered, crabbing, or moving the front or hind legs out of line. This latter is probably the most common consequence, and means that the front feet and hind feet are producing parallel lines of footprints.

Where a dog is balanced and has the correct angulation in both the forequarters and the hindquarters, the dog will move with the maximum length of forward (horizontal) movement and the minimum amount of up-and-down (vertical) movement. To put it another way, the better the

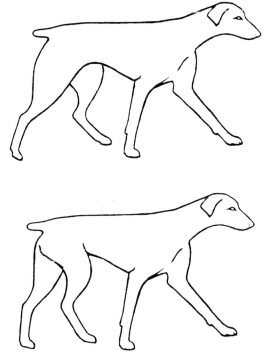

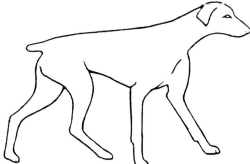

TOP LEFT: When pacing, the legs move in alternate, lateral pairs, giving the dog an ungainly gait.

ABOVE: Under-angulated forequarters make the rear footsteps longer than the front footsteps, resulting in a stilted action.

LEFT: Under-angulated hindquarters make the front footsteps longer than the rear footsteps, resulting in the feet landing heavily.

angulation, the smoother will be the movement. A Dobermann's movement should appear free and effortless. It should be rhythmical and should give the appearance of grace and elegance, which is so much a part of the Breed. It should also be vigorous, giving the appearance of strength and power. The FCI Standard asks for the movement to be "elastic, elegant, agile, free and ground covering", while the USA and UK Standards ask for it to be "free, balanced and vigorous". A dog's movement will only meet these requirements when it is soundly constructed and properly balanced. Judges should therefore use a dog's movement as a barometer of its construction.

When moving there should be good reach forward with the forequarters. As already indicated,

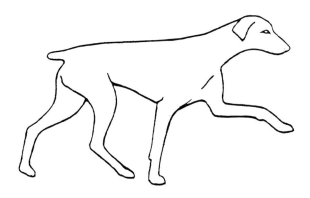

Incorrect: The front feet should not be lifted too high off the ground, resulting in a hackney-like action, and there should be no excessive bending of the pastern joint.

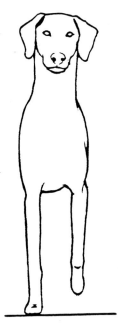

The front legs move in planes perpendicular to the ground and parallel to each other.

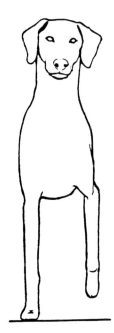

The dog should not move wide in front.

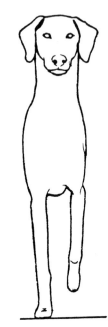

The dog should not move too close in front.

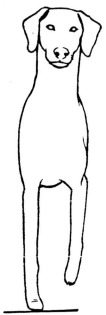

The front feet should not turn inwards.

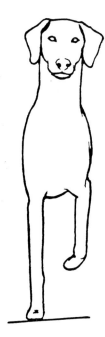

The pasterns should not bend excessively, allowing the feet to flip.

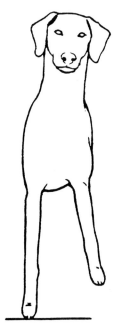

The legs should not be thrown outwards.

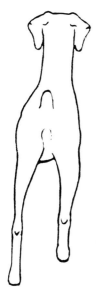

LEFT: The hind legs should remain parallel to each other when moving, and should move in planes perpendicular to the ground.

RIGHT: If the hocks are not parallel to each other, the dog will be cow-hocked, resulting in poor hind movement, and a loss of driving power and symmetry.

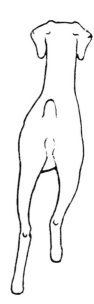

this will occur where the shoulder joint angulation is about 90 degrees. As the angle increases, the forward reach will be reduced. The ability to reach forward is also dependent on the hindquarters being correctly angulated, or the reach may have to be adjusted to match the rear movement. The FCI Standard asks for the front legs to reach out as far as possible, and for the hindquarters to give far-reaching drive. This would seem to be at odds with its requirements of a 110 degrees shoulder angulation and a 130 degrees stifle angulation.

The hind legs should drive powerfully and smoothly with a distinct rotary action, resembling a bicycling movement. Since a true rotary action would produce a circular but static movement, this was qualified by the addition of the word "apparent" when the UK Standard was revised in 1986.

The front legs should move in planes perpendicular to the ground and parallel to each other. The pasterns and feet should move in the same vertical planes as the legs. This correct movement will result in the dog moving in single track position. Where a dog moves wide in front, it suggests that it is loose in elbow or has too much spring of rib. In extreme cases, the front feet will tend to cross each other. Where the front legs move too close to each other, the dog is likely to lack forechest or brisket. The front feet should not toe-in or turn out. Weak pasterns may cause a dog to toe-in, or may be revealed by the dog bending the pastern joint when the foot is in the air, then straightening it out before landing. Dogs which do this are said to have 'flippy pasterns'.

Just as the front legs should remain parallel with each other while the dog is moving, so should the hind legs. Where the hocks incline towards each other, the rear pasterns will not be parallel and the dog is said to be 'cow-hocked'. This is an undesirable fault, both because of the loss of driving power and because it is visually unattractive. If the dog is driving properly the pads of the hind feet should be visible as the dog moves away from you.

The need for tight, cat-like feet has already been emphasised. If the feet are loose, open or splayed, the dog will appear to flop along. This not only detracts from the elegance of the dog, but reduces the efficiency of the movement and the dog's endurance. The topline of the dog in movement should remain firm. This is particularly important so far as the visual impression is concerned. A topline which dips or roaches is not acceptable, as it indicates that the shoulders are faulty, the dog is too long in the body, or lacks the necessary strength and muscle.

COAT

It is the smooth, short coat and distinctive colour pattern which, more than anything else, gives the Dobermann its distinctive appearance. The FCI, USA and UK Standards are similar in that they ask for the coat to be smooth, short, hard, thick and close-lying. These requirements are fairly precise and leave little room for doubt. The Dobermann has a single coat, lacking the woolly undercoat of some breeds. This enables it to lie close to the body. The short, hard hairs enable it to lie flat, giving it a soft, smooth appearance. Any softness of the hairs themselves would result in them not lying flat and giving a woolly appearance. The FCI Standard specifically identifies a long, soft, curly coat as a fault.

The coat should be thick in order to give as much protection as possible from the weather. The thickness of the coat may be influenced by its colour. The black coats are the densest, while the blue and fawn coats are weaker. These dilute coat coloured dogs tend to lose coat on the back and flanks from about three years of age. This is a genetic factor linked to the recessive dilutant colour gene. A Dobermann's coat is a barometer of condition. If the coat is harsh and staring or lacks lustre, it indicates that the dog is out of condition. The FCI Standard states that a thin coat and bald patches are faults. It also includes pronounced thin coats and large bald patches as disqualifying faults. This would appear to invite disputes and debates as to the degree and extent of any coat loss, particularly as these problems can be of a temporary nature.

A grey undercoat is sometimes found on the neck. This is specifically allowed by the USA and UK Standards. Any such undercoat should be concealed by the top coat, i.e. it should be imperceptible. The pre-1986 UK Standard was similar to the USA Standard, in that it referred to it as "invisible grey undercoat". If it was truly invisible, it would not be capable of being seen. For this reason the revised UK Standard refers to it as an "imperceptible" undercoat. The FCI Standard states that undercoat is not allowed. However, it includes a visible undercoat as a fault. It must therefore be assumed that the FCI requirement is the same as that in the UK and USA Standards.

The UK Standard states: "hair forming a ridge on back of neck and/or along spine highly undesirable". A ridge is a line of hair which stands upright, or grows in the opposite direction from the remainder of the coat. It is considered to be a fault because it spoils the clean outline of the dog. A ridge is not considered a fault in the USA. A ridge is only a fault in the UK when it occurs along the back of the neck and/or along the top of the spine. This means that ridges which occur elsewhere, such as along the top of the muzzle, on the forechest or on the brisket, are not faults.

Cowlicks and whirls are similar to ridges but affect much smaller areas. They invariably occur on the neck or shoulders. They are small areas of hair lying flat to the coat, flowing a little to the left or right, instead of straight. The UK Standard does not specifically refer to cowlicks. These should probably be penalised in the same way as ridges, as they have the same visual effect, and ridges and cowlicks may not always be capable of being distinguished. It should be noted, however, that cowlicks on the shoulders are not faults, as they do not occur on the neck or the spine.

COLOUR

The UK and USA Standards identify four acceptable colours. These are Black, Brown, Blue and Fawn (Isabella). The FCI Standard does not accept the Fawn (Isabella) colour. While the UK Standard identifies brown dogs as Brown, they are referred to as Red in the USA Standard and as Dark Brown in the FCI Standard. The Standards do not discuss what shades are desirable. The darker colours are generally accepted as being better than the lighter colours, e.g. dark brown is more desirable than light brown. This is implied in the FCI Standard, which specifically asks for Dark Brown. Browns may be too dark in colour, when they may appear to be neither brown nor black. The actual shade of the colour is probably less important than its uniformity. There should not be any patches of lighter colour on the coat, since this adversely affects the overall appearance of the dog.

The UK Kennel Club's attitude towards colour is that it is a matter of fashion and that no colour will be made a disqualifying fault. This means that a dog of any colour, including white, may be shown, and it is up to the judge whether or not such a dog is placed. However, the 1986 review of the Standard qualified the four acceptable colours with the word "only". This would appear to imply that only the four stated colours are acceptable and that other colours are not acceptable. This is probably the nearest that the Kennel Club is likely to go towards a disqualifying fault. The USA Standard specifically makes any colour other than the four stated colours a disqualifying fault. This means that, unlike in a UK show ring, a white Dobermann could not win a class, even if it was the only entry, since it would be disqualified and so would not be eligible to be placed. Interestingly, the FCI standard merely states the three acceptable colours without specifically making the other colours, such as Isabella, a fault.

The tan markings of the Dobermann are an essential part of the colour pattern. The USA Standard requires Rust coloured markings, while the UK and FCI Standards ask for Rust Red markings. The absence of the word Tan is interesting when it is realised that all Dobermanns in the UK are invariably registered as "Black/Brown/Blue/Fawn and Tan" and the colour of the markings

A ridge is a line of hair that stands upright, or grows in the opposite direction from the remainder of the coat.

A cowlick is similar, but it is a small, circular area of hair lying flat to the coat.

is always referred to as "Tan". It is also interesting that in the UK Fawns may be registered either as Fawn or as Isabella, depending upon which colour is put down on the registration form. However, if they are registered as Fawn they are annotated as 'Fawn and Tan', but if they are registered as Isabella they are annotated as 'Isabella', not as 'Isabella and Tan'.

The tan markings should be a rich dark tan, since this gives the most pleasing appearance and the best colour contrast with the basic coat colour. The FCI Standard includes "markings too light" as a fault. The markings should not be too dark, however, as they would then tend to merge with the base coat colour. The markings should always contrast with the coat colour. This is particularly important on the muzzle, where the clean-cut expression of the head would be lost. The tan markings should be clearly defined and not merge into the base coat colour. The FCI Standard identifies markings which are not sharply defined as a fault.

The locations of the tan markings are set out in the breed Standards. The USA, FCI and UK Standards all ask for the markings to be on the muzzle, above the eyes, the throat, the forechest, the forelegs, the feet, the inner side of the hindquarters and below the anus. It is generally accepted that the chest markings should comprise two clearly defined patches. These should not merge to form a continuous blaze across the forechest, nor should they be so small as to appear missing. The markings on the muzzle should include a clearly defined spot, which should be separate from the remaining markings and not appear as an extension to them. The FCI Standard specifically asks for this spot on the cheeks, and for the two spots on the forechest. The markings over the eyes, on the legs and on the feet tend to vary very little from dog to dog.

Black ticking sometimes occurs on the feet. This is not considered to be a fault and can, in fact, often be very attractive. These markings are often quite pronounced at birth but largely disappear as the puppy grows. The FCI Standard indicates that a "big, black spot on the legs" is a fault. It is not clear whether this refers to this ticking or to something more significant.

The occurrence of white markings, particularly on the forechest and the brisket, is not uncommon. This may vary from a few white hairs to a wide white flash. White markings on new-born puppies can appear to be frighteningly large, but it is surprising how their size can decrease as the dog grows. Some quite large white marks on puppies at birth can end up as no more than a few white hairs when the dog is fully grown.

The UK Standard considers that white markings of any kind are highly undesirable. The USA Standard accepts a white patch on the chest, provided that it does not exceed half a square inch. The FCI Standard includes "white spots" as a disqualifying fault, but their location is not stated, so it must be presumed to apply to any white spots appearing on the dog. White hairs may sometimes occur as a consequence of injuries received, such as from fighting. Such white hairs are not part of the dog's normal make-up, and as such should not be considered to be a fault when judging.

A white toenail occurs on some dogs, usually on one of the hind feet. This can apparently be traced back to the beginning of Dobermann history and would seem to be carried genetically in some bloodlines. White toenails are probably of little concern, and do not merit consideration in the Breed Standards, which are only concerned with coat colour. The FCI Standard does, however, require the toenails of both front and rear feet to be black.

SIZE

The question of what is the correct height for a Dobermann is always one of the most controversial parts of the Standard, as it frequently comes down to a matter of personal preference.

The UK Standard states that the ideal height is 69cm (27 inches) for males and 65cm (25½ inches) for females. This means that dogs of these heights are more correct than dogs of greater or lesser heights. It also means, however, that dogs of heights other than these ideals are acceptable. The Standard then adds that "considerable deviation from this ideal undesirable". It does not define 'considerable deviation', which effectively leaves it to the discretion of individual judges. This may be seen as a dangerous situation, as, if deviations in height are ignored, the uniformity in size of the Breed could be lost. It also increases the risk that attempts will be made to revise the Standard to fit the dogs that are being bred, rather than breeding to the Standard. Conversely, it would be unwise to define the limits of deviation, otherwise they would soon become the accepted degree of deviation. The USA Standard states that males should be 26 to 28 inches, with an ideal of about 27½ inches for males and 24 to 26 inches, with an ideal of about 25½ inches for females. The USA Standard thus gives a range of heights which are acceptable, and then gives an ideal height. Interestingly, it qualifies these ideal heights by stating that they should be "about 27 inches" and "about 25½ inches", thereby building in further flexibility.

Presumably this flexibility is limited to half an inch, otherwise it would allow heights greater than the 26-to-28-inch and 24-to-26-inch ranges which are given for Dobermann height. It should be noted that the ideal height for males in the USA Standard is 27½ inches, which is half an inch greater than the 27 inches provided for in the UK Standard.

The FCI Standard states that males should be 68cm to 72cm, and that females should be 63 to 68cm. This is qualified by a statement that medium size is desirable. It also provides that deviation by up to 2cm above or below the Standard is a fault, and that deviation in excess of 2cm above or below the Standard is a disqualifying fault. One can envisage this leading to disputes as to the precise height of dogs which may only be resolved by actually measuring them in the ring, since this would be a matter of fact rather than opinion.

If these FCI Standard heights are converted into inches, rounded to the nearest quarter of an inch, these heights become males 26¾ inches to 28¼ inches, females 24¾ to 26¾ inches. Heights which are faults are between 26 inches and 26¾ inches, and between 28¼ inches and 29 inches for males, and between 24 inches and 24¾ inches, and between 26¾ inches and 27½ inches for females. Disqualifying faults are below 26 inches or above 29 inches for males, and below 24 inches or above 27½ inches for females.

The USA and UK Standards are very similar in their requirements, though the USA ideal height for males, at 27½ inches, is ½ an inch more than the UK Standard height of 27 inches. The FCI Standard does not fit quite so happily with the USA and UK Standards. The USA range of heights fall within the FCI acceptable range of heights, but the FCI requirements are slightly higher at each end of the range for both males and females. The result of this is that male heights between 26 inches and 26¾ inches, and female heights between 24 inches and 24¾ inches are faults in the FCI Standard, but are within the acceptable range of heights in the USA Standard. Conversely, the FCI heights which are faults due to dogs being too tall, are all outside the upper heights set out in the USA Standard. The FCI Standard disqualifies males below 26 inches and females below 24 inches; these two heights are the lower ends of the acceptable USA range of heights. The conclusion must be that the FCI Standard requires or accepts taller dogs than the USA Standard, and the USA Standard accepts lower heights, which are considered faults by the FCI Standard.

The UK Standard height requirements of 27 inches for males and 25½ inches for females are both within the FCI height range, but the 27 inches for males is only ¼ of an inch above the bottom of the FCI range. Since the UK Standard provides for some deviation from these heights, any males which are more than ¼ of an inch below the stipulated 27 inches, would fall within the fault range of the FCI Standard. Females in the UK would need to be more than ¾ of an inch below the required 25½ inches before falling into the FCI fault range. Males more than 1 inch below the required 27 inches, a deviation which may well not constitute "considerable deviation," would be within the FCI range of disqualifying faults. The conclusion must be that, while the required heights for females are generally compatible, the FCI Standard requires or accepts taller males than the UK Standard, and that the UK Standard accepts shorter heights for males, which would be considered faults or even disqualifying faults under the FCI Standard.

The pre-1986 UK Standard was headed 'Weight and Size', but then never mentioned weight! The present Standard does not refer to weight. This probably matters little, as it would be impractical to weigh Dobermanns in the ring. Nevertheless, the dog should look right and should be in proportion. The Dobermann is a working dog, so should have sufficient bone and substance for the purpose, and not be overweight, or appear flabby and out of condition, which would also mean a loss of the clean-cut outline. Allowance should be made for bitches with false pregnancies, since these are hormonal and temporary; even so, a judge must always judge a dog as seen on the day. A dog may be too thin, particularly young active males. It is my view that conformation and soundness should take priority over condition when judging, though condition cannot be ignored. The FCI Standard attempts to give more specific guidance as to weight by indicating that males should be between 40-45kg and females between 32-35kg.

ENTIRETY

The UK Standard includes a note which states that "male animals should have two apparently normal testicles fully descended into the scrotum." A dog which only has one testicle descended is generally referred to as a monorchid. A dog which has neither testicle descended is generally referred to a cryptorchid. Technically, both these terms are incorrect, since they refer to the total absence of one or both testicles, whereas the dog normally does have the 'missing' testicles, though they are retained in the groin area, so are not descended into the scrotum. The correct terminology should be 'unilateral cryptorchid' and 'bilateral cryptorchid'. Nevertheless, the terms 'monorchid' and 'cryptorchid' are in wide general use and are understood by everyone.

The USA Standard contains no reference to entirety. The FCI Standard identifies both monorchidism and cryptorchidism as disqualifying faults. Monorchids and cryptorchids are considered to be serious faults because they are believed to be hereditary and reduce the dog's ability to reproduce. It is worth noting that no corresponding check is carried out to see whether bitches have two ovaries.

FAULTS

UK breed Standards no longer include specific faults as they did prior to the 1986 review. The Standard now includes a general statement to the effect that anything which deviates from the ideal as described in the Standard is a fault and the greater the deviation, the worse the fault. The USA Standard contains a similar phrase, though it is more strongly worded, in that it states that any deviation from the Standard "must" be penalised to the extent of the deviation. The USA Standard goes further than the UK Standard in that it includes four disqualifying faults. These are mouths which are overshot by more than 3/16 of an inch or undershot by more than 1/8 of an inch, four or more missing teeth, and dogs not of an allowed colour. The FCI Standard takes a different approach in that it schedules an extensive list of faults, many of them disqualfying ones.

The Faults section of the Breed Standard, particularly in the UK and USA Standards, is effectively a pulling-together of the whole Standard. It requires a judge to assess every aspect of the dog against the Standard; to make subjective judgements as to degrees of conformity; and to assess each dog against each other dog, thereby having to make subjective judgements as to the relative seriousness of different faults.

In a way, this rather general statement is not much help, in that it states the obvious, and gives no guidance as to the relative seriousness of different faults or on the accumulative effect of different faults. The UK Standard gives further guidance, in that specific points are identified within the Standard. These are categorised as 'Undesirable', 'Highly Undesirable' and 'Very Highly Undesirable'. In a sense these could be seen as comparable to the FCI Standard's schedule of faults, though it divides them into three degrees of seriousness. These faults highlighted in the Standard are:

Undesirable: Dewlap and loose skin on neck; Considerable deviation from ideal height

Highly Undesirable: Light eyes in Black dogs; Undershot, overshot or badly arranged teeth; Long, weak or roach backs; Long, flat, deviating feet; Weak pasterns; Hair forming a ridge on back of neck and/or along spine; White markings of any kind.

Very Highly Undesirable: Shyness or viciousness; Head out of balance in proportion to body, dish-faced, snipey or cheeky.

This is an illogical schedule of faults in that it fails to include a number of serious constructional faults, e.g. bad shoulder angulation, shallow chests, loose elbows, poor fronts, bad rear angulation, cowhocks and low croups. The implication must be that the UK Standard considers those faults specifically identified as being more important than the constructional faults that I have identified. This considerably weakens the general Faults clause, which indicates that all faults must be taken into account. The USA Standard is much stronger, in that it does not include any hierarchy of specific faults. The FCI Standard is also stronger, in that its schedule of faults is relatively comprehensive, though it gives little guidance as to the relative seriousness of the different faults.

The apportionment of the faults in the UK Standard within the three categories is also illogical, e.g. considerable deviation in heights is only considered undesirable, whereas any form of poor head is considered very highly undesirable.

As I suggested at the beginning of this Chapter, it is open to question whether the UK breed Standard describes the ideal Dobermann as a dog which is most able to fulfil its role as a working dog, or as a dog in the show ring competing in a beauty contest. In other words, which faults are more serious – constructional faults or cosmetic faults? An analysis of the schedule of faults extracted from the UK Breed Standard would seem to give greater priority to cosmetic faults than to constructional faults. I believe that this is wrong and that conformation should always take precedence over cosmetic faults.

When considering the UK Standard it is necessary to consider also the Kennel Club Regulations. These give additional guidance on cropped ears, deafness, blindness, de-barking and entirety.

The Regulations stipulate that cropped dogs are not eligible to take part in any Kennel Club licensed activity. This means that they cannot be shown at any Kennel Club licensed show; this includes 'not for competition' entries.

The Regulations on disqualification state that a dog may be disqualified from any award, whether an objection has been lodged or not, if it is proved to have been totally blind or deaf. While this would seem to make blindness and deafness disqualifying faults, it does include the qualification 'may', so introducing a degree of uncertainty to the regulation.

De-barked dogs can only be shown with Kennel Club approval. Applications for this approval need to be supported by a certificate from a veterinary surgeon.

The Kennel Club now allows a dog which has 'undergone an operation to prevent breeding' to be shown, provided the Kennel Club has been notified first. No instruction has been given to judges to disregard the requirement for entirety, however, so the dog is most unlikely to win in the show ring. This must be correct, otherwise monorchid dogs could be castrated, so becoming eligible to be shown without penalty.

The AKC Regulations also need to be taken into account, in that they state that any male which is not entire will automatically be disqualified. This stance means that no reference to entirety is needed in the USA Breed Standard.

SCALE OF POINTS

The UK Standard used to be accompanied by a scale of points in the 1950s and 1960s, which gave a guide to the relative importance of the various parts of the dog, but it appears to have fallen into disuse since then. It is interesting that this same scale of points was used with the USA Standard as set out by William Schmitt in his book, *The Dobermann Pinscher in America,* which was published in 1940. It has certainly passed the test of time.

While this scale of points may be useful as a guide, it could never be used as a basis for judging, since it does not take into account the relative seriousness of different faults or the inter-relationship of different faults. It does, however, teach one not to fault judge.

Chapter Six

SHOWING AND WORKING

Dog showing is one of the world's great hobbies. In almost every country where dogs are kept and bred, there are organised dog shows. It is a hobby which has no barriers, in that it embraces the young and the old, the rich and the poor, and can be enjoyed by those owning almost any kind of dog, whether pure-bred or crossbreed, Kennel Club registered or not.

There are many reasons why people show dogs. At one end of the scale there are serious breeders using the show ring to monitor the quality of their dogs. If their dogs are not good enough to win, then they need to consider how they can improve their stock. At the other end of the scale, there are many people who own dogs which have no pretensions to being top class show dogs but, nevertheless, enjoy competing for relatively modest awards.

For some people showing becomes a very serious matter, with winning as the sole objective. For such people showing becomes a mania, and they lose sight of the principal objective – namely, to enjoy themselves. Showing must be fun; it must be enjoyable. Never let winning become too important. Many people use it as a release from the normal pressures of life. At a show they can relax with their friends, have the fun of showing their dogs, enjoy it as a social occasion and know that, win or lose, they actually have the best dog in the world. The term 'show dog' is much abused. *A show dog is merely a dog which goes into the show ring.* Most show dogs are only in that role now and again, and are family pets the rest of the time.

Those who do find showing taking hold of them in a big way will probably end up trying to buy a dog with real show potential, and competing at Championship shows. These are very important for all breeds of dog, including the Dobermann, since the winning dogs are likely to be the ones which are used for breeding and for maintaining the quality of the breed. And, of course, it is only by winning at Championship shows that dogs can achieve the coveted title of Champion. Many of the dogs with the best show potential, however, are never shown, being family pets only.

Just as the owners enjoy showing, so do many of the dogs. They enjoy the excitement of the travelling, they enjoy being the centre of attention, and certainly expect all the fringe benefits of showing. I have had several Dobermanns who have learned to recognise ice-cream vans and expect to receive a treat every time they pass one. Dogs also make their own friends and it is surprising how quickly Dobermanns recognise dogs that they meet on a regular basis. They also remember exhibitors who have nice things, such as ring-bait, in their pockets. Showing also makes a pleasant break from the routine of life in the house or in a kennel. Some dogs, of course, do not like showing, and generally make their feelings known by not co-operating and looking thoroughly miserable. Such dogs rarely win and are usually withdrawn from the show ring fairly quickly.

THE ATTITUDE OF JUDGES

While showing is a hobby, it is also a competitive sport and whether or not a dog wins on the day may depend on the judge. Different judges will assess the same dogs in different ways and so end up with different winners. It is this uncertainty that makes dog showing so interesting and exciting. A dog may win Best in Show under one judge one day, but fail to win even a place at the next show under a different judge. The results also depend on other factors, such as which dogs are present and how well they show on the day.

Your objective is to convince the judge that your dog is the best one in the class you have entered. To do this you will need to present and show your dog to the best possible advantage. The judge will assess each dog against the breed Standard and against every other dog in the ring. Judges do differ in their interpretations of the breed Standard.

UK SHOW CATEGORIES

There are three main categories. Exemption shows are run by individual persons, usually in aid of charity and are generally held in village halls or on the local playing field, and are extremely informal. Then there are Open shows, which probably account for the majority of shows held and are, by definition, open to all dogs who are registered with the Kennel Club. Championship shows are similar to Open ones, except that they tend to be much larger events, classifying a wider range of breeds and providing many more classes, which are generally divided for dogs and bitches. The key difference is that at these shows Challenge Certificates (CCs) are awarded to the best dog and best bitch in each breed.

SHOWING IN THE USA

This is very different from showing in the UK. There are only two types of show held in the USA under the auspices of the American Kennel Club – Licensed or Member shows and Sanctioned Matches. Shows may be either a Member show, which is run by a club or association which is a member of the AKC, or a Licensed Show, which is run by a club which is not a member, but which has AKC licence to hold shows where Championship points may be earned. These are why these shows are sometimes called "point" shows.

Championship points are computed on the basis of the number of dogs *actually* competing in the ring, so does not include absentees. The number of points to be awarded in each breed varies with the size of the entry as laid down in the 'Schedule of Points', which is revised annually by the AKC. This schedule is a scale of how many dogs have to be exhibited for different numbers of points to be awarded. The schedule varies from one part of the USA to another, and is based on entries made the previous year. This means that, in some parts of the country, more dogs will need to be beaten in order to gain each point than in others. To obtain the title of Champion, a dog must win fifteen points under three different judges. These must include at least two majors won under two different judges. A 'major' consists of three, four or five points won at a single show, by virtue of the size of the entry. The number of points won can be increased by successive wins at a show. If Winners Dog wins two points and Winners Bitch wins four points, the dog will also win four points if he wins Best of Winners. His points score can increase further – up to a maximum of five points – if he subsequently wins the Group or Best in Show, and, in the process, beats a Best of Breed winner who has won a five point major.

PRESENTATION

Dog showing is a beauty competition so, while the conformation of the dog is paramount, presentation and performance are also extremely important. This means the dog must be well-

TOP: British style: The Dobermann is shown on a loose lead, with the handler attracting attention. Ch. Sallate Black Magic of Coltrac (Ch. Sallate Feris – Brookmans Princess Stephanie). Bred by Mrs G. Hunt, owned by Colin and Hazel Watson. Winner of 9 CCs, 6 Reserve CCs, 5 Ch. Show Best of Breeds, including Best of Breed at Crufts 1994, Top Dobermann Bitch 1994, Best in Show Welsh Dobermann Club Ch. Show 1992, Reserve Best in Show NE Counties Dobermann Society Ch. Show 1994.

Photo: Dean Sawyer.

RIGHT: American style: The Dobermann is stacked and held in position on a taut lead. Am. Ch. Barricini dob Mann. Owned by Edd and Irene Bivin.

trained, to show off attributes to advantage. A well-trained dog makes showing look easy. However, this is a deception, as showing is not easy and is the end-result of a great deal of hard work.

If you have acquired or bred your Dobermann with the intention of showing, you should start show training as early as possible – seven weeks is the ideal age, or eight weeks, if that is when the puppy comes to you. Begin by standing the puppy on a table. Initially the puppy will object and want to get down. The puppy must become accustomed to being stacked up, that is having the legs positioned so that the puppy is standing four-square, with the front legs at right angles to the ground and parallel to each other, and the hocks of the hind legs also at right angles to the ground and parallel with each other.

Hold the puppy's head with one hand and lift the tail into a position just above the horizontal with the other hand. The puppy will learn to accept this 'top and tail' method of being stacked up very quickly. *Do not overdo the training – a little and often is the best way.* When the puppy is a few weeks older and has accepted wearing a collar and lead, you should teach the puppy to accept being stacked on the ground. You should also introduce the commands Stand and Stay, and practise using your voice to give praise and encouragement, making sure you use a tone with gives reassurance that everything is well. Once the puppy has learned to stand four-square and is willing to hold this pose after being stacked, you can begin to introduce the idea of ring-bait. Initially this can be anything the puppy finds attractive, such as cheese, liver, sausage or a piece of biscuit. Hold this in front of the puppy's nose, who will then pull forward in the hopes of obtaining it. The art of using ring bait is to get the dog to pull forward to accentuate flowing lines and an alert look, while still maintaining the pose. If you use ring bait in the show ring, do it discreetly. Do not scatter it round the ring, which will put off other dogs, and do not stuff food into your dog's mouth just as the judge want to examine the teeth. Make sure you can show your dog without bait if the need should arise, as some judges will not allow you to use it.

Once your puppy has learned how to stand in show-pose, and has completed all the primary vaccinations, you will both need to go to show-training class, sometimes referred to as a ringcraft class. These are similar to obedience training classes but with the emphasis on the arts and skill of showing. They will give your young dog experience of being handled by strangers and will generate something approaching a ring atmosphere. In many ways it is the socialising aspect of these ringcraft classes which is the most valuable. Your Dobermann needs to get used to being among other dogs and people at an early age. Most Dobermanns love training classes, which eventually become social evenings for both dogs and owners. Training at home should continue in parallel with the classes. While you are busy training your future show dog, you should also be learning the breed Standard and be able to assess your dog against it, in order to discover any faults and virtues. If you are new to the world of dog showing you will not find this easy and will probably only be able to spot your dog's virtues. Part of your learning process should be to read as much as you can about Dobermanns, to look at pictures of winning dogs and to attend shows. Remember this learning process never ends and, if you ever think you know it all, you are almost certainly deceiving yourself. Also beware of those instant experts in the breed who think that they know it all after a mere year or two. They have already deceived themselves, but don't let them deceive you.

ENTERING YOUR FIRST SHOW
Once your puppy is relatively well-behaved and will show well you should consider entering your first show. These early shows are really an extension of your training, and you should treat them as such. Do not expect to win, though you are entitled to hope that you might. Whatever training you have done, there is no substitute for actually being in the show ring, and this experience is essential for you both. Do not worry if you or your puppy make mistakes; it really doesn't matter. Everyone makes mistakes when they begin. The important thing is to learn from them. Never be afraid to talk to your fellow exhibitors, most of whom are very friendly and willing to give help and advice.

Before setting off, think of all the things that you will need to take with you. It is also important to think about what you are going to wear. For example, ladies should always wear something comfortable, avoiding long, flapping dresses and high-heeled shoes. Men should also wear something comfortable, and make sure their trousers are a light colour, so that the Dobermann shows up well against them. The outline of a black dog can be lost against dark-coloured clothing.

Above all, handlers must be clean, smart and tidy. While it is the dogs that are being judged, handling and presentation are both important. I am sure that there are occasions where two dogs are relatively close in terms of their conformation and it is the better dressed handler who will be the winner. This may be a subconscious decision by the judge but it is, I suspect, human nature. In any case, you owe it to your dog to be well-groomed. You must, of course, ensure that your dog is also well-groomed and presented. There is no point in spending months on training and then not presenting the dog in perfect condition. Teeth and ears should be cleaned, toe-nails clipped and coat brushed. If necessary give the puppy a bath the day before, though too much bathing is counter-productive as it will take out the natural oils and leave the coat dry and harsh. Just before you go into the ring, quickly spray the dog's coat with something to make it gleam and shine, then give it a quick rub over with a velvet pad or a piece of chamois leather. Many exhibitors consider it necessary to trim the dog's whiskers, but my view is that this is not necessary. Keep a small swab of cottonwool handy, soaked in cooking oil, which can be rubbed over the toe-nails, nose and any scars to enhance the overall appearance of a well-groomed dog.

IN THE SHOW RING

Once you actually get into the show ring, try to remember everything you have learned and practised at home. Don't be nervous, although most exhibitors are to begin with. This wears off after many years. But you must learn to control nerves. I well remember being told at the beginning of my show career that, by being nervous, I was being conceited and that I had no right to be conceited, as the judge was looking at my dog, not me. I am not sure whether it helped me, but I never forgot it. The real problem with being nervous is not only that it prevents you from showing your dog to the best of your ability, but it goes down the lead to your dog, who then loses self-confidence and all too soon you are feeding off each other's nervousness and tension.

The normal procedure is for the judge to walk round the ring to look at each dog in the class quickly, to gain a general impression before starting on a detailed assessment of each dog. You will need to get your dog stacked up and looking smart and stylish for this preliminary examination. Once the judge starts going over each dog individually, you can let your dog relax until your turn comes.

When this happens you will need to stack your dog again. You will by now have decided whether you are going to top and tail the dog, or free stand. Whichever method you use, have a quick look from all angles to ensure that you really are presenting your dog to the best possible effect. The judge should always approach from the front. Keep your hands on the dog to increase the dog's self-confidence, give the command Stay and words of encouragement. While the judge is assessing the head, you should stand along side the dog's shoulder, so as not to interfere with the judge. When the examination is extended to the shoulders and body, you should move forward towards the dog's head, maintaining the physical contact and the verbal encouragement. Showing is teamwork – you and the dog, and you must do your bit.

Once the physical assessment has been completed, the judge will stand back and look at the dog in order to assess the overall picture. You should therefore make sure the dog is properly stacked up at this critical moment because, if the judge sees your dog standing badly, it may create an unfavourable impression which will be very difficult to change later.

There are a number of points for which you should watch. Avoid the temptation to overstretch the back legs, which will make the dog look long in the body, show loose elbows and give a rocking-horse appearance. Try to hide any faults by careful presentation. Show off the dog's virtues and, above all, do not show faults which do not really exist, purely through poor handling. Check that the dog is standing in a straight line. A dog not doing this is likely to move, possibly when you least want this to happen. Never drop the lead in the ring as you immediately lose your control over your dog; you would be penalised for this in any handling competition.

Learn to stack your dog the 'wrong way', i.e. facing to the left while you are standing behind. While you will initially feel awkward and clumsy and the dog will feel uneasy, it is something that you must both learn to do. If you are on sloping ground, never stand your dog down the slope, as you will lose the elegant outline. If necessary, face the dog in the opposite direction, standing up the slope. That way the dog will look even better than if the ground was level. Always ensure that your dog is between you and the judge. Learn to read the ground; look for the undulations and work out where to stand your dog for the best possible effect. Avoid over-handling – once the dog is stacked, leave well alone.

HANDLING TECHNIQUES

The actual way in which the Dobermann is handled in the USA and the UK is not dissimilar. In the UK some handlers use the top-and-tail method, others combine this with baiting the dogs, while some handlers free-stand their dogs and bait them from the front. Each handler adopts the method which will present the best image to the judge, and the same handler may use a different technique for different dogs.

In the USA the method of handling is more uniform, and is best described as being an exaggerated top-and-tail method, with the chain held short around the nape of the neck.

In Europe dogs are shown free-standing on long leads. In the USA and UK the handlers attempt to hold the dogs' interest, and make them look alert, by using bait. In European countries this is achieved by means of double handling – the dog is held in the ring by one person, while the owner stays outside the ring and attempts to attract the dog's attention, to create an alert expression. This is done by calling the dog, bouncing rubber balls, using squeaky toys, or employing any other tactic to achieve the objective. Double-handling is not allowed in the USA or UK.

Always make sure that you have plenty of space in which to show your dog; avoid getting hemmed in or crowded out. Exercise your dog before going into the ring; it is most embarrassing if the dog misbehaves in the ring. If your dog backs away from the judge while being examined, you are unlikely to win. Allowance will be made for inexperience, particularly with puppies, but not for older dogs. Ring-shyness needs constant training and a lot of experience to overcome. Many Dobermanns go through a silly stage at about nine to twelve months, after which they become more adult and self-confident

Once the standing assessment has been completed, the judge will want to assess your dog moving. This is done at the trot. The normal procedure is to move the dog in a triangle, across the ring and back, or in a circle round the ring. You may only get one chance, so you must make it count. Always make sure that you are moving in a straight line, with the dog on a loose lead. Do not let the dog crab across the ring. Move back straight towards the judge, rather than to one side – unless you are trying to conceal a faulty front or poor front movement. Movement is an important part of the judging process as it enables the judge to assess the dog's conformation. Many faults which can be concealed by careful handling will be revealed when the dog is moved. Train your dog to move on either side of you, as you may be required to move across the ring and back, with the judge watching in profile. As with the standing, always keep the dog between you and the judge. When moving, try to maintain a continuous flow rather than doing a series of disjointed short runs. Keep talking to your dog, both to encourage and command. Anticipate the dog's actions as you approach any point at which you need to change direction, and get a firm command in before any mistakes are made. Make sure that your dog is not pacing. This is an economical movement and can become a bad habit. The judge will not be able to assess conformation while

Eng. and Ir. Ch. Pompie Sea Jade of Chancepixies (Ch. Flexor Adonis – Ch. Pompie Alcyone). Bred by Hilary Partridge, owned by Dave Anderson and Jean Frost. The UK's current Dobermann bitch breed record holder with 24 CCs, 7 Reserve CCs, 6 Irish Green Stars, 17 Championship Best of Breeds, 1 Working Group, 2 Reserve Working Groups, 3 Best in Shows and 2 Reserve Best in Shows at Breed Club Shows, Reserve Best in Show, Darlington Ch. Show 1986, Top Dobermann bitch 1985 and 1986, and Irish Annual Champion 1985.

Eng. Ir. Ch. Caspajacks Secret Affair (Ch. Crossridge The Jazzman – Electras Dark Secret). Bred and owned by Muriel Hughes. Winner of 3 CCs, 1 Reserve CC, Working Group and Reserve Best in Show WELKS Ch. Show 1991, Dog World Top Bitch 1991; in Ireland 5 Green Stars, 3 Reserve Green Stars, 1 Group and 2 Reserve Group wins.

Ch. Jowendys Tokyo Joe At Damarills (Marienburg Firedanza v. Tavey [USA import] – Jowendys Into Jazz). Bred by Wendy Burge, owned by Karen Brown. Winner of 5 CCs, 2 Reserve CCs, Top Puppy 1990, and winner of the Dobermann Club's Coronation Cup.

Ch. Tudor Tarrados (Ch. Sallate Ferris – Lady Myfanwy Talbot), bred by Mr T. and Mrs R. Allen, owned by Richard and Caroline Newman. Winner of 6 CCs, 1 Reserve CC, Junior Warrant, 3 Ch. Best of Breeds, Best in Show Birmingham and District Dobermann Club Ch. Show 1993.

Photo: Trafford.

Ch. Fugelow's Starlight Express of Vidal (Marienburg Firedanza v. Tavey (USA import) – Vidal's Alsia). Bred by J. and N. Perks, owned by Rosemary Hooper. Winner of 3 CCs, 3 Reserve CCs, Best in Show SE of England Dobermann Club Ch. Show 1994.

Ch. Chater The Ferryman (Achenburg Andrew – The Lotus Eater Of Chater. Bred and owned by Vicki Philip. Winner of 4 CCs and 5 Reserve CCs, Joint Top Puppy of the Year 1984, Best Puppy in Show National Working Breeds Show 1984.

Photo: Dave Freeman.

Ch. Mabaro Swanky Sue (Red Rebel of Chequers – Mabaro's Dragon Dancer). Bred by Aline and Bryan Langton, owned by Angela Kirkby. Winner of 4 CCs, 4 Reserve CCs, Junior Warrant, Best in Show Dobermann Club Ch. Show 1989.

Ch. Sallate's Ferris (Ch. Perihelias' Resolution – Sigismund's Ice Cool Kate). Bred by Mrs G. Hunt, owned by Mr and Mrs Y. Bevans. The Dobermann breed record holder with 42 CCs, 24 Reserve CCs, 9 Working Groups at Ch. Shows, including twice at Crufts, 4 Best in Shows at General Ch. Shows, Junior Warrant – a truly remarkable show record. Photo: Jordan.

the dog is moving in this way. It can be overcome either by starting off with a sharp jerk and a fast first step, so forcing the dog to lead off with one foot, or by taking the dog around you in a tight circle and leading straight off with one foot. When moving, make sure that you are at the correct speed. This is something you will learn from your training class. As I have already stressed, do not overwork a young or inexperienced dog too hard initially. The dog must find showing an enjoyable experience if it is to be done properly. Let the dog relax when you can, only concentrating at key moments. Even so, keep an eye on the judge, who may look around the ring when you least expect it, thereby catching you off guard and spotting all those faults that you tried so hard to conceal when you presented your dog. Also, remember that many of your future judges may be watching at the ringside and will be quick to spot the defects in your perfect puppy.

FINAL ASSESSMENT

Once all the individual assessments have been completed the judge will once again view all the dogs in the class in order to decide on the final placings. You will need to get your dog properly stacked for this. In a big class, the judge may select a few dogs for further assessment, possibly watching them move again. Eventually, after what might seem an eternity, five dogs will be placed, the awards being first, second, third, reserve and very highly commended (VHC). Having received your prize card, you leave the ring to await your next class, or even your next show.

JUDGING

Once you have been showing your dog, or dogs, for several years, you may be invited to judge Dobermanns. If you decide to accept an invitation to judge, make sure that both the invitation and the acceptance are in writing, which can avoid all sorts of problems. Do remember this is a contract which you should not break unless there are genuine reasons. Failure to honour a judging contract can incur penalties from the Kennel Club.

On the day of the show, arrive in good time and report to the Secretary or the Show Manager, who always like to know that their judges have arrived. Find out where your ring is located and who is to be your steward. Dress smartly but sensibly, no wide-brimmed hats, flapping skirts or high-heeled shoes; no ties that dangle over the dogs during the inspection. Avoid sunglasses, which can put dogs off and may lead the exhibitors to question your ability to see the dogs properly. Also avoid perfume as many dogs will not like it and will react to it.

Always look self-confident, even if you are not. You are on show and must look the part. Be happy, cheerful, polite and pleasant. This costs you nothing and makes everyone's day that much more enjoyable. Before you start you will receive your judging book. Check this to see how many dogs you will have to judge in how many classes. Pace yourself to ensure that you have adequate time for all the dogs. Time always seems to go so quickly, and there is nothing worse than a judge who takes too long to do the earlier classes and then has to race through the later ones.

Always be considerate to your exhibitors. While it is their responsibility to be in the ring when required, they may be needed to be in two rings at the same time. Be patient and tolerant, as they have paid to enter under you for your opinion. An exhibitor who is required in two rings at the same time should tell the two ring-stewards, who will ensure that you will receive your missing dogs with the minimum of delay. The steward should also ensure that the system is not being abused, such as where an exhibitor keeps a dog cool in the shade until most of the class has been judged.

You must always be fair and only judge the dogs as you see them, without being influenced by outside factors. And remember that you are being judged by the ringsiders: they are normally only too well aware whether you are judging well or badly.

Ch. Bledig Bugatti (Ch. Crossridge The Carbon Copy at Lynfrds – Ch. Twinglo Le Juice at Bledig), bred and owned by Richard and Angela Braver. Winner of 3 CCs, 8 Reserve CCs, Top Puppy 1989, and the Dobermann Club's Coronation Cup.

Ch. Autolander General, owned by Debbie Horsman. Winner of 22 CCs, 14 Reserve CCs, 16 Best of Breeds, including Crufts 1992 and 1993.

It is the normal procedure to write a critique on your winning dogs, which is for publication in the specialist canine press. I always remember one piece of advice about this: "to their faults be blind, to their virtues be kind". It is interesting that in the UK there is no check on the performance of judges. No training is required before being allowed to judge at a Championship show, merely an agreed amount of experience at Open show level, and an agreed level of breed experience. This is in complete contrast to some other countries, such as Germany, where the judge is expected to follow a set procedure and meet the approval of a panel of experts. While this system ensures a more consistent standard of judging, it could be said to have the disadvantage of removing the judges' free-will.

Ch. Sinjaris Betty Boo (The Jhidda From Halsband – Halsband's Shin-Shu). Breeder/owners Sue and David Johnson. 3CCs; 5 Res. CCs.

THE EUROPEAN SYSTEM

In the UK, the judge sets out to place the dogs in each class in their order of merit, irrespective of their quality. This means that a dog could have any number of undesirable characteristics but, in a class of one, would win it. In European countries, Dobermanns are judged against the Breed Standard rather than against each other. In other words, judging is based on a quality grading system. Under the European system, the judge must write a full critique on each dog, which is typed up at the ringside and then posted up for all to see. These are not the brief write-ups which are seen in the UK, which rarely do more than mention some of the dog's attributes. They are full and comprehensive and include details of all the dog's faults as seen by the judge. Having completed these critiques, the judge then gives each dog one of four possible grades, but only dogs which are graded 'excellent' are invited back into the ring for the final assessment. No dog under fifteen months of age can receive an 'excellent' grading, or go on to win a Challenge. The best dog and the best bitch are awarded a Challenge, referred to as a CAC. Challenges are given for the best dog and bitch of each of the three accepted colours, which would be considered totally unacceptable in principle in the USA or UK, where all colours must compete against each other in equal competition. In Europe this is not so important, because each dog must be graded 'excellent' before even competing for the CAC. To become a Champion, a dog must win at least four or five CACs, depending on the regulations in different countries. There must always be a minimum of twelve months between the first and last CAC and the dog must win his last CAC after twenty-seven months of age. Each European country has variations to these rules, but the general principles are similar. One important difference, however, is that in Austria and Germany a dog must have won a working certificate, such as Schutzhund or IPO (International Working Certificate), before being eligible to claim the title of Champion. A similar situation applies in France, where a dog has to pass a special working test, the TAN. A working qualification is not required in all European countries, for example not in Holland.

To become an International Champion a dog has to win at least two International Challenges (CACIB) in two different countries and hold a Schutzhund or an IPO qualification. Twelve months

South African Ch. Danika Vom Norden Stamm (Atilla vd Piratenburg – Int. Ch. Nicole Vom Norden Stamm). Imported into South Africa by Marc de Chalian. She began her career by winning Best Opposite Sex under two specialist judges in one day – a South African record – and she achieved her Championship on the day she was 18 months old, the minimum age under Kennel Union regulations.

Ch. Metexa Miss Brodie (Quanto Vom Haus Schimmel (imp) – Metexa Midnight Surprise). Breeders/owners John and Irene McManus. 3CCs; 3 Res. CCs; Multiple Best of Breed and Group winner at general open shows.

Am Ch. Julmar's Siboney (Ch. Agape The Lion of Judah – Ch. Marienburg Comanche Firebird): Now a Champion-producing sire.

Ashbey photography.

Irish Ch. Andalucia's Great Expectations (Rosecroft By The Way To Bilsam [USA import] – Wild Amber Star to Andalucia). Breeders Margaret and Arthur Hall. Owners Kath and John Brooks. 1 CC; 65 Best of Breeds at Open shows; Junior Warrant; 8 Green Stars; 4 Res. Green Stars in Ireland.

Ch. Swnydwr Storm Bearer (Ch. Crossridge The Jazzman – Stevely's Black Jezabel). Breeders/owners Milton and Jean Quigley. 8CCs; 3 Res. CCs; 5 Best of Breed at Championship shows.

must elapse between the first and second Challenge. This emphasis on the working side of the Dobermann is very important in most European countries and is applied not only to the showing of the dogs, but also to their breeding. Any dog or bitch used for breeding in Germany must have passed the 'fit for breeding' or ZTP test. This requirement for Dobermanns to prove their ability to work before being able to gain their championship title has never gained favour in the USA or the UK. As a result, the working side of the Dobermann tends to be practised by a relatively small band of enthusiasts.

WORKING TRIALS

If you are interested in utilising your Dobermann's intelligence to the full, you should consider the working side. Working Trials are, in essence, an extension of the obedience exercises that you will already have done, and in which your dog will have needed to have achieved a reasonable degree of proficiency. Classes are run by Working Trials Training Clubs and by some of the Dobermann Clubs. Most people want to enter competitions, or qualify their dogs at the various Working Trial Stakes, so the training you receive will be directly related to the exercises you would do in Working Trials competitions.

There are three categories of Working Trials. The Championship Working Trials are Open Trials at which Kennel Club Working Trial Certificates are offered. Open Working Trials are open to all, subject to the limitation of the maximum number of dogs permitted to take part. Members Working Trials are restricted to dogs owned by members of the club promoting the Trial.

The actual Working Trial competitions are called Stakes and are, in ascending order of difficulty, Companion Dog (CD), Utility Dog (UD), Working Dog (WD), Tracking Dog (TD) and Police Dog (PD). A dog has to have achieved a certain level of success in one Stake before being able to compete in a higher one. The Kennel Club Working Trial Regulations set out the precise exercises that each dog must perform in each Stake, and the marks that are available. These exercises are included within three or four groups, depending upon the Stake. Dogs which obtain 70% or more marks in each Group of exercises in the Stake entered are awarded a Certificate. If they achieve 80% or more of the total marks they are awarded a Certificate of Merit and gain the additional qualification "Excellent". Three groups of exercises are common to all five Stakes. These are Control, Agility and Nosework. Control covers the basic obedience exercises; Agility includes the scale, clear jump and long jump; Nosework includes search and tracking. In the CD Stake there is an additional group covering the Sit and Down elements of the basic obedience exercises, and in the PD Stake there is Patrol. In the Agility Group a Dobermann would be required to scale a six-foot high plank barrier, clear jump a three-foot high hurdle and long jump a distance of nine foot. In all Stakes, except CD, the dog must show steadiness to gunshot, so must have a sound temperament. The search element of Nosework requires the dog to recover four articles in five minutes from a twenty-five yard square search area (three articles within four minutes from a fifteen yards square area for CD Stake). The tracking element of Nosework involves the dog following a track laid by someone not known to the dog, and to recover a specified number of articles placed along the track. The dog will track wearing a harness and a tracking line.

The exercises within the Patrol group include quartering the ground, in which the dog is required to locate a missing person or criminal; a test of courage; search and escort, which includes protection of handler from attack; and manwork, in which the dog is sent after a fleeing criminal whom the dog is required to stop and to release on command. You will find that your Dobermann will love tracking and will do it with great enthusiasm. It can be a severe test for a Dobermann though, as the dog's objective is to reach the end of the track in the shortest distance and time possible. The Dobermann may, therefore, cut corners, or even track slightly downwind, since the

Bronco von der Kunigundenhohe At Heimdall, owned by David Stafford, shows the strength and agility of the Dobermann as he clears the long jump, with encouragement from Wendy Crick.

scent will often drift slightly, thereby failing to find the articles laid on the track.

Your Dobermann will also enjoy jumping and be very easy to teach. Unless you intend to do Working Trials, however, do not teach this, otherwise you will find your fences at home being jumped. A Dobermann can clear a six-foot high fence with apparent ease.

Manwork is the last exercise you will be allowed to teach your Dobermann in Working Trials. Very few Dobermanns ever reach the high standard of training needed to even contemplate doing this. Never teach it to your Dobermann unless you are doing it under careful instruction within a training club, and you are seriously doing Working Trials. If you teach your dog manwork, you will have a terrible liability. You will have a dog who knows how to attack someone, and who will probably enjoy doing it, and you will not have sufficient control to prevent it.

As I have already indicated, the working ability of the Dobermann is considered to be of extreme importance in many European countries, particularly in Germany, where the breed originated, and where control of all matters relating to registration, breeding and the showing of Dobermanns is in the hands of the Breed Club, rather than the Kennel Club.

The situation is very different in the USA and the UK, where there is total freedom for anyone to breed a litter of puppies, using any stud dog of their choice, and any resulting puppies will be registered by the Kennel Club, provided both parents are themselves registered. The Kennel Club has never supported the idea of working dogs needing to have proven working ability before being allowed to become Champions. Attempts have been made to introduce Schutzhund training into the UK, but these have been discouraged by the Kennel Club, no doubt mindful of the current climate, which is in favour of considerable dog-control, particularly in respect of dangerous or aggressive dogs.

Chapter Seven

COLOUR IN THE DOBERMANN

DOBERMANN COLOURS

The Black and Tan colour pattern is probably the most striking single feature of the Dobermann, giving the Breed its unique identity and making it immediately recognisable. However, there are actually four recognised Dobermann colours – Black and Tan, Brown and Tan, Blue and Tan, and Fawn and Tan. The Fawn is often referred to as Isabella.

When the first Breed Standard was drawn up in Germany in 1899, only the one colour, Black and Tan, was considered acceptable. A number of the early Dobermann fanciers objected to other colours being allowed. Opinion must have changed fairly quickly, however, as the Standard was revised in 1901 and included the Brown and Tan and Blue and Tan colours as well.

As will have been seen from the discussion on the origins of the Dobermann, we do not really know what breeds of dog were responsible for its creation, even though the breed is barely one hundred years old. Equally, the source of the different Dobermann colours is not really known. Early writers have put forward various theories, some of which seem to be more credible than others.

It seems likely that the foundation for the Dobermann was the Thueringen Pinscher, sometimes referred to as the German Pinscher. This breed is now extinct but seems to have had many of the basic characteristics of the modern Dobermann, including the black colour and smooth coat, as well as the tan markings which varied from straw yellow to red. It is probable that this Thueringen Pinscher also provided the basic genetic pattern for the four possible coat colours. Certainly, all four Dobermann colours were recorded very early on in the life of the breed.

An alternative hypothesis is that the Black and Tan and Brown and Tan colours came originally from the Rottweiler, then known as the Butcher's Dog, with the dilution factor for the Blue and Tan and Fawn and Tan being supplied by the Thueringen Pinscher. Although rarely seen today, brown Rottweilers have been recorded.

The Beauceron is believed by some experts to have played an important role in the origin of the Dobermann. This claim is certainly enhanced by the fact that both the Beauceron and the Dobermann share the same genetic pattern of coat colour inheritance. Both breeds are most commonly Black and Tan, but Brown and Tan, Blue and Tan and Fawn and Tan colours also occur. This common inheritance would not only account for the origin of the four Dobermann colours, but would provide a convincing argument to support the suggested close relationship between the two breeds.

EARLY DEVELOPMENTS

During the early development of the Dobermann, breeders used the Black and Tan Terrier and the

Greyhound to improve the breed. The Black and Tan Terrier was an English breed of dog, which became known as the Manchester Terrier in 1923, when the first breed club was established. According to Otto Goeller, who was one of the earliest Dobermann breeders, the Black and Tan Terrier had not been introduced into Thuringia by 1890, when the first Dobermanns had become established. There is good documentary evidence of cross breeding with the Black and Tan Terrier around the turn of the century, however, and it would seem likely that this led to a considerable improvement to both the coat and the colour of the early Dobermann. Prior to the introduction of the Black and Tan Terrier, the Dobermann was said to have a thick, woolly undercoat and light tan markings which were not well defined. The darker tan markings of the Black and Tan Terrier were dominant over the lighter colour of the Dobermann, and very quickly resulted in the darker and well-defined tan markings of the Dobermann, as we know them today, becoming established.

Apart from coat and colour, the Dobermann is said to have inherited a number of other desirable characteristics from the Black and Tan Terrier, including alertness, expression and manoeuvrability whilst moving fast. Speed was actually obtained from the introduction of Greyhound blood around the same period, in the early years of the twentieth century. One interesting consequence of the use of the Greyhound was the appearance of brindle-coloured Dobermanns. Checks were also recorded at about the same time.

Otto Goeller wanted these other colour combinations to be recognised. He refrained from taking the necessary action as he feared that it would fail, even though there appeared to be some support for this move. The main objection seems to have been that it would have necessitated the provision of additional classes in which they could be judged, for the different colours were judged separately rather than competing together against one another. It is interesting to speculate whether the recessive genes for brindle Dobermanns are still being passed on from generation to generation, and may one day reappear when two dogs carrying them happen to be mated together.

Goeller considered that the introduction of the Blue Great Dane was responsible for bringing the Blue and Tan colour into the breed. This theory has never been well supported and is not substantiated by any records of cross breeding. Interestingly enough though, I know of a Great Dane breeder who bred a litter of Fawn Danes, two of which had a full set of Dobermann tan markings.

An alternative theory is that the recessive genes for Blue and Fawn were introduced by cross breeding with the Weimaraner, but even this is questionable. The Weimaraner was also considered to be responsible for the introduction of the white marks which sometimes appear on the chest of our Dobermanns today, and also for the white toenail which is still occasionally seen.

THE FAWN (ISABELLA) COLOUR
The early Dobermann breeders produced Fawns but they did not realize that this was a genuine colour. They thought it indicated weakness and degeneration and that it resulted from inbreeding. For this reason, Fawn was not included in the 1899 or 1901 German Breed Standards. In fact, it was never included on any standard until becoming an accepted colour in the USA in 1969. What is more surprising is that there was only one standard which considered it necessary to include it as a fault, or as being undesirable in any way. This was the USA Standard of January 1935, which stated "Light Fawn (or Isabella) prohibited". This was one of a number of faults set out in capital letters, which were described in a note to the Standard as being major faults evidencing degeneration of the Breed. The Fawn did not remain in the USA Standard as a fault for very long, however, as again there was no reference to it in the next Standard which was adopted in 1948. Why it should have only been included as a fault in that one Standard, which had a life span of a mere thirteen years, is not clear. Possibly the true genetic basis of the colour had become

recognised, or maybe Fawns were being produced and it was realised that the earlier belief that the colour was associated with degeneration was simply not true.

The first move towards Fawn becoming an accepted colour occurred in the USA when a Fawn bitch by the name of High Halo's Calypso won Reserve Winners Bitch at the Mississippi Valley Kennel Club Show in 1966. Not surprisingly, this win caused some confusion, since Fawn was not mentioned in the Standard. The AKC was consulted on the matter and ruled that: "The Standard for the Dobermann Pinscher Breed does not state that an Isabella colour is disqualifying. Therefore you would be permitted to show such a colour." The AKC also stated that: "A protest could not be lodged against an Isabella because of its colour."

There are a number of theories as to how the name Isabella, which has no genetic validity and can hardly be said to suggest a specific colour to anyone not familiar with the term or the Breed, came to be applied to the Fawn Dobermann. One suggestion is that it is derived from the Latin via the French word 'sable', which means sand. The word therefore suggests a sandy colour. There are two theories relating to Queen Isabella of Spain. One suggests that she ordered that all Spain's royal horses should be of her favourite colour, which was a sandy-yellow colour. As a result of this, horses throughout Europe became known as 'Ysabellas' in her honour. We now refer to horses of this colour as Palominos, which are actually a bright gold colour with a metallic sheen, with the mane and tail being white. The alternative theory is that when her capital city was under siege, she refused to change her linen until the siege was lifted. In the event, the siege lasted three years, by which time her linen was the colour of parchment, since when the colour has been described as Isabella.

FAWNS IN THE USA

The Fawn Dobermann had been the subject of detailed consideration in the USA for several years prior to Calypso's win in 1966. In July 1960 Dr John Colmore, Head of a DPCA Committee to study the Blue and Fawn colours and make recommendations, gave a lecture which was illustrated with colour slides showing all four colours. This was later printed by the DPCA, along with pedigree charts, and distributed to the entire membership. In 1961 ballots were mailed to the membership to vote on one of the following:
1) to leave the 'allowable colours' in the Standard unchanged;
2) to disqualify the Isabella;
3) to disqualify both the Isabella and the Blue;
4) to include the Isabella as one of the Standard colours.
The voting was overwhelmingly in favour of including the Isabella.

However, it was voted to allow another year for study and to send out a simple 'yes' or 'no' ballot to be reported on at the 1962 Annual Meeting. This vote resulted in 187 in favour of the Isabella and 119 against. The Meeting voted to accept the Report and request AKC approval of the change.

At the 1963 Meeting the AKC had not yet come to a decision. In 1965 a Committee on the Clarification of the Standard was appointed under the Chairmanship of Mrs Rhys Carpenter, one of the few surviving members of the Committee which drew up the (then) current Standard in 1948. In January 1966 Mrs Carpenter sent a report of her Committee's meeting of October 1965, and stated that they hoped to submit a clarified revision of the present Standard at the October 1966 Meeting, including an unambiguous stand with respect to the Isabella for the vote of DPCA members. She further stated: "In our Breed we have four, not three, colours! We are most fortunate that the colour inheritance pattern is definite and genetically simple. Strangely, the colour question has aroused more heated emotional discussion than any other point in the Standard, perhaps because few people have ever seen an Isabella." The Fawn (Isabella) colour was added to the Breed Standard by the AKC in October 1969. Following the addition of Isabella to the Breed Standard, the first Fawn to complete its championship in the USA was the bitch, Ch. Aventine's Gabrielle, who was sired by Ch. Tarrado's Corry, in September 1972.

The acceptance of the Fawn in the USA led to a number of other countries adding the colour to their breed standards. One was Ireland, though it is doubtful that this led to any Fawns actually being shown in that country.

FAWNS IN THE UK

Although Blues and Fawns occurred occasionally in the UK, they really made their appearance in the late 1970s and early 1980s following the importation of the bitch, Kayhills Outrigger, by Phil and Eileen Edwards, from Jane Kay in the USA. She was imported in whelp to Ch. Tarrado's Corry and whelped in quarantine. Two of the dog puppies in that litter, Phileen's American Express and Phileen's Duty Free of Tavey, were subsequently shown to carry the recessive dilutant gene and between them they effectively established the Blue and Fawn colours in the UK.

Phileen's American Express was the only Black male in the litter and produced two Blue dog puppies to a Brown bitch, Frankskirby Red Christel, owned by Bernard and Joyce Spaughton. The Spaughtons kept one of these two dogs, and the other, Frankskirby Jubilee Blulad of Roanoke, came to me at the Roanoke Kennels. Blulad had a highly successful show career, gaining his Junior Warrant and becoming the first Blue male to win a CC in the UK, at the Welsh Kennel Club Championship Show in 1978.

Probably because of the impact that Blulad made in the show ring, it was realised that the emergence of Fawns of a Show Standard was a distinct possibility. The possibility of adding Fawn to the Breed Standard was considered by the AGMs of the then four member clubs of the Dobermann Breed Council in the spring of 1978. As two clubs voted for accepting the colour and two clubs voted against, the final decision fell to the casting vote of the Chairman, Richard Jackson. He adopted the conventional procedure of voting for the status quo, so voted against acceptance of the colour. The issue was reconsidered by the four clubs again the following year, 1979, when the membership of all four clubs rejected any inclusion of the colour into the Breed Standard. Shortly afterwards, Derek D'Cruze (Twinglo) bred a Fawn dog puppy in a litter sired by Pompie Rouge Warrior out of a Brown bitch, Marrions Rusty Ballerina. Both dogs were descended from Phileen's Duty Free of Tavey, one of the Brown males from the Outrigger litter. Duty Free was owned by Fred and Julia Curnow of Tavey fame, and was the second dog from that litter which was proved to carry the recessive dilute coat colour gene. This Fawn puppy, Twinglo The Silver Wraith of Roanoke, was born in 1979 and also joined the Roanoke Kennels. At the request of the four member clubs of the Dobermann Breed Council, the UK Kennel Club was asked why Fawns were allowed to be registered when they were not on the Breed Standard. The Kennel Club's response was: "The Breed Standard is a guide to the Breed and it does not in any way indicate that any dog of that Breed that does not conform to the Standard is not eligible for exhibition, therefore if the owner of a Fawn Dobermann wishes to enter it for competition, they may do so, and it is left to the Judge to decide, and if by chance the Judge does in fact favour the Fawn and award it a Challenge Certificate, no action will be taken by the Kennel Club."

Because the Isabella issue had become so political and controversial and had the potential to be so divisive and damaging to the Dobermann Breed, I decided that Silver Wraith should be shown and that I should actively campaign for the colour to be added to the Standard as an acceptable colour. Silver Wraith made his debut at the Midland Dobermann Club's Championship Show in November 1980, winning a Very Highly Commended (fifth place) in his class in an entry of sixteen dogs, under Judge John Cave. I doubt if the winning of a VHC has ever been the subject of so much interest or controversy.

The Dobermann Club lodged a formal objection against John Cave to the Kennel Club. It is probably the only time that such an objection has ever been lodged in respect of a VHC, but there was clearly a principle here which needed to be resolved.

Silver Wraith continued to be shown selectively, mainly under championship show approved judges, and was placed by nineteen out of twenty-three judges prior to the whole Isabella issue being resolved. He won a number of Firsts, was a Best of Breed winner and even won Reserve Best in Show at the Clacton and District Canine Society's Open Show in July 1981.

The issue finally came to a head when the Breed Council formally requested the Kennel Club to amend the Breed Standard to make any other colour 'highly undesirable'. The Kennel Club considered the Breed Council's request but did not accept the proposed addition to the 'colour' section of the Breed Standard. It then considered a report on the genetic inheritance of coat colour in the Dobermann prepared by Dr Malcolm Willis, an expert geneticist and then adviser to the Kennel Club. It found the evidence irrefutable for the acceptance of the Fawn, which was thus added to the Breed Standard as an acceptable colour in December 1981.

THE FAWN IN EUROPE

It is now only the European countries using the FCI Standard which do not accept Fawn as a permitted colour. It has even been suggested that these countries may move in the opposite direction by deleting Blue from the Standard. This would appear to be a retrograde step, though it would be logical insofar as it would make both dilute colours unacceptable but, as Dr Malcolm Willis explained, it will not eliminate Blues and Fawns. To do that one must also exclude Browns and aim to produce only the BBDD (Type 1) Blacks. In the process, one would probably cast aside a large percentage of the potential breeding stock, possibly losing many desirable breed characteristics in the process, and risk setting back the progress of the Breed by many years.

One has only got to think of the loss to the Dobermann Breed in both the USA and the UK if the Americans had adopted such a policy in the 1960s. That fabulous Blue Champion, Felix vom Ahrtal, would never have been allowed to win his Championship or to produce such a dynasty of top dogs through his son, Ch. Tarrado's Corry. This would seem to be a high price to pay in order to eliminate two colours which have always existed as part of the Dobermann Breed, one of which, the Blue, has been included in every Breed Standard produced since 1901.

GENETICS OF COAT COLOUR

Coat colour is one of the most important things to be considered by anyone thinking of buying a puppy. It is also of great interest to many people when they breed litters of puppies, since they often either want to produce, or to avoid, specific colours, or at least to have some idea of what will be the colour of the puppies that they are likely to obtain from any specific mating.

The inheritance of coat colour in the Dobermann is a subject that generates a great deal of interest, but is one which appears to be little understood by many people. This may be because it involves the study of genetics, which always manages to seem extremely complicated. In actual fact, it is very straightforward, once the basic principles involved, and some of the more important terminology, have been learned.

Genetics may be defined as the science of heredity, which is the study of how qualities of all kinds are transmitted from parent to offspring. Before being able to understand the basic principle of genetics, it is first necessary to know something about the cell and how it divides.

The cell is the basic unit of life, and consists of a nucleus in the centre, with cellular matter (cytoplasm) around it. Any organism is the result of the fusion of two cells (the sperm and the ovum). The organism then grows by the division of this cell into two cells, and the subsequent division of these two cells into four cells and so on, with the process continuing throughout the growth of the organism. During this growth process different cells become specialised for different purposes, e. g. skin cells, nerve cells, liver cells, etc.

The nucleus is the most important part of the cell, because it contains all the genetic matter of the organism in thread-like structures known as chromosomes, which occur in pairs. In the dog there are 78 chromosomes, occurring as 39 pairs. Attached to these chromosomes, somewhat like beads on a string, are the genes which collectively represent a complete blueprint of the organism. It is estimated that each gene is about 0.00003mm in size, and that a human being has 100,000 genes in each cell. Each one of these controls some facet of the organism, such as shape, colour, hair, features, etc. In some instances, genes may work in conjunction with one another, as will be seen later. When one refers to a gene one should really refer to a pair of genes, since they are always present at the same point on the same chromosome.

When a cell divides, the nucleus divides into two equal halves, after which the cytoplasm surrounding the nucleus also divides, half going with each of the newly formed nuclei. Although this process of cell division, known as 'mitosis', is a very complicated one, with the division of the nucleus going through several clearly definable stages, what is really important is what happens to the contents of the nucleus during this division.

When the nucleus divides, each chromosome divides longitudinally, rather like splitting a hair into two down its length. The genes also divide into two, so that each half-chromosome contains the full gene complement. As the division proceeds, the nucleus takes the shape of a dumbbell, with the two halves from any one chromosome going to opposite ends. The dumbbell eventually separates in the middle, giving two nuclei. As a result of this chromosome and gene division, every cell nucleus contains the same genetical make-up.

The sex cells, however, divide by a process known as 'meiosis'. This is really a two-stage division, with the first stage being the same as for a normal cell division. The two newly-formed nuclei, each with a full set of chromosomes and their complement of paired genes, then goes through a second division, which differs from the earlier division in one very important respect. While the chromosomes divide as before, the genes do not do so. Instead, one gene from each pair goes with each half-chromosome. As a result of this, each newly formed cell will contain a full set of half-chromosomes, but only half the normal complement of genes. These cells, containing only half the genetic matter, are the sperm in the male and the ova in the female. During reproduction there is a fusion between a sperm and an ovum, as a result of which the newly formed cell once again has a full set of chromosomes and genes, half having come from each parent, and it is these genes which determine the animal's characteristics.

Although it is the genes which produce the individual features and characteristics of an animal, they produce different results depending on what other genes are present. The presence, or absence, of one gene may not only affect those characteristics that it normally controls, but it may also influence characteristics controlled by other genes as well. Thus several genes may be responsible for producing a given characteristic. This means that for any individual species not only are there a virtually infinite number of possible genetic combinations, but there are also a virtually infinite number of possible gene interactions. This makes it very unlikely that any two animals will have an identical genetic composition and so produces the slight variations that can be seen between members of the same species. They will resemble their parents fairly closely, though, since they derive their genes from them.

THE INHERITANCE OF COAT COLOUR

Once the basic principles of genetics are understood, it is possible to apply them to the inheritance of coat colour in the Dobermann. As already indicated, there are four Dobermann colours, Black, Brown, Blue and Fawn, sometimes referred to as Isabella; it is important to realize that both Blue and Fawn (or Isabella) are not really actual descriptions of a dog's colour, but genetic terms to define the colours resulting from certain genetic combinations.

There are two pairs of genes which are involved in determining coat colour. One pair determines whether the dog is basically Black or Brown, while the second pair determines whether the coat colour is dense (Black or Brown) or dilute (Blue and Fawn). For the sake of simplicity, these genes are given symbols, which are in universal use and are widely understood. The Black/Brown pair of genes are referred to as the 'B' genes, while the Blue/Fawn genes are referred to as the 'D' genes. There are undoubtedly other pairs of genes which have some effect on other aspects of coat colours, such as the darkness and evenness of the coat colour, the shade and extent of the Tan markings, etc., but it is not necessary to consider them.

A gene may be either 'dominant' or 'recessive'. A dominant gene is one which suppresses the effect of its partner, whilst a recessive gene is one whose effects are masked by its partner, unless both genes of the pair are recessive. This means that if a pair of genes consists of one dominant gene and one recessive gene, the dog's colour will reflect the presence of the dominant gene and not that of the recessive gene.

GENES FOR BLACK AND BROWN

Applying this principle to the Dobermann colours, Black is a dominant colour, whereas Brown is a recessive colour. In the language of genetics, a dominant gene is identified by a capital letter and a recessive gene by a small letter. A dominant Black gene is therefore given the symbol 'B' and a recessive Brown gene the symbol 'b'. If a dog has a dominant B gene, it must be Black; the other gene may be either another dominant B gene or a recessive b gene. This means that a Black dog must be BB or Bb. It equally follows that a Brown dog cannot have a dominant B gene, or it would, by definition, be Black. A Brown dog must be bb, i. e. it must have two recessive genes. The actual colour of the dog is referred to as its phenotype. There are thus four phenotypes, namely the four Dobermann colours. A Black dog may be BB or Bb, and whichever option it has is referred to as its genotype.

It was shown earlier that when the sex cells are produced during meiosis, each cell contains only half the normal genetic material. This means that with a Black dog (BB) each sex cell produced must contain a B gene. Equally, with a Brown dog (bb) each sex cell must contain a b gene. With a Black dog (Bb), however, there is a 50/50 chance that any individual cell will have either a B gene or a b gene. It follows from this that a mating between two Black dogs, both of whom are BB, can only produce puppies who are themselves BB, since both parents can only produce B genes. This can be illustrated as follows:

BB (Black) x BB (Black)
BB BB BB BB

What this actually means is that there are four possible combinations of genes that any puppy could inherit but, in this case, they are all the same.

Similarly, a mating between two Brown dogs can only produce Brown puppies, since both parents only produce b genes, which means that the puppies can only acquire a b gene from each parent. Using the same means as before, this can be illustrated as follows:

Twinglo The Silver Wraith of Roanoke (Pompie Rouge Warrier – Marions Rusty Ballerina): The first Isabella (Fawn) Dobermann to win in the UK show ring.

Black and Tan is the most striking of the Dobermann colour patterns. Ch. Sallate Hollywood (Ch. Holtzburg Mayhem – Sallates Qala at Stroudley). Bred by Mrs G. Hunt, owned by Sandra Goodwin. This dog gained his title in 12 weeks at 21 months, making him one of the youngest male Champions.

bb (Brown) x bb (Brown)
bb bb bb bb

Where two Black dogs are mated, one of which carries a recessive b gene, the following situation occurs:

BB (Black) x Bb (Black)
BB Bb Bb BB

This means that all the sex cells from the BB dog must be dominant B genes, whilst those from the Bb dog have a 50/50 chance of being B or b. The mathematical probability is that 50 per cent of the puppies will be BB and 50 per cent will be Bb. They will, of course, all be Black.

If a Black dog (BB) is mated to a Brown dog (bb) the following genetic combinations will occur:

BB (Black) x bb (Brown)
Bb Bb Bb Bb

This means that all the sex cells from the BB dog must be dominant B genes, while those from the Brown, bb, dog will be recessive b genes. The puppies will all be Black, with the genotype Bb. They will therefore all carry a recessive b gene. From this it can be seen that to produce Brown puppies, both parents must carry a recessive Brown gene. Furthermore, a dog who has two dominant Black genes can never produce Brown puppies.

If the Black dog is Bb, however, and is mated to a Brown dog, the genetic combinations become:

Bb (Black) x bb (Brown)
Bb Bb bb bb

This produces a 50/50 ratio of Black and Brown puppies. Obviously, this is a mathematical probability and the actual ratio may vary one way or the other.

It is possible to produce Brown puppies from two Black parents, providing both parents are Bb. Such a mating would produce:

Bb (Black) x Bb (Black)
BB Bb Bb bb

By the same mathematical probability this would produce three Blacks and one Brown, i.e. a 3:1 ratio. From the above it will be readily apparent that you can tell a lot about the genetic make-up of a dog from its colour and the colour of its parents. If it is a Brown then it must be bb. If it is Black it can be either BB or Bb; if one of its parents was Brown, however, it must be Bb, since that parent could only have given it a recessive b gene. Only where both parents are Black will it not be possible to say whether the dog is BB or Bb. The only way to find out would be to mate it with a Brown dog. If the resulting litter produced some Brown puppies, you would know that the dog was Bb, since a Brown puppy can only be produced when both parents carry the recessive b gene.

GENES FOR BLUE AND FAWN

So far, only the Black and Brown genes have been considered. It is now necessary to look at the dilute coat colour genes which are responsible for Blue and Fawn. The same genetic terms are used as before, 'D' being dominant and 'd' being recessive. Where a dog has the dominant D gene, i. e. it is DD or Dd, it will have a dense coat colour which will be either Black if it is BB or Bb, or Brown if it is bb. Hence a Black or Brown dog must have a dominant D gene but may be DD or Dd. It is only when a dog has two recessive d genes (dd) that it will be either Blue instead of Black, or Fawn instead of Brown. This means that Blue is recessive to Black and Fawn is recessive to Brown.

This may become clearer by illustrating which genetic combinations produce which colours. There are actually nine genetic combinations, four of which produce Black, two produce Brown, two produce Blue and one produces Fawn. These nine genotypes have been given type numbers by the Dobermann Pinscher Club of America for convenience.

Type 1   BBDD Black
Type 2   BBDd Black
Type 3   BbDD Black
Type 4   BbDd Black
Type 5   BBdd Blue
Type 6   Bbdd Blue
Type 7   bbDD Brown
Type 8   bbDd Brown
Type 9   bbdd Fawn

This categorization is extremely helpful as it enables one to describe a dog's genotype quickly and simply in a way which everyone knows and understands. Advertisements for stud dogs in America frequently include the dog's genotype using this system. It has never really been used in the UK, however, possibly because there are very few Blue or Fawn Dobermanns and relatively few dogs which carry the recessive diluting d gene. It is also probably true that breeders in the UK rarely deliberately set out to breed Browns or to avoid breeding them. The result of this is that the actual genotype is not of particular interest.

The results of various matings can be calculated in exactly the same way as before, though it becomes slightly more complicated since we are dealing with two pairs of genes. As an example, consider a mating between a Type 4 Black dog (BbDd) and a Type 6 Blue bitch (Bbdd). The Black dog will produce four possible gene combinations in its sex cells in approximately equal numbers, namely BD, Bd, bD and bd. The Blue bitch will also produce four possible gene combinations which would be Bd, Bd, bd and bd. In this case there are two combinations which are actually different, each occurring in approximately equal numbers. Each of the four gene combinations from the dog could combine with each of the four gene combinations from the bitch, which means that there are 4x4, or sixteen, possible combinations which will be received by the puppies. Which of these sixteen combinations will occur is a matter of chance, but each option has the same mathematical probability of occurring.

The simplest way of considering these sixteen options is to present them in the form of a grid. The grid has the four gene options from the Black sire across the top and the four gene options from the Blue dam down the side. The sixteen squares of the grid are then filled in, combining the two genes from each parent each time. The colour which each of the sixteen options would produce is then added. This shows that for this mating, the mathematical probability is that there would be six Blacks, two Browns, six Blues and two Fawns, i. e. a ratio of 3:1:3:1 in the litter.

BLACK DOG (BbDd)

		BD	Bd	bD	bd
	Bd	BBDd Black	BBdd Blue	BbDd Black	Bbdd Blue
BLUE **BITCH** **(Bbdd)**	**Bd**	BBDd Black	BBdd Blue	BbDd Black	Bbdd Blue
	bd	BbDd Black	Bbdd Blue	bbDd Brown	bbdd Fawn
	bd	BbDd Black	Bbdd Blue	bbDd Brown	bbdd Fawn

The various colours are unlikely to occur precisely in accordance with this mathematical ratio, due to the random gene associations referred to above. What is important is that such a mating is potentially capable of producing all four colours.

While it is possible to work out the likely results of various matings in the same way, space does not allow this to be done here. However, various factors become evident from an analysis of the mating already considered in detail. For this mating it was assumed that the full genetic make-up (the genotype) of both parents was known. Very often only that part of the genotype which is evident from the dog's actual colour (the phenotype) is known, with maybe a little extra information from one's knowledge of the parents' genotype and phenotype.

If one is aiming to breed a dilutant colour (Blue or Fawn), it is necessary for both parents to carry a recessive d gene. Obviously, if both parents are Blue or Fawn, then all the puppies will also be Blue or Fawn, the ratio depending on the Black/Brown genotype of the parents. If one parent is Blue or Fawn and the other is Black or Brown, then Blue or Fawn puppies will only be produced if the Black or Brown parent carries the recessive d gene. However, all the offspring of a Blue or Fawn parent will inherit a recessive d gene, so will be capable of producing the dilutant colours themselves.

The problem arises when two non-dilutants (Black or Brown) are mated. Even if they both carry a recessive d gene, i.e. they are both Dd, there will be a 3:1 ratio of Blacks/Browns to Blue/Fawns; of the Black/Browns two-thirds will inherit a recessive d gene, so will be Dd, but one-third will be DD, and not inherit the recessive d gene. The only way to tell whether one of these Blacks/Browns has a recessive d gene is to mate the dog to a Blue or Fawn dog and see what colours are produced. If Blues and Fawns are produced, then the dog is Dd; if only Blacks and Browns result, the dog is DD. Equally, a dog which is mated with a Black or Brown which is known to be Dd, i.e. one that has a Blue or Fawn parent, will also produce Blues and Fawns in a 3:1 ratio of non-dilutants to dilutants if Dd, but will only produce Blacks and Browns if DD.

BREEDING FOR COLOUR

If it is desired to breed Blues and Fawns, this can be done in two generations. A Black or Brown bitch mated to a Blue or Fawn dog will result in a litter of puppies all carrying a recessive d gene. If one of these is kept and then mated to either a Blue or a Fawn, or to a son/daughter of a Blue or Fawn, the resulting litter should contain Blues and Fawns. If the original Black or Brown bitch happens to carry a recessive d gene, it will produce Blues or Fawns in one generation.

Breeding specifically to produce the Blue and Fawn colours can be very fascinating, but should never be done at the expense of soundness, type or overall quality. There is no point in producing these recessive colours if the resulting puppies are of poor quality or have bad temperaments. The recessive dilutant gene would need to be bred into a bloodline of known quality, in the hope that the eventual Blues and Fawns will be up to the required standard. This does mean, of course, that a reasonably sound Blue or Fawn dog is required which also has a sound pedigree in the first instance.

The danger of breeding for recessive colours is that the potential pool of breeding stock which carries the required recessive genes is always likely to be small. This means that the choice of dogs for breeding is likely to be limited and the end result may be that an inferior dog is used, thereby producing puppies of lower quality. It would be equally wrong, of course, to breed so as to deliberately try to avoid certain colours, since again the potential pool of breeding stock would be reduced. If you succeed in breeding Blue or Fawn puppies you will find that there is a limited demand for them, since Black is by far the most popular colour.

COAT PROBLEMS IN BLUES AND FAWNS
Most Blues and Fawns tend to suffer from a thinning of the coat once they reach about three years of age, typically starting along the topline and spreading around the flanks. The outer guard-hairs disappear, leaving a softer undercoat, which gives the appearance of being lighter in colour. It is a gradual process which takes place over a period of years, and tends to be most noticeable at times of moult, with the loss being partly recouped when the new coat comes through. The rate and extent of coat loss varies from dog to dog. Some lose their coats over a very short space of time and are almost bald on the back and flanks, whereas others tend to lose it more slowly and appear to have a moth-eaten coat rather than being partly bald. There are some Blues and Fawns, however, who do not lose their coats at all, but unfortunately I have found that this does not mean that their offspring will inherit good coats. There appears to be no way of predicting which Blues and Fawns will retain good coats. The vast majority, however, will not do so.

COAT CARE FOR BLUES AND FAWNS
I have owned many Blues and Fawns over the years, and most of them have suffered from some loss of coat and a dry, scaly skin to some extent. Although the loss of coat may not be preventable in the long run, I believe that, with a little care and attention, it can be delayed. Basically, this involves treating the coat and the skin to prevent it from drying out. This treatment should be both internal and external. The internal treatment should include the addition of a tablespoon of vegetable oil, preferably corn oil, each evening on the dinner. Alternatively, give the dog a lump of margarine; approximately one-eighth of a half-pound block would be a reasonable daily amount. In addition, try to increase the fat content of the diet by feeding something such as breast of lamb. This may be given either raw or roasted. About half a pound given three days per week would be adequate. Breast of lamb is also excellent for putting body on dogs or for encouraging fussy eaters. Do not give the dog any of the larger rib bones, particularly if cooked, but the softer cartilage will not cause any problems. Vitamin B and Vitamin C should also be given daily, since both of them are beneficial to skins and coats. I have always used Vitamin B Compound tablets, which contain a range of the B vitamins, and Vitamin C (Ascorbic Acid) tablets. Be careful about the Vitamin C tablets; they are easily available from a chemist but are produced in a wide range of strengths. There is little danger to the dog if too much of these vitamins is given, since they are water-soluble and any excess can simply be excreted. Even so, it is always a wise precaution never to overdo any

supplementation. Both Vitamins B and C are relatively inexpensive to buy. I have heard of other additives being proposed from time to time. One that comes to mind is the use of brewer's yeast, which Audrey Kelly (Rathkeel) always gave her Blues and Fawns.

Feeding also plays a part in this coat care issue. I have found that a frequent cause of coat loss is the use of complete flake foods, which contain a high level of maize. While they are probably very good foods in themselves, they do seem to play havoc with the more sensitive skins and coats of the Blue and Fawn Dobermanns. The dogs seem to eat the food readily enough, and do well on it for a period of time but then suddenly come out with spots, particularly along the back and the flanks and even on the legs, which is an allergic reaction to the flaked maize, to which the dogs seem to build up an intolerance. In my experience, the cooked and extruded pellet-form of complete foods do not seem to cause this problem. Any allergic reaction should be treated with cortisone to alleviate the spots or rash and the dog should be put onto a different feeding regime. Unfortunately, an allergic reaction such as this can trigger off a more rapid rate of coat loss than would otherwise occur. I have always found liquid paraffin, readily obtainable in bottles from a chemist, very effective for the external treatment of the coat. This should be gently massaged in, particularly along the back and the flanks. Baby oil is also most effective, and helps to keep the skin moist and supple.

WHITE DOBERMANNS

There are a number of White Dobermanns in the USA. I have no record of White Dobermanns appearing elsewhere in the world, though there were strong rumours about one having been seen in West London in the early 1980s. The first White Dobermann to be recorded was a bitch, Padula's Queen Sheba, bred by Mrs Ray Potter in 1977 and owned by Helen and Joseph Padula of Norfolk, Virginia. She was mated to a Black dog, Satin's Black Raven, and produced a litter of Black and Tan puppies. Two of these puppies, one of each sex, were retained for breeding and a mating between them produced a litter of ten puppies, including two Whites. The male was also mated back to its mother, Sheba, and this mating also produced two White puppies.

A number of subsequent matings took place, with the initial objective of testing the genetic mode of inheritance of the white colour, and they showed conclusively that it was the result of a single pair of recessive genes. Some of these test matings were carried out using dogs purchased by the DPCA, which set up a White Dobermann Research Committee for the purpose. This course of action by the DPCA must be seen as highly commendable, irrespective of any individual opinions on the colour, or of its value to the Dobermann breed.

Dr J.P. Scott, Professor of Psychology Emeritus at the Bowling Green State University in Ohio, prepared a report on the White Dobermanns for the DPCA, which was reproduced in the UK in the North of England Dobermann Club's 1982 Yearbook. It suggested that these White Dobermanns are not true albinos as they are not completely colourless. The pair of genes involved is, therefore, probably not the C series, in which the recessive cc produces an albino, which totally lacks pigmentation and in which the eyes are pink. Dr Scott tentatively designated the genes as the W series, in which the double recessive ww produces white and masks the four colours that would otherwise have been produced by the B and D genes in the dog's genotype. Where a dominant W gene is present, the white does not appear and the dog's colour depends on its B and D gene combination. This should not be confused with the white marks which sometimes appear on Dobermanns, usually on the forechest, of otherwise normally coloured dogs. This is caused by a separate genetic factor.

The most likely origin of this recessive w gene is that a mutation occurred in a remote common ancestor of Sheba's sire and dam. The recessive w gene would then have been passed on from generation to generation, with each carrier passing it on to 50% of its progeny, until one day a mating took place between two apparently unrelated dogs which both carried the recessive w gene and, hey presto, out pops a White puppy.

A description of these White Dobermanns was given in an article by Judy Doniere in the USA, reproduced in the UK in the Midland Dobermann Club Yearbook in 1983. The coat colour is described as varying from a very pale cream, or having a slight yellow tinge to a light buff colour. All have dead white markings where the tan markings would normally be found. The lips, eye rims, pads of feet and the nose are bright pink, which varies from deep pink when the dog is active, to pale pink when at rest. The coats are very dense and clearly do not suffer from the alopecia which afflicts the Blue and Fawn coats. There are no apparent physical defects, such as deafness, associated with the white colour, apart from photosensitivity of the eyes, in that they squint in bright light and the pupils contract to a very small aperture of approximately one-sixteenth of an inch in diameter. Indoors the eyes are normal, although the pupils appear to be somewhat more contracted than those of a dark-eyed dog. There is no indication of defective vision.

The AKC is willing to register White Dobermanns, though this caused some surprise and even some disappointment initially. They are *not eligible for exhibition*, however, following the AKC's agreement to amend the breed Standard to make any colour other than the four acceptable colours a disqualifying fault. There is no restriction on the use of White Dobermanns for breeding, in that their offspring can be registered and, if they are of the four acceptable colours, they can be shown. Without the ability to register White Dobermanns, this would be difficult, if not impossible, to achieve.

Chapter Eight

BREEDING DOBERMANNS

In practical terms, anyone who breeds a litter of puppies may be defined as a breeder. However, this is a very simplistic dictionary definition and is not really sufficient. To qualify as a breeder, one should be attempting to produce Dobermanns of as high a quality as possible, taking great care about the way the puppies are reared and how they are eventually homed. Someone who simply breeds for the sake of breeding, possibly for financial gain, is not a true breeder – they are better described as a producer.

EXAMINING YOUR MOTIVES
Before considering the various aspects of breeding in detail, ask yourself whether you should really be breeding a litter of puppies. Are your motives right? Are you breeding in order to produce a litter of good-quality puppies in order to perpetuate your bloodline, or to achieve a potential show winner – or are you simply planning to produce more dogs of a questionable standard simply by using a convenient or cheap stud dog?

Are you able to devote the necessary time and resources to looking after a bitch in whelp, supervising the whelping, rearing the puppies and finding them suitable homes? If you cannot commit yourself totally to what may well be a time-consuming responsibility, then don't consider breeding. Is your bitch of a sufficiently high standard to justify breeding from her? If not, then don't breed from her. Is your bitch of a suitable breeding age and in proper breeding condition? If not, then do not breed from her.

Do you really want to breed a litter, or have you been told that every bitch should be allowed to have one litter? *There is no necessity to breed from a bitch.* Many lead full and healthy lives without ever having puppies. Are you planning to breed for financial profit? If so, forget it. You may be lucky and make a bit of money, but if you rear your litter properly, or have a small litter, then it is more than likely that it will cost you money.

Are you sure that there will be a demand for the puppies that you breed? You should certainly check whether you are likely to be able to provide good, loving homes for your puppies before you bring them into the world. There is nothing more dispiriting than finding that no-one wants them. Are you of a nervous disposition? Do you panic easily? If you fall into these categories, then you should only breed if you are sure that you can call upon the services of an experienced breeder or vet to guide you.

If you feel that you really are a suitable person to breed a litter of Dobermanns, and that your motives are honourable, then proceed. The first thing to realise is that breeding is not simply a matter of putting a dog with a bitch, allowing them to mate, and then rearing the resulting litter of puppies. Breeding is both an art and a science. Many breeders have spent a lifetime studying this subject and trying to breed better-quality Dobermanns. One of the first things to understand is that the more one knows, the more one realises how much there is still to learn. Nobody ever knows it all. The other thing is that nature has a happy knack of springing the unexpected. The only consolation is that the more you know, and the greater your experience, the more able you are to deal with all eventualities.

Having decided that you are going to allow your bitch to produce a litter, you must decide which stud dog you are going to use. This is probably the most important decision you will need to make, since it will determine, to a very considerable extent, what your puppies will be like, both in terms of their appearance and their temperament. You must remember, of course, that your bitch shares an equal responsibility for the characteristics of the puppies.

BREEDING FOR QUALITY

For anyone wishing to breed Dobermanns with the principal objective of acquiring top-quality show dogs, or of continuing, or even improving, their bloodlines, a great deal more thought about the choice of stud dog is needed. There are many theories about breeding, of which anyone claiming to be a breeder should have, at least, a working knowledge.

These theories are all based on the relationships of the dogs in the pedigrees of both the bitch and the intended stud dog. The more closely related the two parents are to each other, the more alike they will be, and the greater the probability that the puppies will resemble the parents, share their characteristics, and be more uniform among themselves.

The reason for this is that breeding brings together the combination of countless genes, half coming from each parent, which determine the appearance and characteristics of the puppies. It has been calculated that a dog such as the Dobermann has thirty-nine pairs of chromosomes and that each chromosome contains more than twenty-five thousand genes. The possible combination of genes is, therefore, virtually infinite. If the two parents share a common ancestor, the puppies will inherit many of the same genes from both parents. The result will be that the puppies are more likely to resemble their parents and each other than where there is no common ancestry in the parents' pedigrees.

Am. Ch. Tarrado's Corry (Am. Ch. Felix v Ahrtal – Am. Ch. Highbriar Jasmine). Owned by Frank and Eleanor D'Amico. This dog has had a tremendous impact on the UK Dobermann, being the foundation for many of the top winning dogs and bloodlines of the 1980s and 1990s.

Ch. Holtzburg Mayhem (Ch. Perihelia's Resolution – Ch. Dizown I Can Boogie Too With Holtzburg). Bred and owned by Fiona Field. Winner of 7 CCs and 7 Reserve CCs. One of the breed's outstanding sires, and winner of the UK's Top Stud Dog All Breeds 1993.

The main methods are known as line-breeding, inbreeding and outbreeding. These terms are the subject of varying definitions, which merely illustrates the degree to which they are frequently misunderstood. There are also a number of beliefs and old wives' tales associated with them, some of which are misleading and incorrect.

INBREEDING

Inbreeding is the mating of closely related individuals, i.e. father-daughter, sister-brother, thereby concentrating the genes of the two parents in the puppies. It may concentrate desirable genes in some puppies, but there is also the risk that it may have the same effect with undesirable genes in other puppies. Also, both desirable and undesirable genes may occur in the same puppy. Where the parents both carry the genes for desirable traits, it is reasonable to expect these to be transmitted to the puppies. The problem is that if they both carry recessive genes for an undesirable trait, these will also come through to the puppies, again doubled up.

When inbreeding, it is necessary to monitor carefully the resulting puppies, to select those that have the desirable traits and to reject those that exhibit undesirable ones. The great advantage of inbreeding is that you not only double up, and so perpetuate, desirable type and temperament, but such dogs become prepotent for these traits and are much more likely to pass them on when they, in turn, are used for breeding.

Inbreeding is best left to the more experienced breeders who are fully aware of the potential risks and possibilities of inbreeding within a particular bloodline. It is usually done to intensify an ideal feature within that bloodline. It is often believed that inbreeding is harmful and should always be avoided. This is not true. Used properly with the right dogs and with the ability to assess the resulting offspring, inbreeding can be a very powerful weapon for a breeder. The risk is with any undesirable recessive genes carried by the two parents. A serious breeder should know, or want to know, what undesirable traits are being carried in his bloodline. It must be borne in mind that these only manifest themselves when they are already being carried by the two parents.

Ch. Perihelia's Madame Rochas (Ch. Tavey's Gridiron – Jadan Aravorn The Huntress of Perihelia). Bred and owned by Mrs E. and Miss D. Lonsdale. Winner of 6 CCs and 6 Reserve CCs. She is the dam of Ch. Perihelia's Resolution and grand-dam of Ch. Holtzburg Mayhem.

Ch. Dizown Street Legal (Marienburg Firedanza v. Tavey (USA import) – Dizown Daisy Brown). Bred and owned by Di Patience. Winner of 6 CCs, 3 Reserve CCs, and the sire of 5 UK Champions.

LINE BREEDING

Line breeding is a form of breeding, in which the parents have one or more common ancestors in the first three generations. The term inbreeding is normally applied only to matings between father and daughter, mother and son and brother and sister. Line-breeding is usually considered to be a mating such as son to grandmother, daughter to grandfather or half-brother to half-sister. Line breeding has the same potential advantages as inbreeding, in that it increases the genetic relationship between the puppies and the desirable common ancestor to which the litter is being line-bred. Unless some form of line-breeding is carried out, it will only be three or four generations before the genetic contribution of even the most outstanding ancestor is diluted to the point where it makes very little contribution.

Most breeders prefer to linebreed rather than inbreed, since it is more likely to produce the desired results. The basic objective is to keep the overall relationship to common ancestors high by line-breeding back to them in successive generations. This process is the most likely way of preserving breed type and the desired conformation. Line breeding will only be successful, however, if the dogs to which one is line breeding are sound, since any faults will be concentrated, as well as any virtues. It is therefore no good considering line breeding back to a stud dog which carries faults which you do not want to perpetuate, particularly if the bitch has the same fault. Line breeding also presupposes that there is a suitable dog to which you can linebreed back: this is more likely to be the case where the bloodline is a strong, well-established one. Where the available dogs to which you can line-breed are relatively unknown and have little merit to commend them, then there is little point in breeding to them.

OUTBREEDING

The opposite to inbreeding is outbreeding, which may be defined as the mating together of two dogs which are less closely related than the average of the population. This effectively means that

Ch. Crossridge The Carbon Copy At Lynfryds (Ch. Findjans Chaos – Dizown Copy Cat). Bred by Messrs Crossley and Dethridge, owned by Fred and Linda Wilkes. Our Dogs/Pedigree Petfoods Top Sire 1989, Dobermann Club Top Sire 1990 and 1992. Sire of 3 UK and 1 Irish Champion, as well as Am. Ch. Findjans Outrage CD, ROM, CGC, GHC, the first Dobermann in the USA to gain his Championship with uncropped ears.

Am. Ch. Electra's The Windwalker: Sire of over 80 Champions. Owned by Judith Bingham.

Marienburg Firedanza v. Tavey (Marienburg's Don Diego – Ch. Marienburg Topaz Flame). Bred by Mary Rodgers of Montana, USA, and imported into the UK by Reg and Mary Barton. He is the sire of 7 UK Champions, and one South African Champion.

both sire and dam have no common ancestors in the last four or five generations and are not themselves line-bred. Outbreeding may be used as a means of trying to correct a particular fault on the bitch by using a dog which is strong on that point. The problem with outbreeding is that there is likely to be very little doubling-up of dominant genes and a high preponderance of recessive genes. This results in a considerable variation of type among the puppies, with little resemblance between them and the parents. It is therefore not a recommended method if you are interested in breeding for known type and temperament or if you are attempting to establish a blood-line.

OUTCROSSING
A breeding system which is used much more frequently is outcrossing. This is similar to outbreeding, except that both the bitch and the stud dog may well be line-bred for several generations. Outcrossing a line-bred bitch to an unrelated dog will introduce fresh genes into the blood-line, and can be used to try and improve on certain features. It may also be necessary where the bitch is so line-bred that it is difficult to find a suitable sire within the same blood-line. Having produced an outcross litter, one then has the option of line-breeding back to either side of the pedigree in the next generation.

Occasionally top-quality dogs are imported from overseas in order to expand the gene pool available. Perez vom Franckenhorst at Barrimilne (Int. Ch. Dutch/German/French Fela vom Franckenhorst – Int. Ch. Dutch/German Golda vom Franckenhorst. Imported and owned by Margaret Bastable.

Photo: Sally Anne Thompson.

If you are considering using an outcross sire in order to improve a particular feature, you will need to be sure that he is not only strong on that particular feature, but is passing it on to his progeny. You will also need to bear in mind that such a mating may well introduce a whole range of new faults into your blood-line, possible in the form of recessive genes. Clearly, the more the sire and the dam are line-bred, the less likely it will be that undesirable traits will be passed on, and the easier it will be to predict the likely outcome of the mating. An outcross mating to a sire which is not line-bred – hence has little prepotency – will make it less easy to predict the outcome. In this situation it will be necessary to select carefully the best of the progeny and then line-breed back to the bitch's pedigree in the next generation.

CHOOSING A STUD DOG

You should make a decision as to which stud dog you would like to use well in advance of the anticipated time that you will mate your bitch. Some stud dog owners do not take kindly to being asked on the telephone if a bitch can be brought to one of their dogs in about two hours time! To help in making the decision, visit a number of the major dog shows, see some of the winning dogs, and arrange to visit kennels who offer dogs at stud so you can look at their available stock. This will enable you to assess the conformation and the temperament of their dogs, and possibly other members of the same family. You should also study pedigrees, and obtain copies of them for those dogs in which you are interested. If your bitch is descended from a particular bloodline, or has been bred by a knowledgeable breeder, then consult them, as they will be able to give you useful advice, possibly suggesting dogs you may not otherwise have considered.

CHECKING FOR TEMPERAMENT

Many occasional breeders, certainly in the UK, are more concerned about the temperament of the dogs they produce than their conformation, providing they are of a reasonable standard. If this is a major consideration, then you should check the temperament of your chosen stud dog and as many of his close relatives as possible, to ensure that they meet your expectations. This will give you a good guide as to the likely temperament of your puppies. *Do remember that your bitch will contribute as much to the puppies as the stud dog*, so you will need to bear in mind that, if there is any questionable temperament – or indeed conformation – in her breeding, this will come out in the offspring. Seek out a kennel which has a reputation for producing dogs with good temperament.

As you will already have realised from the consideration of breeding methods, it is not always the top show winner which will give you the best puppies. The best producer may well be a close relative which will carry similar genes but be just that bit more dominant in certain characteristics, or more able to stamp his type on his progeny. If you have the opportunity to study the outcome of various litters, it may be possible to identify a sound, well-bred dog who is not a show winner but who has what it takes to be a good producer.

Halsbands Manhatten with four of her offspring, who are all Champions. They are: Ch. Halsbands Redwing, Ch. Halsbands Bugenhagen, Ch. Halsbands Wicked Wizard and Ch. Halsbands Helmsman. Manhatten is owned by Roger James and June Lewis.

THE TERMS OF THE MATING

Having decided on your stud dog, approach the owners and seek their approval to the prospective mating. You should discuss the terms, if the owners are agreeable, though you may not receive an outright acceptance unless you, or your bitch, or her breeding are known to them. The normal arrangement is that you will pay a pre-arranged stud fee once the mating has taken place. Most owners have a fixed fee which can vary considerably from dog to dog and from kennel to kennel. Unless there are exceptional circumstances, you should not let the level of the stud fee decide whether or not to use a particular dog. At the time of the mating, you should also receive a copy of the dog's pedigree, which you will need to enable you to prepare pedigrees for your eventual puppies. You will also need the stud dog owner to sign the relevent paperwork, required by your national Kennel Club for registration purposes. You should also make sure that you obtain a receipt for the stud fee, particularly if you pay in cash.

Both the brood bitch and the stud dog should have had their hips X-rayed before being considered as breeding stock. The results of these X-rays should be available to all puppy purchasers. In the USA visiting bitches should be tested for Canine Brucellosis. This is a highly contagious disease (unknown in the UK) which leads to the abortion of foetuses.

MAKING ARRANGEMENTS FOR THE MATING

You should arrange to contact the stud dog owner on the first day of the bitch's season. This is generally taken as the first day a discharge of blood is seen. You will then be able to make the necessary arrangements regarding the intended mating. Check that the dog will be available on the day, or days, that the mating will need to take place, and that a written reservation is made.

It is normal procedure for the bitch to visit the stud dog. This is because males are always more confident on their own territory. However, experienced stud dogs may become sufficiently self-confident to mate bitches away from their own premises. If, for any particular reason, you want the dog to visit the bitch, or for both to meet on neutral territory, then you should make quite sure that the stud dog owner is agreeable and that the dog is likely to perform. Over the years I have heard of a number of matings which have been carried out at mutually convenient locations, but probably none more strange than one which took place in the vaults of the Bank of England!

Before arranging for your bitch to be mated, you should ensure that she is fully registered with the national Kennel Club, that she has had her hips scored, and in the USA, been tested for Canine Brucellosis.

KEEPING RECORDS

It is always a good idea to keep careful records of your dogs. This is particularly true with regard to the seasons of your bitches. Note the date that each season starts, when the bitch appears to be ready for mating, how long the season lasts and any other facts you think may be useful for the future. You should also keep careful records of all matings, the puppies born and any problems that you had, as well as any veterinary treatment given. It is surprising how often notes made at the time can be of benefit to you in the future. You should also keep careful records of vaccinations, wormings and other notable events, such as any veterinary treatment.

BREEDING AGE AND FREQUENCY

The earliest age at which a bitch should be mated is often the subject of discussion and controversy. It is generally accepted that a bitch should not be bred from until she is mature, both mentally and physically, which is at about two years of age. This is now enshrined in the codes of ethics of most of the Dobermann breed clubs in the UK, who insist that no bitch is allowed to produce a litter until she is two years of age or more. It is considered to be a serious offence for anyone to deliberately breed from a bitch who is under two years old.

Some authorities state that a bitch may be used for breeding at the third season. It is not safe to express breeding age in terms of the number of seasons, as the third season can occur as early as eighteen months of age. It is far better to stipulate it in terms of the actual age of the bitch.

The frequency of breeding from a bitch is possibly even more controversial than age. When I first came into the breed, it was the recognised procedure among the principal breeders that a brood bitch was bred on two consecutive seasons, then rested on the third. It is now generally felt that breeding from a bitch on consecutive seasons amounts to exploitation and it is discouraged. Several of the Dobermann clubs in the UK have incorporated this into their codes of ethics, either by insisting that bitches are not bred on consecutive seasons, or that they should not have two litters within a twelve month period. A blanket ban on breeding from a bitch at the season following a litter is perfectly reasonable where a bitch has had a good-sized litter, or has had a difficult whelping. However, it is not nearly so clear-cut where a bitch has, say, one or two puppies. In such cases, it may be argued that it is not unreasonable to breed the bitch again at the next season. This course of action would be supported by many vets on the grounds that it would not be detrimental to the health of the bitch in any way. The problem is to decide how many (or how few) puppies constitutes a 'small' litter. Allowance must always be made for those bitches who only come into season once a year.

Fixing an upper age limit for breeding a bitch is much more difficult. Seven is probably a reasonable rule-of-thumb age, but the general health and condition of the bitch is far more important. While I would never advocate breeding from a bitch who is over seven, it may well be that a bitch only five or six years old may not be in sufficiently good condition for breeding. Bitches who are fat and flabby, or lacking in muscle tone, are much more likely to have whelping difficulties and should only be mated after the most careful consideration.

Young bitches are always likely to whelp more easily than old bitches and it is probably unwise to try and breed a first litter from a bitch who is over five years old. Again, no precise age can be laid down, as it depends so much on the individual bitch, her condition and state of health.

Health checks are rarely carried out on bitches before they are used for breeding in the UK. In the USA, however, it is normal to check for heartworm in areas where this is a problem, and for brucellosis. It is always wise to ensure that the bitch has had the appropriate booster vaccinations, and has been treated for roundworms.

THE OESTRUS CYCLE

The pattern of a bitch's seasons is known as the oestrus cycle. It has four stages, pro-oestrus, oestrus, metoestrus and anoestrus. Pro-oestrus is the onset of the season and is considered to start when the first dark red, bloody discharge is noticed. The vulva becomes firm and swollen. The bitch begins to become attractive to males during pro-oestrus, due to the secretion of a pheromone with the urine. Oestrus is the period during which the bitch is receptive to males. She begins to flirt, raises her tail and flags it to one side, and presents her vulva when a hand is run down her back. The vulva itself becomes softer and the discharge changes from bright red to a pinkish, straw colour. Many bitches exhibit male mounting and thrusting actions, particularly if there are several bitches in season together. This is perfectly normal behaviour, so if you find that you have an excellent stud-bitch, don't be alarmed! This activity may occur at any time during the bitch's season. Oestrus probably lasts from about the ninth day to the fifteenth day of the season.

Metoestrus begins once the bitch refuses to continue standing for the male and is the time when she may be said to be coming towards the end of her season. The discharge will still be present but will gradually reduce in quantity until about the twenty-first day, when the season is generally considered to have finished. Metoestrus lasts for about eighty days and covers what would be the normal sixty-three day gestation period.

Anoestrus is the period of reproductive rest which lasts from the end of metoestrus until the onset of the pro-oestrus, when the next oestrus cycle begins again. Bitches do not have a menopause, continuing to have seasons all their lives, unless spayed.

FERTILISATION

Once the ova are released from the egg follicles, they are attracted to the opening of the fallopian tubes, which lead from the ovary to the uterus. They must mature in the female for about seventy-two hours after being shed before they are ready to be fertilized by the sperm, which is deposited at the front of the vagina. Through a combination of being washed forward by the prostatic fluid, their own swimming actions, and the contractions of the muscles of the vagina and the uterus, the sperm travel along the uterus, up the uterine horns and into the fallopian tubes, where fertilization takes place. The sperm can survive in the female for three or four days after a mating has taken place, thereby helping to ensure that, even if the eggs are not fully mature at the time of mating, they can still be fertilized a day or two later.

Once this has happened, the ova begin to grow by means of cell division. They remain in the fallopian tubes for about four days, then pass into the uterine horns. They become attached to the walls of the uterine horns about fourteen to eighteen days after fertilization. From then until about the thirty-fifth day, they grow very little, but the cells reorganise themselves in such a way as to form recognisable individuals. Once they reach this stage of development, they can legitimately be referred to as embryos.

THE GESTATION PERIOD

The gestation period is normally considered to be sixty-three days from the day of the mating. The actual period may vary, since fertilization may not be on the same day. Most of the growth of the embryos takes place during the last three or four weeks of this period. It is during this time that the bitch will visibly thicken in the flanks and then the underline will begin to drop. Dobermann bitches seem to be able to keep you guessing right until the last moment, but if the bitch has a reasonable number of puppies, she will become quite matronly from the seventh week onwards. Heavy bitches, or bitches with small litters, may be able to keep you guessing even longer.

During these last few weeks of the pregnancy, the bitch should slow down somewhat. However, not all pregnant Dobermann bitches do so, which means that you have to think for them. Do not let them over-exercise. Do not let them play rough with other dogs. Avoid anything which may result in the bitch being banged, since this may damage the puppies.

NUTRITIONAL REQUIREMENTS

Since the developing embryos grow relatively little during the first five weeks, their nutritional needs are not very great. This means that it is not necessary to give the bitch extra food during this period. There is a great temptation to think that, because the bitch has been mated, she must be in whelp and so needs extra food. Most Dobermanns would welcome this suggestion, whether or not they are in whelp. The result will be a very happy Dobermann, but quite possibly one which is overweight and, if this is accompanied by a lack of the normally required exercise, an out-of-condition one as well. This should be avoided, as such bitches do not whelp as easily as those that are in peak condition.

During the last four weeks of the pregnancy, the bitch will begin to need extra feeding. You will notice that the normal Dobermann request for any extra food that might be in the offing will be replaced by an urgent demand for more food. During this period, the bitch should be given two meals per day, possibly reducing the quantity for the main evening meal, but ensuring that the total amount of the two meals exceeds the normal main meal.

It is difficult to be too precise about what you should be feeding the bitch, since there are so many different feeding methods. If the bitch is being fed a good-quality complete food, with a protein content of about twenty-five percent, then it is sufficient to simply increase the quantity. If the bitch is being fed on a meat and biscuit type diet, then it would be helpful to increase the amount of meat or at least the protein element of the diet, to something approaching a fifty-fifty ratio of protein to carbohydrate. This assumes that the normal ration of meat to biscuit is about one to two. Whatever the feeding regime, towards the end of the pregnancy, it is not a bad idea to give the bitch some milk every day, but this should not exceed one litre, since milk tends to give Dobermanns diarrhoea. It is better to give the milk in a cooked form, such as in a milk pudding. Rice, macaroni or tapioca puddings are all acceptable and most Dobermanns do not seem to have a preference, though I find that the macaroni is always well-received. Other high-protein foods which can be given include eggs and cheese, but neither should be given to excess, with eggs being rationed to a maximum of two per day.

It is my belief that the use of supplementary vitamins and minerals is frequently overdone. Most good-quality complete foods contain a balanced diet and include all the vitamins and trace elements that a Dobermann requires. There is no need to supplement this, even for a pregnant bitch. At best, you are simply wasting money, as the bitch will excrete any surplus and, at worst, you may be creating problems, particularly with those vitamins where any excess is stored in the body rather than excreted. I am even doubtful about the need to give additional calcium, though it is often argued that the bitch needs this for the growing puppies and that it helps to build up the bitch's own calcium level, thereby avoiding eclampsia. On balance, I think that it is a wise precaution to give a small amount of calcium powder on the dinner once per day during the final two weeks. One teaspoonful should be adequate. Care should be taken not to give too much, as it is known that excess calcium can have the effect of depressing a bitch's ability to mobilise it once she has whelped.

VACCINATIONS

When to vaccinate is one of those questions to which there is no single, correct answer. The bitch should be given the necessary booster vaccinations before she is mated, in order to maintain her antibody levels. This will enable the puppies to acquire a reasonable level of maternal antibody protection which will last until they are about twelve weeks old, at which time they should be given their own primary vaccinations. This whole subject is one on which veterinary opinions differ, and if you are concerned as to whether the bitch has the required protection, you should discuss it with your vet. If necessary, a blood test can be carried out to ascertain the bitch's antibody levels before deciding what, if any, boosters are required. This will also ensure that boosters are not given which will generate a level of maternal antibody protection to the puppies which is so high that it will not have worn off prior to giving them their primary vaccinations. This can be a problem with parvovirus, where very high antibody levels can be achieved, and the take-up of the vaccination by the puppies is not always good. Vaccination theory, and the vaccines themselves, are always being improved, but your vet will be able to keep you abreast of current developments. Any boosters should be given to the bitch before she is mated, as it is not a good idea to give boosters to a pregnant bitch.

THE WHELPING DATE

The date that the bitch is due to whelp – i.e. sixty-three days after the mating– should be etched on your brain and written in large letters in red on the calendar. Even so, there is a fair chance that she will not actually whelp on that day, since most Dobermann bitches seem to come early, frequently one or two days, but it is not uncommon for them to whelp as much as seven days early. The earliest that I have ever experienced was a bitch who whelped a litter of five puppies ten days early. In this instance the puppies were a good size, fully developed, and all survived without too much trouble. The moral is quite simple: be ready for your bitch to whelp well in advance of the due date. Even if you are caught out, you should be able to get the bitch and the necessary equipment into the whelping room with the minimum of delay.

ALERTING YOUR VET

I have made a number of references to the need for you to consult your vet and it will, by now, be fairly obvious that you may need his help, or at least his reassurance, during the time that your bitch is whelping. You should, therefore, contact him and forewarn him that your bitch is due to whelp on a particular day and ensure that you can enlist his assistance whenever you need it. Some bitches produce a slight whitish discharge a few days prior to whelping. This is quite normal and should be no cause for alarm. If the bitch starts losing a blackish discharge, this signifies that there may be a problem and veterinary advice should be sought. This blackish discharge should not be confused with the greenish-black fluid which will probably be present during and after the whelping. This is caused by the break-down and decomposition of some of the blood-vessels of the placenta. Again, it should not be seen as a discharge any length of time before the bitch begins to whelp.

PREPARING FOR THE WHELPING

The first decision to be made is the location for the whelping. This is important as it will be the bitch's sanctuary for the next few weeks, where she will rear her litter. It does not matter if the chosen whelping room is inside the house or in a kennel, providing certain criteria can be met. It is frequently more convenient inside the house as it is easier to keep an eye on the whelping and, subsequently, on the puppies. Once the puppies are mobile at about four weeks old, however, they can become very messy and it is then desirable to relocate them to an outside kennel.

Whatever location is chosen, the whelping room should be relatively small, in that the bitch should feel that it is her private room. This will give her a sense of security and allow her to be more relaxed. It should be quiet and private, since there is nothing worse for a bitch who is whelping or rearing a litter than to be constantly disturbed by people coming in and out, or by excessive noise. It should be a room in which you can control the temperature, which should be kept at an average of about seventy degrees Fahrenheit, and this is easier to achieve in a small compact room than it would be in, say, a garage or a barn. It should also be capable of being cooled, if the temperature gets too high. It should be convenient, both for you, in that you will want to be able to exercise regular supervision, and for the bitch, so that she can go outside whenever the need arises but not be too far from her puppies.

THE WHELPING BOX

The most important item of whelping equipment is the whelping box. If you are likely to breed several litters over a period of time, it would be worth making one, or having one made, and keeping it as part of your kennel equipment. I have always found that a wooden whelping box is ideal, as it can be washed down after use, and stored ready for the next time it is needed. The ideal size is about three foot six inches by three foot six inches. Although this may seem too large, you should envisage the bitch with ten puppies of three weeks of age having to fit into it. Equally, the box should not be too large, or the puppies may get lost in it, particularly when they are very small. The box should be about ten inches deep, in order to give good protection from draughts. The back and the two sides should be fixed, but the front should be open, but capable of being closed by sliding boards across it. These can be removed when you want the puppies to be free to come and go, or alternatively, they can be slid into place if you want to prevent the pups from falling out when they are still small.

The box should be fitted with a pig rail on the two sides and the back. This is a wooden rail designed to prevent the bitch from being able to squash the puppies against the side of the box. It should be fixed at a height at which the bitch will lean against it when lying down but under which the puppies will be able to crawl if necessary.

A separate bed should also be provided for the bitch, which will enable her to get away from the puppies if she needs to do so. This is normally necessary once they reach about fourteen days old. It should be raised off the ground, to prevent the puppies climbing in once they are mobile.

HEATING

The ideal means of heating the whelping room is an infra-red electric fire, fitted with a thermostat. This should be fixed to the wall, so as to keep it well above the reach of the bitch and well clear of anything inflammable. I have always found a one-kilowatt infra-red strip heater is adequate. It is always useful to hang up a thermometer in the room to give you a check on the room temperature. Suitable thermometers can be purchased from any garden centre and need not be unduly costly. Do watch where you hang it, though, as I have had several chewed up by bored residents, and mercury is a hazard.

In addition to keeping the room itself at a steady seventy degrees Fahrenheit, additional warmth will be required for the puppies themselves. I have always found an overhead infra-red lamp to be ideal. This should be hung from a hook in the ceiling, using a length of chain, which can then be raised or lowered as required.

OTHER EQUIPMENT

You will need a large supply of newspapers, some paper sacks, such as dog-food bags, some clean blankets, both for the whelping box and the incubator, a roll of absorbent kitchen paper, some writing paper and a pen, several towels, washing facilities such as a bowl, soap and a jug of water (unless these are already close to hand) a small stool, and a clock. As far as medical equipment is concerned, I would never be without a pair of scissors, a pair of artery forceps, methylated spirits, a clinical thermometer and a night-light. For this I use a builder's inspection lamp, which can be plugged in wherever needed, with a low-wattage bulb, from five watts to twenty watts. These are often sold as nursery bulbs. A night-light should be left on from the time the puppies are born until they are about six weeks old and can be guaranteed to find their way to the bed, even in the dark.

You will also need to provide yourself with a camp bed, or a chair of some kind, as you will be spending many hours and nights with the bitch while she is whelping and for the first few nights thereafter.

Chapter Nine

WHELPING AND REARING

THE ONSET OF WHELPING

You will not know precisely when whelping will begin, but there are a number of pointers to watch for. The most obvious is the behaviour of the bitch, who will become very restless, wandering from room to room, and unable to settle down in any one place for more than a few minutes at a time. This is likely to be particularly noticeable during the final two days prior to the whelping, though if she is carrying a large litter, and is particularly distended, she will be restless, to some extent, for the final two weeks, which is a good time to introduce her to the whelping quarters and box.

Dobermann bitches tend to become more loving and affectionate during the final few days, although this is sometimes noticeable quite early on during the pregnancy – almost as if the bitch is looking to you for support and comfort, and to share the responsibility with you, which is a very good thing. It enables you to give her the reassurance that she needs and lays the foundation for you to stay with her during the whelping and to assist whenever necessary. This teamwork is very important, as she should know that you are helping her and are willing to share the work and the pleasure of the litter with her.

Some people have the idea that whelping is a natural, instinctive action, and that the bitch will quite happily whelp on her own without any help or interference. I believe this to be not only misguided but irresponsible. Whilst many bitches are able to manage by themselves, there are a number of things that can go wrong, which you can put right simply by being there. Your failure to be in attendance could well be putting not only the lives of the puppies at risk, but the life of the bitch herself. If you care so little for the well-being of the bitch and her litter, then you should not be breeding.

While supervision is important, you should not over-react or upset the bitch. It is important to remain cool and calm, giving her reassurance when necessary and help when needed. Hopefully, the bitch's natural instinct to whelp and to care for the puppies as they are delivered, is functioning properly. This is important, as the puppies have to be attended to quickly after they are born, if they are to survive. You should discourage anyone else being present during the whelping; this should be a time when the bitch has no unnecessary disturbance. Too many people watching can unsettle a bitch, make her nervous and have an adverse effect on the whole procedure.

A bitch may go off her food. This can occur up to two days prior to whelping but is usually only evident on the day. If the evening meal is rejected, it is a fair bet that she will whelp that night but, like everything else in nature, there is no guarantee that this will happen. I well remember a bitch who was whelping during feeding time and was mortified to think that she might be missing her dinner. She ended up eating the dinner and whelping at the same time. There always has to be one,

I suppose! The one thing that all bitches will do shortly before whelping is to experience a drop in temperature, which goes from a normal of 101 degrees F to 101.5 degrees F (37.7 degrees C - 38 degrees C) to about 98 degrees F (36.6 degrees C). The temperature usually drops about six to eighteen hours before whelping starts and is the most certain and reliable indicator of its onset. It is therefore useful to include a rectal thermometer as part of your dog equipment. As the temperature drops, the skin will feel cold and clammy to the touch and have a detectable twitch and superficial muscle fibrillation, due to physiological attempts at body temperature elevation.

THE START OF LABOUR

These various activities by the bitch take place while the cervix is dilating, which is necessary to allow the puppies to pass out of the uterus. This is generally known as the first stage labour, which usually lasts for twelve to twenty-four hours. The length varies, and tends to be shorter for the more tranquil and stable bitches. First stage labour is accompanied by muscular contractions in the flank region, which are initiated as a direct response to uterine distension, and gradually increase in both intensity and rapidity.

They are followed by the more definite and stronger contractions of the second stage labour. These contractions are much more purposeful and differ from the earlier ones in that they are voluntary, forceful, abdominal muscle contractions, initiated by the conscious effort of the bitch, in order to expel the puppies. This is normally considered to be the labour, and the transition from the first stage to the second stage may not be easy to identify. The contractions will gradually become more severe, and will be accompanied by further bed-making and periods of lying down. Bitches often pant quite noticeably during this stage, though they may well not want anything to drink. The infra-red lamp can well be raised a little at this time.

These firm contractions indicate that the first puppy is on the way. Now is the time to dry off the scissors and the artery forceps, which will have been standing in methylated spirits to sterilise them, and have them close to hand, together with several sheets of kitchen tissue and some cottonwool. And it is the time for patience. You must sit and wait, giving the bitch your encouragement in order to put her at ease, as far as possible. The time scale between the onset of these contractions and the appearance of the first puppy will vary from as little as ten minutes to as much as two hours.

THE BIRTH OF THE FIRST PUPPY

The contractions cause the puppy and its associated membranes to separate from the uterus wall, push through the dilated cervix and into the outside world. The allantochorion ruptures inside the uterus, but the puppy is usually born in the inner bag, the amnion. The placenta may come out still attached to the umbilical cord and the puppy, or it may separate and come out later. A puppy may be preceded by a bubble of water protruding from the vagina. This will then burst. When this happens, the water is said to have broken. A puppy will follow very shortly.

The puppy, on arrival, will look like a small black sausage, usually enclosed in the bag. If the umbilical cord and the placenta are still attached, the first action to be taken is to break open the bag, which is a thin membrane of skin tightly enveloping the puppy. This can be done with your fingers. Once the bag is removed, wipe any mucus away from the puppy's mouth and nose with a small swab of cottonwool, which will ensure that the air passages are clear and that the puppy will be able to breath. The cord should be clamped with the artery forceps, about one inch from the puppy, and cut on the placenta side of the forceps, which can then be removed. The act of clamping the cord is sufficient to cause the blood in it to drain back. If the cord is just cut, there is a risk that it might bleed. The puppy's arrival is often accompanied by a considerable amount of fluid, which is dark red in colour. The puppy, once detached from the cord, should be moved on to a dry patch of paper close to the bitch's head, so that she can be encouraged to lick her offspring dry. You will need to help her with this task by briskly rubbing the puppy with sheets of the absorbent kitchen tissue, which will also stimulate respiration and get the puppy breathing air properly. Both these objectives are important, so this rubbing dry and licking by the bitch should be done as quickly as possible once the puppy has been born. A cold and wet puppy is at considerable risk of dying from hypothermia. The stimulation of rubbing or licking is necessary to get the heart and the lungs functioning. The puppy, once relatively dry, should be encouraged to start sucking milk as quickly as possible by being held close to one of the teats. If necessary, gently open the puppy's mouth and place it on the teat, holding the puppy in place until sucking has started. Sometimes puppies do not suck immediately after being born. This does not matter, so long as they begin within an hour or so. Maybe they need to get over the shock of being born first! You will not always know in advance how the bitch is going to react to the birth of the first puppy. If it is also her first litter, she may not know what has happened or what to do. I well remember one bitch, on hearing her first puppy cry, wanting to run away, as she was frightened. Usually, however, bitches seem to know instinctively what the puppy is and what needs to be done.

THE REST OF THE LITTER
Once the first puppy has settled down, it is time to tidy up the whelping box and prepare for the next one. Put additional layers of newspapers on top of the bloody discharge from the first puppy, in order to provide a dry base for the next arrival. I always keep a plastic or paper sack in the corner of the whelping room ready to receive any such paper or other rubbish. This enables it to be removed hygienically and be disposed of once the whelping has finished.

As the second puppy is about to be born, the first puppy should be quickly transferred to an incubator, away from any possible harm if the bitch suddenly gets up or shuffles around the box or starts scratching up the bed. The incubator can be as simple as a cardboard box with a blanket in it. This will also prevent the puppy getting wet again and gives you and the bitch a clear working area. Once the second puppy has been safely attended to in the same way as the first one, and more clean paper put down, then the first puppy can be returned to the whelping box and the bitch can attend to both puppies. Again, make sure that both puppies are sucking and, if they are not, then try and hold them onto a teat until they do.

There will be an interval of waiting until the third puppy arrives. It is not unusual for three or four puppies to be born fairly quickly, say over a period of two hours, followed by a period of rest of anything up to three or four hours. This period of inactivity is not a matter for concern, provided the bitch is resting and is not contracting hard without any results. Prolonged periods of unproductive contractions may require investigation. The third and subsequent puppies will be born, cleaned up and introduced to the milk-bar in the same way as the first two.

PLACENTAS
As already indicated, the placenta may be passed still attached to the puppy and needs to be detached. Frequently, the puppies are born already separated, in which case the placenta will be expelled independently, sometimes intermittently with the puppies, or after the last one has been born. It is important that all the placentas should be passed, as their retention can cause major problems. It is therefore always a good idea to keep a log of the whelping. Write down the times of each birth, the sex of the puppy, and whether the placenta has been passed. It is also worth noting anything else which happens – such as any treatment given, any apparent problems, etc.

Left to themselves, bitches will normally eat the afterbirths and clean up as much of the fluid discharges as they can. While this practice may seem distasteful, it should not be discouraged. Apart from it being the natural instinct of the bitch to keep the nest area clean and to hide the scent of the new-born puppies from any would-be predators, the placentas provide a high-grade source of protein, and contain hormones that will stimulate contractions and milk-flow. Eating too many placentas, however, will certainly give the bitch diarrhoea, so I normally let her eat some of them and, if it is a big litter, remove the rest to the paper sack.

Whether the cords are severed by the bitch or cut by you, they begin to dry off very quickly. They should be trimmed back to about half an inch in length as soon as possible, as they tend to get wrapped around everything if left too long. The bitch must be watched, as she will often pull the cords and nibble them whilst cleaning up her puppies. This should be discouraged, as it may make them bleed and could cause an umbilical hernia. The remnants of the cords will dry up and disappear within about twelve hours of the birth.

WHELPING PROBLEMS

I have always considered that the Dobermann is a breed which whelps easily. I express this as a matter of opinion rather than as fact, as I am aware that some of my fellow breeders take a very different view, having encountered serious problems more often than not. I do not know why one breeder should always experience problems whilst another rarely does. However, it indicates that one should never be complacent. Always be watchful and ready for the unexpected.

The four main danger signals to watch for can be summarised as follows. One is a prolonged period of time elapsing after the first stage labour, without the onset of any second stage labour contractions – though, as noted already, it is not always easy to tell when a bitch progresses from first to second stage labour. As a rough guide, a delay of four hours should be taken as a maximum; any longer than that is suggestive of primary uterine inertia.

The second danger signal is repeated severe and abortive straining in an attempt to give birth, followed by physical exhaustion. A reasonable time must be allowed, but about two hours should be taken as the maximum. This is not the time-gap between births, but the duration of severe contractions without leading to a birth. This would suggest a puppy stuck somewhere, wrong presentation, or an over-size puppy. It may also indicate a possible defect or deformity in the bitch, such as a stricture of the cervix, either from birth, or due to an illness or injury, such as a tumour.

The third is the failure of the bitch to continue having contractions before the whole litter has been born. This would suggest secondary uterine inertia.

The fourth is the refusal or reluctance of the bitch to relax completely once the whelping has finished. This would indicate the retention of a puppy, or placentas, or the possibility of an infection.

Most of these problems can usually be resolved by external means. The vet and the breeder will need to consider the situation and make decisions. This will often be whether to be patient a little longer and to continue the external attempts to encourage normal births, or whether surgical intervention in the form of a caesarean is needed.

THE END OF WHELPING

It is never easy to know when a bitch has finished whelping. Usually she will settle down and go to sleep. However, because she has done this, it does not necessarily mean that there are no more puppies to come. It may be possible to feel in her flanks to see if there are any obvious puppy bulges. A vet, who is experienced at checking bitches, may well be able to give a more certain opinion.

Even if the bitch appears to have finished whelping, she may well continue to have contractions and to discharge muck and debris for several hours. This is technically referred to as the third stage labour, during which the remaining afterbirths are expelled. Clean pieces of newspaper should be placed under the back-end of the bitch, in order to keep the bed clean and to prevent her from trying to clean up the mess herself, which may not be her first priority if she is worn out after a long whelping, and has a reasonable size litter.

When the bitch has finished whelping, and settled down with her new family, every puppy should have learned to suck milk from her teats. You will need to ensure that each one is sucking, and that the smaller ones are able to push their way through, past the bigger ones.

The best way to check that each puppy is receiving an adequate amount is by observing the puppies themselves. If they are fat, appear contented, sleep steadily and croon quietly to themselves, then it is reasonable to assume that all is well; but if there is one which appears to have a sunken belly, is thin and obviously not happy, try opening that puppy's mouth and placing it over a teat. Check that the bitch really does have milk, by squeezing her teats gently between thumb and finger – though if lack of milk is the problem, all the puppies would be unhappy. One solitary unhappy puppy suggests that the little thing is either sick or defective. It is certainly worth giving such a puppy supplementary feeding, but don't be too upset if the puppy does not respond and eventually dies.

NEST SENSE

Some bitches have a marvellous nest sense, others simply don't. You will soon find out into which category your bitch fits. Some will step into the nest box very carefully, manoeuvre themselves into a position where they can sit down without disturbing the puppies, then carefully lie down alongside them. Others are not so careful and leap into the box, scattering pups and bedding everywhere, simply flopping down on top of whatever happens to be under them. Such bitches are a nuisance, and if you have one like that, you will need to steady her down and make her get in slowly and carefully. If necessary, quickly move the puppies to one side so that they are clear of her feet, then put them alongside her once she has settled down.

For the first three weeks of their lives, the puppies are entirely dependent on their mother's milk. Ch. Remesca Firelight, owned by Allison Moss, is pictured nursing her puppies, sired by Ch. Jowendys Kilowatt.

Some bitches wash and clean-up their puppies very carefully without rolling them too far away. Others wash them with such enthusiasm that they end up in the far corners of the whelping box, then look helpless and worried when the puppies cry. Some bitches are clever enough to nuzzle, or even pick-up and retrieve, such stray puppies, but some will shuffle around the whelping box to get close to the stray and, in the process, disturb all the others and you will end up with a box full of crying puppies and a frantic and unsettled bitch.

With a bit of encouragement and plenty of reassurance from you, these excitable or inexperienced bitches soon learn the necessary basic nest sense and usually become reasonably good, if not expert, mothers. Again, the key to their learning is your patience and help and that all-essential teamwork between you and the bitch.

CLEANING THE PUPPIES
Most bitches instinctively know how to clean the puppies and to lick them in order to stimulate them to urinate and defaecate. Puppies cannot do this for themselves until about two weeks old, and rely on the mother doing it for them. Occasionally, one comes across a bitch who is not willing to attend to this necessary function, so they have to be encouraged by holding the puppy in front of them. If they will not co-operate, then it will be necessary to gently massage the puppies with a swab of cottonwool, moistened with water, to mimic the mother's tongue. You will need to do this at regular intervals if you ever hand-rear puppies. Generally speaking, it has to be done after every feed. Sometimes bitches are reluctant to clean their puppies at the outset but do so later.

THE VETERINARY CHECK
You should arrange for the vet to see the puppies as soon as possible after the whelping, and certainly within twelve hours. The vet will be able to check that the bitch has finished, by feeling and palpating her flanks, reassure you that all is well and give the bitch an injection, often referred to as 'pit'. It is actually a hormone called oxytocin. In the USA, this injection is known as the 'cleanout shot', which describes very well why it is given. It causes contractions, which will push out anything remaining in the uterus, be it a puppy, dead or alive, or afterbirths, it reduces the surface area of the uterus, thereby reducing the risk of infection, and it stimulates milk flow. Pituitrin may also be given during the whelping, when the bitch has clearly not delivered all her puppies but has gone into a state of prolonged dormancy. It will cause contractions to ensure the speedy birth of the remaining puppies. It should not be given when the bitch is contracting and whelping normally, or when a puppy is stuck and the bitch is already contracting, and should only be administered by a vet or an experienced breeder, in order to avoid inadvertent misuse.

FEEDING THE BITCH
After they have whelped, some bitches eat very little for several days, and quite possibly for as long as two, or even three weeks. They are obviously in some pain or discomfort following the ordeal of whelping, their digestion will be unsettled from eating the placentas and other whelping discharges, and they are cleaning up after their puppies. The stools will therefore be loose, possibly for the three weeks that they will be feeding the puppies. This is the time to pamper the bitch, by offering her things that may tempt her to eat. There is an element of trial and error involved in this, as different bitches are tempted by different things. It is always worth trying the usual dinner first, as there is always the exception to every rule and some bitches will continue eating normally.

Once the bitch is eating again, you should feed her two meals a day. If necessary, adopt a 'feed when you like' regime, by leaving food in the whelping room. Once the bitch has settled down, she may help herself if she is hungry. One word of warning – never leave any food in the whelping box. Most bitches will guard the food, even from tiny puppies, whether or not they actually want it. Always ensure that the food is left away from the whelping box, but where it is accessible to the bitch.

POST-CAESARIAN CARE
The bitch who has had a caesarian will probably suffer after-effects from the anaesthetic for up to twelve hours and will need to sleep until these have worn off. She may also suffer from post-operative shock, characterised by coldness to the touch and shivering. She should be put in the whelping box, or some other warm resting place, with the overhead infra-red lamp. As a result of the operation, she will lose much of her milk supply, though this will return fairly quickly. The puppies should be kept away from her for the first twelve to twenty-four hours, until she has fully regained consciousness and has recovered from the shock. They should then be put back with her on a regular basis for feeding, providing she has sufficient milk, since this will not only ensure the well-being of the puppies and give them the colostrum, which is rich in food value and antibody protection, but will also encourage the return of the milk-flow. If she does not have sufficient milk, you will need to give supplementary milk, using a baby feeding bottle. This procedure will be very time-consuming, but you must always accept at the outset that these sort of problems may arise when you mate your bitch. If you can't manage to rear the litter if there is a problem, then you should not breed your bitch.

DEFECTIVE PUPPIES
Deformed or defective puppies are occasionally born. These are not common, and you must consider yourself unlucky if there are any in your litter. If you breed litters on a regular basis, then there is a strong probability that sooner or later you will see one.

Cleft palates: These occur when the roof of the mouth is incomplete and the milk that the puppy sucks tends to get into the nostrils and out again through the nose, rather than all going into the stomach. **Hairlips** are sometimes found. These defects are obvious at or very soon after birth. Such puppies are not viable and should be put down as soon as possible If you cannot bring yourself to do it, then ask the vet to do it for you.

'Squealers': Some defects become evident shortly after birth, once the puppies have begun to grow. One such defect is where there is a problem with the balancing mechanism in the ears. Such puppies are unable to get off their backs, and squeal continuously. When placed feet down, they simply roll over onto their backs again. Such puppies are generally referred to as squealers. They can suck normally if helped and can reach three weeks of age, but when a normal puppy is learning to walk, squealers are unable to do so. They should, therefore, be put down as soon as possible rather than reared. They are also extremely disruptive in the whelping box, as the bitch is always ill at ease with their constant crying.

Swollen heads: These are found occasionally. They are soft and spongy to the touch and can look really unpleasant and, in my experience, are best left alone. The condition does not seem to upset the puppies, who suck and grow normally. The swellings seem to be re-absorbed by the time the puppies are two weeks old.

Deaf puppies: There are some defects which only come to light once the puppies have been weaned and are mobile. These have to be assessed as and when they become evident. The key test is whether or not the defect is such that the dog will be able to live a reasonably normal life. Deafness becomes obvious once the puppies are four to five weeks old. Normal puppies will leap out of the whelping box to greet you as you enter the room, but a deaf puppy will remain asleep, oblivious to your presence. Once suspected, it is easy to confirm by veterinary diagnosis.

Weak puppies: Sometimes a puppy is born apparently normal, but does not grow, appears to lose body weight rather than gaining it, does not seem to be able to suck with any great vigour, and generally has no vitality. Such puppies are probably defective in some way and usually die within the first seventy-two hours. Do not be upset about losing such puppies. It is not a reflection on you in any way and no amount of supplementary feeding, warming in the incubator or trying to make them suck is going to make any difference. Simply accept that they are defective and not viable, and give your attention to those that will survive. There may be occasions when pups will reach four to five weeks old, then appear not to grow, and steadily get thinner and weaker and eventually fade away. Again, such puppies almost certainly have some major defect and it is better that they die early rather than after they have been homed. An alternative would be to cull such puppies once their defect became obvious, if they have not died naturally. Do not confuse defective puppies with puppies which are simply small – these often grow up to be as big as the others. You will also notice that it is always the small bitch in any litter which has the most character and personality. I do not know why, but it always seems to be the case.

These weak, defective puppies often make a bitch unsettled. She senses something is wrong, because of the puppy's lack of vigour, coldness and feel to the touch. She will continue licking the puppy, which will get pushed away from the teats in the process. Normal puppies will very quickly find their way back to the teats, but defective pups won't, probably because they don't have the strength. This gives the appearance of the bitch rejecting them, though I doubt whether she is actually doing so as she will sometimes hold a weak puppy in her mouth. Fortunately, once such puppies have gone, the bitches very quickly forget them.

Umbilical hernias: These appear as holes in the abdominal wall where the umbilical cord was attached. They can be felt very easily with the fingers and are often noticed as a slight bulge where the skin hangs down. If the hernia is fairly small, say the diameter of a pencil when the puppy is four to five weeks old, it will probably disappear by the time the puppy is six months old. If the hole is larger, there is a danger that the intestine can drop into it and become trapped, which may lead to peritonitis. This should be corrected once the puppy reaches twelve weeks of age and can be vaccinated against any infection that might occur on the vet's premises and is old enough to withstand the anaesthetic. It is a very simple operation, since it is really only skin-deep and puppies recover very quickly.

CULLING PUPPIES

Most breeders would accept that it is reasonable, and probably humane, to cull weak or defective puppies, as the weaker puppies will fade away and one or two may be killed as a result of accidents in the whelping box. Culling is the normal procedure in some countries, such as Germany, where the Breed Club has total control over the breeding and registering of puppies. This is based on the principle that a bitch should not be expected to rear more than about six puppies if she is not to be overworked and the puppies are to be big and well-reared.

FADING PUPPY SYNDROME'

There is nothing more upsetting than to see a litter of lovely, apparently normal, healthy puppies begin to weaken, stop sucking and simply fade away one by one, usually before they are three days old. Sadly, this is something which does sometimes happen. It is generally referred to as 'fading puppy syndrome. No one cause for such puppy deaths has ever been satisfactorily isolated, though a considerable amount of research into the subject has been carried out. Two theories which seem to offer the most likely explanation are a low-grade infection derived from the mother and the use of antibiotics on the bitch during the last few weeks of pregnancy. Where a bitch has an infection in the uterus, such as a streptococcal infection, this could be passed to the puppies. Although post-mortems may well not conclusively identify this, it is always worth bearing the possibility in mind if a litter is lost. It is difficult to check the bitch for such problems, as a swab will only identify what is in the vagina, for access to the uterus is not normally possible. Where a bitch has lost a litter, it is always worth giving her a course of broad-spectrum antibiotics a few weeks before she is due in season. This will kill most bacterial infections which may be present and will reduce the risk of the next litter being lost through an infection. There are a number of reports indicating that when post-mortems have been carried out on faded puppies, not only has no bacterial infection been identified, but no bacteria of any kind have been found in the digestive tract. This phenomenon has been linked to the giving of antibiotics to the bitch shortly before she whelps, which has the effect of removing all bacteria, beneficial and harmful alike, from the digestive tract of the puppies. Since some bacteria are needed to ensure digestion, it is possible that a total lack of bacteria means that normal digestion is unable to take place. If it is suspected that this is the cause of the problem, or it is known that the dam has been receiving antibiotics, then the normal flora of the puppies' stomachs can be replaced by giving oral doses of lactobacillus acidophilus. Where the bitch has been treated with antibiotics, it can be given to the puppies as a precaution before evidence of a fading problem is noticed. It has also been suggested that lactobacillus helps to avoid the bacteria which cause enteritis.

ECLAMPSIA

One problem which you will always need to be on the look out for is eclampsia. This is also known as hypocalcemia, or milk fever, which is caused by a drop in the blood calcium level below a critical threshold, due to the milk being drawn off by the puppies and the inability of the bitch's body to replace it sufficiently quickly. The symptoms are very characteristic. The bitch becomes very restless, is hot and pants a lot, and exhibits a staggering, unco-ordinated movement due to muscle spasms, twitching muscles and a high temperature. If the bitch appears to be too hot, give her a cool drink and check that the infra-red heater, or the room temperature, is not causing this. If these are eliminated as the cause, then eclampsia should immediately be suspected. This must always be treated as an emergency, and the vet should be requested to attend to the bitch as quickly as possible. Failure to treat the bitch can result in her getting progressively worse, having convulsions and dying. Treatment consists of an injection of calcium borogluconate Once the injection has been given, the symptoms disappear as if by magic, in as little as fifteen to thirty minutes. I have found Dobermanns to be very prone to eclampsia and am more surprised when a bitch does not get it, then when she does. Eclampsia normally occurs during the first five days, and it may occur more than once.

CAKED BREASTS

A regular check should be kept on the bitch's breasts to ensure that all is well. Sometimes, hard lumps can form. This condition is referred to as Glactostasis, or, more commonly, caked breasts. It is caused by the bitch producing too much milk in the mammary glands, either due to over-production or because the puppies are not sucking properly. It normally only affects one or two breasts and is usually due to a deformed nipple or a small litter, where some teats are simply not sucked. I have found it in bitches who consistently lie on one elbow, with the corresponding top breast unavailable to the puppies. If these lumps are detected, they should be treated, since severe cases can cause the bitch discomfort and lead to acute mastitis. The lumps should be massaged twice per day, possibly with a suitable ointment which your vet will supply, and the surplus milk should be drawn off, possibly by getting the puppies to suck the affected breasts.

MASTITIS

Glactostasis is a form of mastitis, but acute mastitis is a lot more serious. It is an infection of the mammary glands due to bacteria gaining access to the breast tissue, possibly as a result of scratches by the puppies. For this reason, as well as for the general comfort of the bitch, the toe-nails of the puppies should be trimmed on a regular basis. This can be done very simply with a pair of scissors. If one blade of the scissors is held under the nail, and slid along towards its end, it will catch on the sharp overhang. This is what needs to be cut off and there is no risk of cutting the quick.

With mastitis, the mammary gland becomes swollen, extremely painful and reddish-blue in colour. The milk may be contaminated with pus, which will cause the puppies gastro-enteritis. It will possibly be discoloured and is likely to be too acid, with a pH in excess of 7.0. The bitch will appear off-colour, feverish and lack appetite. She may well also reject the puppies because of her pain. Veterinary treatment is necessary, usually with antibiotics and ointment for the breasts. The puppies will need to be removed and hand-reared until the condition has improved.

REARING THE LITTER

For the first three weeks of their lives, the puppies will be totally dependent on their mother, who will be solely responsible for their well-being. In a way, this is the easy period for the breeder, as there is very little to do, other than ensure that the bitch is given everything she needs, and to exercise a supervisory role. It is necessary to ensure that the room temperature is comfortable, that the puppies are all sucking and that they are not tucked behind the bitch or buried in folds of the bedding. If all goes well, you will not need to do anything for the puppies during this time, apart from admiring them, which is always guaranteed to do the bitch's ego a power of good.

DOCKING

You will need to decide where or not you want the tails to be docked. In Britain, this needs to be done by a vet, and, in most cases, the third day is preferable. However, this can be left until the fourth or fifth day if the puppies are very small or premature.

DEWCLAWS

Dobermanns invariably have dewclaws on the two front feet, which correspond to the human thumbs. These are normally removed on about the third day, usually at the same time as the tails are docked. This is done because they are very prone to getting caught up in things and damaged. They also tend to spoil the clean-cut outline of the dog. If they are not removed, they must be clipped on a regular basis, as they can grow very long and into the dog's flesh. The Breed Standard specifically requires them to be removed, so any dog which is shown with them still on effectively has a fault. The extent to which this is, or should be, penalised is subjective.

The wording of the USA breed Standard indicates that dewclaws may occur on the hind as well as the front legs. Having doubted that this ever occurred, I have now found one rear dewclaw on a puppy in one of my litters. It was only noticed when the puppy was about six weeks old, so will not be removed. It certainly looks very odd but is surprisingly inconspicuous. However, in future, I will check more carefully for their presence.

THE DEVELOPING PUPPIES

One of the fascinating things about watching a litter of puppies grow is seeing the way in which the various functions develop. At birth the eyes and ears are closed. The nose is probably well developed at an early stage, since the puppies need to be able to find the teats as soon as they are

Dobermann puppies soon learn to use the trap-door in their kennel door. This enables the pups to go in and out without having to leave the door open.

born. The eyes open at about ten days old and begin functioning at about two and a half weeks. Occasionally, when the eyes open, they will be gummed up with a discharge. This may be due to a slight infection but is rarely a serious problem. The affected eye should be gently wiped with a swab of cotton-wool moistened in water. A small amount of eye-ointment should then be squeezed into it. The ears gradually open up and are probably functioning at about two and a half weeks of age. When the puppies reach three weeks of age, everything begins to change. This is when weaning should start and it should be completed by five, or possibly six weeks of age. This is a transition period, during which the puppies will change from being wholly dependent on the bitch, to being entirely self-sufficient, in that they can survive without the mother. It is also the age at which the puppies become aware of their surroundings and react to people coming to see them. They are also beginning to become mobile, so will need to be allowed out of the whelping box.

By five weeks of age the puppies will need to be able to run around fairly freely in order to exercise, play and generally develop. Weather permitting, this should include access to an outside run or to the garden. However, if you do not want your puppies to assist you with the gardening, confine them to a particular area or give them a run. This does not need to be too substantial a construction as it will be needed for only a limited period, unless you anticipate breeding a number of litters. Outdoor exercise is also necessary, because a litter of Dobermann puppies confined to a room in the house will very quickly make their environment both messy and smelly.

Until they are about six weeks old, the puppies will return to their bed quite regularly to rest and sleep, so it needs to be available to them at all times as it is their secure and familiar sanctuary. The overhead lamp should be maintained until they are about six weeks old if the weather is cold. If the weather is hot, then it can be turned off either during the day, or permanently. The best way to ensure that your puppies remain fit and healthy is to feed them well, keep them dry and keep them warm. I always leave a night-light on until the puppies are about six weeks old to ensure that nobody gets lost in the dark. A bowl of clean drinking water should be provided for the puppies from three weeks of age, which should be broad, shallow and heavy to ensure that the puppies can neither fall into it or knock it over.

WEANING

Weaning puppies is a time-consuming, frustrating and messy occupation. Nevertheless, it is a critical stage of the puppies' development. One seems constantly to be preparing beautiful puppy meals, only to find that they pick at them and tread them down to a solid mass, ending up with more of it on them than in them. No matter, it is all part of their learning process. Hopefully at each meal they will eat something, and will gradually learn to eat. They know full well that there is always mum to fall back on for a proper meal at this stage. In return for providing this supplementary feeding service, most Dobermann bitches will expect to be allowed to clean up any food not eaten by the puppies, even if this means getting it off the puppies themselves. It is an interesting observation that very few Dobermanns will eat food which puppies have trampled over, other than the puppies' own mother. Most Dobermanns sniff it thoroughly and leave it, with that look of disdain so perfected by the Dobermann breed.

There are many ways of weaning puppies. In fact, there are probably as many ways to wean a litter of puppies as there are breeders! What this shows is that it does not really matter what you wean your puppies with, providing the food you give them is nutritious and has sufficient puppy appeal. I cannot therefore tell you how puppies should be weaned. I can merely give you a few ideas and describe what I do.

Weaning should start when the puppies reach three weeks of age. By then they will be struggling to survive purely on the mother's milk supply, particularly if there is a large litter, so they will be getting hungry, and this will encourage them to start eating proper food. I am not keen on trying to wean puppies younger than three weeks old, unless there is a valid reason, such as the bitch being unwilling, or unable, to feed them adequately. If you start too early, there is always the risk that the digestive system will not have developed sufficiently to deal with the food which you are providing. The result is likely to be an upset stomach, an unhappy puppy and a set-back which could and should have been avoided.

Most breeders are agreed that fresh, raw minced or scraped beef is the ideal food for the first meal. I have always found supermarket mince to be perfectly suitable, provided it is of prime, lean quality. Mince with too much fat should be avoided. This raw mince should provide the only meal for each of the first two days. I prefer to give it in the evening so that the puppies go to bed on full tummies and sleep through the night. I like to make one pile of mince for each puppy on a dish, so that I know in advance how much each puppy is going to receive. I do not normally weigh the quantities, but each mound is likely to contain about two to three ounces. I like to feed each puppy individually, to ensure that each one has the opportunity to learn what eating is all about and to take as much time over it as is needed.

During the third and fourth days the puppies should be offered two meals per day. They should continue to receive their raw meat in the evening, but should also be fed in the mornings. Generations of Roanoke Dobermanns have been weaned on egg-custard. This is an ideal food as it is semi-solid, so representing a half-way stage between sucking and eating. It is also highly nutritious and is attractive to most puppies.

As with the raw meat, it is a good idea to place a small amount of the egg custard in a dish and individually feed each puppy. Sometimes they are so eager for the food that there is no need to give them the individual treatment. In this case it can be placed in a dish and put in, or near their bed, preferably on a sheet of newspaper. Once they begin to eat it, it is better not to watch them. They will walk in it, sit in it, cover each other and themselves with it and look like the proverbial mucky little pups. The bitch is best removed while this is taking place, as she is more than likely to eat it for them. She should be allowed back in when the pups do not appear to be eating any more of it. She will then not only clean up the remnants in the bowl but will, if you are lucky, also clean up the puppies as well. Once this has been done, I like to make the bitch feed the puppies herself, in order to ensure that they are well-filled. Some bitches will do this naturally, while others are less willing once the puppies reach three weeks old. It does not matter if the puppies do not eat much of these first meals. The important thing is to encourage them to eat. If you fail, no matter. Try again next time. You cannot push the puppies faster than they are able, or willing, to go. An alternative to egg custard is chicken soup, poured straight from the can into a bowl.

By the fifth day the puppies will be more advanced in terms of their over-all development and mobility. They should be eating some of the food that you are offering them rather than relying entirely on their mother's milk. The raw meat should now be discontinued and the number of meals increased to three per day, offered in the morning, midday and in the evening. This will give them time to digest properly between meals. I am not in favour of offering five meals per day for puppies of any age. I feel that they will barely have finished one before being offered the next. At this stage all meals should be on a communal basis. You will need to ensure that there is enough room around the edge of the dish for them all to get at the food. If necessary two dishes can be provided, certainly as they grow bigger and eat more ravenously. Even then Dobermann puppies are always likely to crowd around one bowl, then all move across to the second one when the first has been emptied!

By the time the puppies reach four weeks of age it should be possible to increase the quantities of food being given, and to introduce some solid food into the morning and evening feeds. This can be bread, soaked into the chicken soup, or one of the many complete dog foods on the market. If this is being used, it should be well soaked with hot water before being broken up into small pieces and added to the soup. There are also a number of puppy complete foods which are very well formulated and easy to use. These can be used either as additions or alternatives to the puppy weaning foods and the cooked meats already discussed. I find that different litters seem to prefer different foods. Whatever you eventually decide to dish up, the puppies will continue to appreciate it being more of a drink, with a little solid matter within it, rather than the other way round. They always seem to leave much more of each meal than one expects.

The midday meal should now become the milk-based meal, either egg custard or some other milk pudding. Plain milk or egg and milk can be given, but I am not in favour of giving too much milk to puppies; it is always better in the cooked form. Whatever food is given during this mid-weaning period, it should be high in protein, easily digestible, as nutritious as possible and provide both drink and food. It is better to avoid houndmeal or biscuit meal at this stage as they can be too rough and indigestible.

As the puppies progress towards five weeks of age, their rate of development seems to increase rapidly. They will be much more mobile and will expect to be allowed outside to explore beyond the confines of the whelping room. They will be aware of your presence and will come to the door to meet you. This is the age at which it is essential to begin to socialise puppies. They should be handled as much as possible, so that they learn to associate humans with love and affection. While the personality and temperament of the Dobermann is determined to a large extent by genes, this early environmental influence also plays an important part. Puppies which experience a lot of handling, and are shown gentleness and affection, have a much better chance of becoming gentle, loving and friendly adults. In any event, no-one should need an excuse for cuddling their puppies, as this is one of the joys of breeding Dobermanns.

They should also be exposed to as many of the routine noises and activities of the household as possible, without frightening them, but a degree of initial apprehension is inevitable. I have always found that a wireless playing in the background is beneficial.

WORMING

It is probably true to say that all puppies are born with worms, to a varying degree. In the UK the problem tends to be roundworms, but it can vary depending in which part of the world the puppies are born. They should be wormed as soon as possible after they have begun to eat food, generally at three and half to four weeks of age. There are many different worming compounds available. Whatever you use, it is important to follow the dosing instructions given by the manufacturer. While most worming compounds are relatively safe, it is always a wise policy not to over-dose a dog with any drug. Each puppy should be dosed individually. For this first worming, a chocolate-flavoured worming solution is ideal. It is administered using the barrel of a disposable syringe. Gently squirt the solution into the puppy's mouth, making sure that it is swallowed without choking. It is generally easier to do this through the side, rather than the front of the mouth. Separate the puppies once they have been dosed to ensure that no-one gets a double dose by mistake.

DIARRHOEA

Puppies are very prone to suffering from diarrhoea. If the diet is changed, this often follows. It can also happen after a milk-based meal or if the puppies have been upset by something such as being wormed. Provided the puppies remain normal in their behaviour and give no appearance of being sick, the diarrhoea can be disregarded. It will probably correct itself very quickly and no treatment needs to be given. If it is particularly severe and always follows the milk-based meal, then either reduce the quantity of this or miss it out for a day.

PUPPY STRANGLES

Provided that you keep your puppies warm, dry and well-fed, there is no reason why they should become ill or suffer any serious problems. But this does not mean that things may not go wrong. Nature has a happy knack of catching you unawares when you least expect it, so be vigilant. One problem which caught me unawares in one litter was puppy strangles. This can develop when a puppy is four to five weeks old, and appears as a rash of thick spots around the muzzle, which may spread to the area around the eyes and ears. The lymph glands may also swell. The problem is caused by a staphylococcus infection. While it is most worrying when it suddenly appears it normally clears successfully with treatment. I have heard of this problem with Dobermann puppies in a number of instances, so it is obviously something which crops up with them from time to time.

PUPPY PLAY

One of the problems which always arises with a litter of Dobermann puppies is how to keep them occupied. By the time they reach five weeks of age they are very mobile and very active, wanting to run around, explore their surroundings and play, not only with each other but with whatever makes a good toy. They therefore need to have an area for play. Weather permitting, this should be outside, preferably on grass but with access to their kennel or bed if they want to go back for a sleep. This area will need to be checked regularly to ensure that it is clean and safe. Remove any stones and clear it of all excreta at least once every day. It is a good idea to provide the puppies with some toys. They needs things they can carry, pull or chew. Beef-hide chews, either as knotted sticks or as rings, are always popular and, while you may provide enough for each puppy, they are all going to want the same one! Knotted ropes are sold as dog toys and these are ideal for puppies, as are balls, rings and rubber-pulls. Always avoid toys which can be swallowed, or chewed to produce bits that can be swallowed. Apart from commercially-produced toys, many humble objects such as cardboard boxes and paper are always appreciated, particularly if they can be

These eight-week-old puppies, which include two Blue and Tans, are now fully weaned and ready to go to their new homes.

Photo Steve Nash.

chewed up. Be careful, though, about giving old shoes, slippers or articles of clothing as they give the wrong message to the puppies, who will grow up believing that it is acceptable to chew such items, being unable to distinguish between what is old and what is new.

SELLING THE PUPPIES

For many people, the hardest part of breeding a litter is selling the puppies. It is very easy to form a very strong bond of love and affection with your puppies, particularly if you have spent a considerable amount of time with them. Nevertheless, they should have the opportunity to go to their own home and lead their own life. It is the right of every Dobermann to own a home, a garden and a family. Besides, if someone else had not been prepared to allow their puppies to go to new homes, you would not have a Dobermann now. You must not, therefore, feel too sad as they all go. You will, hopefully, have had a great deal of pleasure in rearing them, the puppies will go to good homes, and you will have made several new friends who, thanks to you, will have years of joy and happiness owning their new Dobermann.

Chapter Ten

THE DOBERMANN'S HEALTH

The Dobermann is a healthy breed of dog. Nevertheless, there will be occasions when your Dobermann is ill, though hopefully these will be minor in nature and short-lived in duration. There are a number of these minor illnesses which you should be able to treat yourself, rather than having to go to the vet. However, if you are ever concerned, or need reassurance that there is nothing seriously amiss, then you should ask your vet to see your dog. It is always better to err on the side of caution.

Over a period of time you will learn to note the subtle changes in behaviour when your Dobermann is feeling off-colour. These may include a slight lethargy, loss of appetite, pus in the eyes, vomiting, diarrhoea, a runny nose, a cough, or even just your own feeling that something is wrong. You will learn to read your Dobermann's body language.

If you suspect anything is amiss, take your Dobermann's temperature by using either a baby's rectal thermometer or one produced specifically for dogs. Shake the mercury well below the 100 degree mark. Vaseline the end and gently inset it into the rectum, for two minutes. Keep the dog steady to avoid injury or damage. Normal temperature for a dog is about 101.2 degrees, so if the temperature is too high, consult the vet.

To give liquid medicine or nourishment to a sick dog, pull out the side of the lower lip and slowly pour about one teaspoon of liquid into the mouth, while at the same time holding the head steady. Assistance from a second person may be helpful – or even necessary – depending on the dog. Do not force the dog's head back as this makes swallowing difficult and could cause choking or liquid going into the lungs. To give pills, place them as far back on the dog's tongue as possible, then hold the mouth closed until the dog has swallowed.

Force-feeding a sick dog is sometimes done, but is generally not a good idea. It is better to tempt them with something which they will eat. Give milk, rather than water. Add honey to it. Not only will this enhance the taste, but honey is a pre-digested food and will give the dog almost instant energy. Try slightly cooked minced beef or chicken, or egg custard, thickened cereal, cottage cheese or broth. Any food given should be lukewarm, not too hot or too cold.

INJURIES: If your Dobermann is injured, you need to make a quick assessment about its severity, and whether or not you can treat it yourself. Consult your vet if you are in any doubt.

Cuts or bites which are bleeding should be washed very carefully in warm water with some antiseptic solution added. If the bleeding persists it can often be staunched by packing the wound with potassium permanganate crystals. If necessary, the wound should be bandaged, to put pressure on the bleeding point, but it must not be tied too tightly or it will act as a tourniquet, cutting off the blood supply and creating a more serious problem than the one you started with.

If the wound is a cut or a tear to the skin, it is much better to ask your vet to stitch it, which will promote quicker healing and result in a less conspicuous scar. Torn ears are always a problem. Where the ear is split, stitching is by far the easiest solution. Where the damage is less severe, bleeding can still be profuse and stopping it is often difficult as the dog will shake its head, starting off the bleeding again. Pack the wound with potassium permanganate or antiseptic dusting powder and cover with cotton wool, which will stick to the blood and eventually form a pad which will stop the bleeding. The ear should be fixed to the side of the head with a bandage which will need to be taken around the dog's head, ensuring that the uninjured ear remains outside the bandage.

If the injury has been caused by something such as a rusty nail or barbed wire which may introduce infection, the wound must be carefully washed, and it is a wise precaution to arrange for the dog to have an injection to counteract any infection. If the dog is in shock, give a tranquilliser to help relaxation and rest.

In the following sections some of the more common health problems are considered, as well as some of the more important problems which could be considered to be specific to the Dobermann.

DIARRHOEA: This is probably the most common problem you will encounter. It is caused by insufficient fluid being removed from the excreta by the small intestines and may be caused by a whole range of things. The commonest cause is dietary, where the dog has eaten too much liver, milk, fat or eggs. Some seem to get it after eating relatively small quantities of some foods. It is not a problem and will resolve itself once the offending food has passed through the system. It is not unusual for youngsters to have diarrhoea after their milk pudding meal. No specific treatment is required in these instances. Experience will tell you what foods are likely to cause problems and are therefore better avoided or fed in very limited amounts. Diarrhoea is sometimes caused by stress or tension, such as when a dog is taken to a dog show. It will probably resolve itself very quickly once the stressful situation has passed. If the diarrhoea is persistent, and lasts for more than twenty-four hours, then you will need to consider whether it is a symptom of something more serious, such as a bacterial infection. If the dog looks dull and listless and is not taking food, then go to the vet, who will probably prescribe a course of antibiotics.

You should always watch for blood in the faeces. A small amount of fresh red blood on the outside of the stool is probably not a problem and only indicates slight damage to the rectum. If this occurs regularly, then veterinary advice might be helpful. Blood within the faeces or the diarrhoea is generally bad news, as it indicates that there is something wrong, such as some bowel or intestinal infection, for example enteritis. You should go to your vet immediately, particularly if a puppy is involved, as it might indicate parvovirus or coronavirus.

It is always a good idea to have a home remedy for the less serious attacks of diarrhoea. Light kaolin is very effective. This is a white powder which can be obtained from a chemist and should be stored in a sealed container to keep it dry. Sprinkle about one tablespoonful on the dinner, or mix it in with a small amount of milk. Or you can get tablets from your vet to keep as a stand-by. If the diarrhoea is not severe and the dog is not ill, then it is probably better not to change the diet. But if it persists, switch to a bland, easily digestible diet and do not overload or overwork the digestive system while the dog is recovering. Do not restrict the intake of water.

PARASITIC PROBLEMS
Fleas: the need to be vigilant has already been stressed. Fleas can easily be identified if the coat is combed with a fine-toothed flea-comb. Not only will the fleas themselves be found, but flea dirt will also be evident. This is actually flea excrement (dry blood) that appears on the skin as a black gritty material. Fleas will also cause the dog to scratch and bare patches may appear, usually on

the shoulders or in the area of the tail. Treatment has been discussed elsewhere. **Lice:** these are greyish-brown, wingless insects that feed on the dog's skin. They lay eggs, which stick to the hair of the dog, generally around the neck and the ears. Lice cannot live off the dog for more than a few days, which means that infection is spread from dog to dog by contact. They cause great irritation and scratching. They can be easily eliminated by spraying with an appropriate insecticide.

Ticks: these can be picked up by dogs from cattle, sheep, rabbits or hares. They are usually found around the head as white or bluey-grey 'warts' attached to the skin. Ticks should not be forcibly pulled off, as this will leave the head and suckers under the skin and cause a festering sore which can take weeks to heal. To remove a tick, soak it in oil, such as olive oil or liquid paraffin, or cover it in grease such as Vaseline or butter. After three minutes, grip the tick firmly and gently pull it out of the skin.

Mites: the need to be vigilant for harvest mites on the feet of your dog has already been stressed. Another mite which can be a problem, particularly with puppies, is cheyletellia. This is sometimes referred to as walking dandruff, which is what it looks like. It causes irritation which results in the dog scratching. Treatment is similar to that for sarcoptic mange.

Sarcoptic Mange: this is caused by a mite which burrows under the skin and causes great irritation. It appears as bare patches down the inside of the forelegs, outside the hind legs and all around the face and ears. The bare patches become red and inflamed, then go bluey-grey, furrowed and sweaty, often with a characteristic 'mousey' odour. Great care should be taken, as it is very contagious. It can be cured with the use of insecticide sprays supplied by the vet. All bedding, sleeping quarters and other areas which the dog frequents should also be sprayed.

Demodectic Mange: this is caused by the Demodex mite, which is present in the hair follicles of most dogs without causing any problems. It can get into the blood stream and so be passed to unborn puppies, which show no symptoms at birth but may break out in the mange when teething. It shows itself as bare patches anywhere on the body. It does not cause the same level of irritation as sarcoptic mange. The application of a mange lotion is highly effective in clearing up the problem. Occasionally the problem does not improve, but gets worse, with numerous patches appearing all over the body, which eventually merge to form large areas which become pustular and reddened, as the skin breaks down. A staphylococcus bacteria is usually present and this makes the condition worse, resulting in sores and bleeding. When the condition becomes extensive it is very difficult to treat and there is no real cure. This problem is sometimes described as folliculitis. Benzene hexachloride, sulphur baths and the continued application of the mange lotion may help. Cortisone will alleviate the skin irritation but will probably be counter-productive, as it depresses the dog's immunity to the mites. Even if the infection is cleared up it is liable to return again, particularly at times of stress or poor health. I have only come across this problem twice with Dobermanns, but in both cases they ended up being put down as it could not be controlled and was too stressful to the dogs. It appears likely that dogs such as these have an immunity deficiency resulting in a lack of resistance, which is probably hereditary, so such dogs should not be bred from. Unlike sarcoptic mange demodectic mange is not contagious.

Ringworm: this is actually caused by a fungus. It is very contagious and is usually picked up from cattle, mice, rats or cats. The hair falls out and round, bare patches of skin are visible. They are very irritating. The condition is highly contagious both to other dogs and to humans and should be treated immediately by the vet.

SKIN CONDITIONS: It has been estimated that about 20 per cent of all visits to the vets by dogs relate to skin or coat problems. The Dobermann is no exception. Skin problems can be due to a variety of causes but the most common are parasitic, fungal, hormonal and allergic. Fungal and external parasitic causes have been considered above, as has the need to control worms on a regular basis, for they also cause dogs to lose condition. A fourth cause of skin problems are allergies. In order for an allergic reaction to occur there must be two specific conditions present: an agent foreign to the body and capable of provoking an allergic reaction, and a specific antibody produced by the body itself. The term allergen, meaning 'allergy generating', is used to refer specifically to a substance that causes an allergic reaction. There are four major groups of allergens that cause dogs problems. These are flea saliva, food constituents, inhaled particles and contact allergies. After flea allergy, inhaled allergy is probably the most common. The allergy may be seasonal, caused by pollen, or be caused by dust, various moulds, dyes, fabric and feathers, either from pillows or from birds which may be kept by the dog's owner. Dogs can also be allergic to cats or other animals and their litter.

Food allergies are very common. The clinical signs of food allergy are no different from those due to other allergies, except that they may be accompanied by digestive upsets. The most usual food allergies are to proteins, particularly beef, eggs, milk and gluten from wheat.

Contact allergens are less common, but can include plants, disinfectants, wool, nylon, dyes, shampoos, ointments and insecticides. With a contact allergen, the reaction will be seen at the points of contact such as on the feet, chin, elbows and hocks, which will aid identification of the cause. With a suspected food allergy the diet should be changed to something that the dog has not eaten before, such as a lamb and rice diet.

CARDIOMYOPATHY: This term covers a number of different heart diseases that occur in animals. Dilated Cardiomyopathy is the specific type usually found in dogs and it affects the Dobermann. Studies of the disease carried out in the USA suggest that it was present in Dobermanns in Europe prior to the 1950s. It is known that some Dobermanns died suddenly, without warning, in the prime of their lives, during this period and were believed to have suffered 'heart attacks'. The problem was introduced into the USA with the importation of certain dogs during the 1940s. A report on cardiomyopathy in dogs in England, which was published in 1984, indicated that it occurred in Dobermanns more than in any other breed. Heredity is involved in the cause of the disease, and line breeding within affected bloodlines is dangerous, as it increases the genetic predisposition in the offspring. For this reason, all dogs with a family history of heart disease should be elimated from any breeding programme. It is a disease of the heart muscle which evolves over a period of two years or longer and results either in sudden death or in congestive heart failure, resulting in weakness, coughing and breathing difficulties, and death after a few days. Some Dobermanns experience one or more episodes of fainting. The cause of this is the same heart rhythm abnormality that causes sudden death, and drug therapy is strongly recommended.

VON WILLEBRAND'S DISEASE: This is named after the doctor who first described the condition. It is one of a number of blood clotting defects which occur in dogs and it is a significant problem in many breeds including the Dobermann. It is similar to haemophilia, except that it affects both sexes. Dogs with the disease suffer from bleeding problems to a greater or lesser extent, and this can vary during the lifetime of an individual dog. When it is severe, the dog will bruise easily and show spontaneous bleeding from the nose, mouth or bladder. Dogs with a moderate to mild degree may only show a tendency to bleed after trauma or surgery.

Dogs can be tested for the disease by taking a blood sample. This will indicate the extent to which a dog is affected by comparing its level of blood clotting factor with a normal dog. Dogs which are bleeding can be treated with drugs to control it. But the more important consideration is how to prevent the disease, which is hereditary. Obviously dogs with a tendency to bleed should be tested and should not be bred from.

HIP DYSPLASIA : The hip joint is essentially a ball and socket joint. In dogs with hip dypslasia there is some displacement and the joint becomes unstable. It is principally an inherited problem, resulting from the interaction of several genes, which means that it cannot be predicted in advance or bred out easily and quickly, as would be the case with a simple dominant/recessive gene.

Dogs with a severe displacement in one or both hips will show some sign of lameness as early as five months of age. Alternatively the lameness may not show until later in life. HD is diagnosed by a physical examination supported by the evidence provided by X-rays. In those breeds which are affected by HD, it is recommended that breeding stock is X-rayed in order to ascertain the degree to which the dog deviates from the ideal. It is rare to see a Dobermann showing any evidence of HD, and statistics suggest that it is not such a problem with them as with many other breeds. However, it would be most unwise to conclude that there is no need to be concerned, and X-rays will continue to monitor the degree to which the breed as a whole, and individual Dobermanns, are affected.

CERVICAL SPONDYLOPATHY: This condition, also known as cervical vertebral instability (CVI), is caused by an abnormality of the neck vertebrae or associated structures Where instability occurs between the vertebrae, pressure is exerted on the cervical spinal cord, which results in hind leg unsteadiness and a lack of rear orientation, so the dog appears not to be aware of its rear end in relationship to the remainder of its body, or one hind leg in relationship to the other. The gait and standing postures are typically wide at the rear and there is often considerable difficulty in turning. There can also be great difficulty in positioning when toileting. Sometimes when walking, but more often when running, the gait appears very stilted and stiff. The fore limbs are sometimes affected, but not always. Sometimes the dog may indicate that there is neck pain. It is this unco-ordinated movement and clumsy, awkward steps that have led to this problem being known as the 'wobbler syndrome' and affected dogs being known as 'wobblers'.

The Dobermann breed clubs became very concerned during the late 1970s when it became known that a number of cases of CS were being reported. A lot of research has subsequently been carried out, which revealed the rather startling conclusion that about 80% of the apparently normal dogs examined had vertebrae that differed from normal vertebrae as found in breeds that did not have a CS problem. This survey, together with subsequent work, has enabled a neck scoring system to be evolved. This allows the necks of individual dogs to be graded, and so dogs which have a high probability of becoming wobblers can be identified. Dogs with seriously defective necks should not be used for breeding. The causes are not entirely clear. It has been suggested that the condition is related to breed conformation and that the position of the head and neck tends to concentrate all the biomechanical forces on the base of the neck, which is where most of the problems occur. Diet is also considered to be important. Feeding a high-protein diet during the two to six months of age period, and the giving of excessive amounts of calcium, are accepted as being partly responsible for producing the condition. There may be a hereditary factor involved, but this has not yet been proven. Although a high percentage of Dobermanns have a neck abnormality, relatively few of them become clinical cases of CS, and those that do occur are usually as a result of some type of accident, such as the Dobermann running into a tree.

PROGRESSIVE RETINAL ATROPHY: This is caused by the degeneration of the cells of the retina of the eye. The first symptom is likely to be the dog's loss of night vision. The condition will then get progressively worse until the dog is blind, or nearly blind. There is no treatment. I have known of cases in Dobermanns, but so few of them that it may be safely taken not to be a breed problem. Affected dogs should always be eliminated from any breeding programme.

PERSISTENT HYPERPLASTIC PRIMARY VITREOUS: This is a congenital eye anomaly in which a plaque of fibrous tissue and blood vessels occurs on the back of the lens of the eye at birth and restricts vision. The disease is congenital, not hereditary. There was concern about it when several Dobermanns were reported to have it in the 1980s, but recent studies suggest it is not a breed problem, though it is wise to have your Dobermann's eyes checked and any affected dogs should not be used for breeding.

CANINE HYPOTHYROIDISM: This is one of the more common hormonal disorders of the dog and the Dobermann is one of the breeds most frequently affected. It normally occurs at between two and five years of age. It arises from a deficiency of the thyroid hormones. The classic symptoms are lethargy, obesity and hair loss, particularly along the flanks. The coat becomes dull and scurfy and the skin appears rougher than normal, bruises easily and is slower than normal to heal. Affected dogs tend to feel the cold more and will sit close to a fire or radiator.

If the condition is suspected, the vet will do a blood test. Treatment is relatively simple but will need to be continued for the remainder of the dog's life.

URINARY INCONTINENCE: The spaying of bitches is a very common operation, involving the removal of the ovaries and the uterus. The advantage is that it prevents unnecessary and unwanted breeding, and stops the bitch having seasons and false pregnancies. It also reduces the likelihood of tumours developing in later life. But there are two recognised disadvantages of spaying: obesity and urinary incontinence. Urinary incontinence can occur in older bitches due simply to muscle weakening with age and natural degeneration, or due to cystitis or kidney problems. However, urinary incontinence following spaying is a real and all-too-frequent problem with Dobermanns.

This means that serious consideration should be given to the possible side-effects before deciding to have a Dobermann spayed unless the operation is necessary for medical reasons. This incontinence is a real problem to owners, as it means their Dobermann will be leaking urine, either constantly or intermittently, in the house. For some owners, this is simply not acceptable and many Dobermanns are put down because of it. For others it destroys the joy of having a Dobermann in the house. Since mammary tumours do not affect all bitches, and even when they do, they are not a great problem, it would seem that it is better to take the risk of these developing than the risk of incontinence. It can be controlled to some extent by controlling the obesity, as bitches who are not over-weight tend to be less inclined to be incontinent. It can also be treated by giving an oestrogen replacement drug, to strengthen the bladder valve. Surgery can also be used to tighten that valve, and it is reckoned to have a success rate of about 80%

EXOCRINE PANCREATIC INSUFFICIENCY: Although this is more normally associated with German Shepherd Dogs, I have come across a number of cases in Dobermanns. It is caused by the cells in the pancreas which produce the pancreatic enzymes being destroyed or wasting away. The problem becomes severe enough to be noticed when about 90% of the cells have died. It is believed to be hereditary. The symptoms are a ravenous appetite accompanied by severe weight loss, a dry and scurfy coat, and faeces that are produced in large quantity, have a cow-pat appearance and are greasy and foul-smelling. The dog may also develop the habit of eating them.

The condition is diagnosed by a blood test and treated by the oral administration of the deficient enzymes, added to the food, which should be given as several smaller meals, rather than one main meal. The diet should be low in fat and high in carbohydrate, using a high-quality protein. The treatment will continue for the rest of the dog's life. It is one of those problems where a Dobermann can look like the classical ill-treated rescue dog, yet still be lively and active with quality of life. Once that fades, or the dog appears to be in pain, then you must consider having the dog put down.

ZINC DEFICIENCY: This is relatively uncommon, so when it does occur it is not immediately recognised. It is caused by the dog having an inability to utilise zinc from high-quality balanced foods, or from dry, cereal foods. The symptoms are quite distinctive. The dog develops small bare patches in the coat, which appear quite suddenly. Usually there is some crusting and scaling of the exposed skin. The dog appears healthy in all other respects.

   The appearance of these bare patches is usually sufficient to give an accurate diagnosis. Treatment is very simple and effective – a daily tablet of zinc sulphate. Interestingly, I have never experienced the problem occurring on the same dog more than once.

SKELETAL SCURVY: Also known as Barlowe's Disease, this is a problem which can affect any of the large breeds, including the Dobermann. Like zinc deficiency, it occurs relatively infrequently and so is not always recognised immediately, if at all. I have encountered it several times in Dobermanns and consider it to be one of the most frightening and upsetting problems that one can encounter. It affects growing puppies in the five to eight month age range. It can appear quite suddenly: a puppy which seems normal one evening can be crippled with it the next morning. It causes swelling of the bone joints, particularly noticeable on the legs. The joints are hot to the touch. Affected puppies are reluctant to get up and walk because of the pain, and will have a high temperature. I have heard of cases where no obvious cause could be identified and the puppies were put down, in order to avoid unnecessary suffering. It is caused by a Vitamin C deficiency or, more correctly, by the over-response of the growing bones to the excessive quantities of food and supplements being given. It has been suggested that the vitamin C is being knocked out by excessive amounts of vitamin D and calcium. The cure is to give the puppy Ascorbic Acid, which is vitamin C. This can be obtained relatively easily from your vet in tablet form. If you buy it from a chemist or from a health shop, be careful of the strength – it can vary enormously. Affected puppies will recover within a few weeks and return to normal. At the outset of the problem it is helpful to give the puppy painkillers and warmth. Aspirin is helpful to reduce the temperature. As it is not an illness in the true sense, conventional drugs such as antibiotics will not help. Under normal circumstances it is not necessary to give dogs vitamin C as they synthesise their own. However, with Skeletal Scurvy, it is quite literally a life-saver.

LICK SORES: Dobermanns do seem to suffer from this problem, which is sore places on the pasterns or the hocks, which are caused by the dog's own constant licking. Quite why they do this is not clear, though they are sometimes referred to as boredom sores. Changing the life-style of the dog may be a possible cure, but in practical terms this is rarely feasible, particularly with an elderly dog, or an active dog who cannot be persuaded to leave the sore patch alone.

   The sores are very difficult to treat. Even if you manage to heal them up the dog invariably licks them raw again at the first available opportunity. I use an antiseptic dusting powder and then cover up the patch with cotton wool, held in place by a bandage, and covered by an old sock, kept in place by wrapping parcel-tape around its top. Over the years I have known Dobermanns who have had a sock on one leg permanently!

Chapter Eleven

THE DOBERMAN PINSCHER IN THE UNITED STATES

By JUDY DONIERE
In the past twenty years we have seen the emergence of many new and very successful breeders. I had only limited space to feature them, but tried to pick out breeders who have continuously bred top-quality Dobermans. With very few exceptions, the Dobermans of today are not kept as kennel dogs. Most are house pets and the breeding programs are limited to one to three litters per year. Some less than that. Gone are the large kennels of ten to twenty dogs or more. We now usually limit our dog population to the average of three Dobermans. Usually one dog and two or more bitches. Beside the Conformation ring, many Dobes are Obedience trained, and now the newest sport, Agility, is really catching on. Tama Johnson is a writer about this sport, as well as Fly Ball. The dogs love it.

ALISATON: GWEN DEMILTA
From the strong foundation of her first bitch, Ch. Arabar's Impertinence, Gwen Satalino deMilta has built a long line of Dobermans easily recognised as Alisaton. Breeding her first litter in 1972, she has bred or co-bred sixty-one AKC champions, dozens of Obedience titlists, and numerous DPCA Working Aptitude Certificate and Register of Merit holders. Alisaton Dobes can be described as usually standard-sized, classic-headed, curvy animals with a gleam in their eye – smart, strong-willed and determined.

Gwen has been the Doberman Pinscher Club of America top breeder, and the owner or breeder of three generations of DPCA Top Producing Dams – Ch. Arabar's Impertinence (six Championships), her daughter Ch. Alisaton's Kinderwicke (fourteen), and Kinderwicke's daughter Ch. Alisaton Bewitches (thirteen). She bred the sire or dam of four DPCA Grand Prize Futurity Winners, bred and owned the 1974 Futurity winner, Ch. Alisaton's Intimate Miss, and co-bred the 1992 Futurity winner, Ch. Datelis Enuf Said Alisaton.

Gwen has bred Group, BIS, BISS winners, Top 20 Dobermans, and top producing dogs and bitches. An historic accomplishment places her in the record books as the breeder/co-owner of the youngest Dobe bitch to finish (eight months and ten days) – Ch. Alisaton Canasta v. DalClar; also the youngest DPCA National Specialty Superior Quality Specimen recipient (nine months and four days). Gwen and Alisaton Dobermans have been a dominant force in America for more than two decades. With many pointed youngsters on the way to their Championships, the future is promising.

BEAULANE: JACKIE BEAUMONT
The foundation of Beaulane was a black bitch, which Jackie acquired in 1963. Through no fault of

Ch. Beaulane The Union Jack: A top-producing sire for the Beaulane kennel.

her own, she did not produce a lot of champions, but what descended from her left a legacy for others to build on. Ultimately, that's what it's all about.

To date, Beaulane has forty champions, but has never really had a "top" show dog. However, this is not something that is important to Jackie, whose concentration has been on the whelping box rather than the show ring. She has striven for a sound, honest, clean dog and has maintained that consistency over the last thirty years.

Her best bitch was Ch. Beaulane Original Sin, a superb animal who is gracing the pedigrees of many of today's Dobermans and leaving a foundation for others. Through her two sons, Ch. Beaulane the Union Jack, and Ch. Beaulane Wind Fall, have descended a line of producing males. Union Jack, the sire of Ch. Zietlins Rogue Force v. Kerri, had numerous champion get stemming from these lines. From Wind Fall came Ch. Electra's the Windwalker, the sire of over eighty champions, including the great bitch Ch. Royal Tudor's Wild as The Wind, whose great grandfather was also Union Jack. Windwalker sired Ch. Beaulane the Nite Ryder, who was lost to the breed at the age of four, but had close to twenty Champions to his name, one of those being Ch. Brunswig Cryptonite (Kafka). In addition to being a number-one show dog, Kafka has some fifty-seven Champions to his credit. Following in his footsteps is his young son, Ch. Primary Caught Red Handed, with eighteen champion get.

Not to be left out are the dams. An Original Sin daughter, Ch. Beaulane Nite Moves, is the dam of Nite Ryder and of the producing Ch. Beaulane Every Nite Josephine, basis for Primary Dobermans. Ch. Beaulane Whisperin' Wind was another producing foundation bitch. Breedings of Ch. Beaulane a Touch of Magic ultimately led to Ch. Beaulane All That Jazz, dam of the current Ch. Beaulane China Beach and the producing Nite Ryder son, Ch. Kalephs Running with the Nite.

Jackie says that when she thinks back now to the black bitch she first bought, there might have been better ways to have conducted her breedings, but in her own way she made a big impact through her descending children. Having good foundation stock is a must and makes breeding a lot easier. Jackie feels that breeders have to concentrate on producing consistent, sound lines for others to continue to build from. The future of the Breed depends on this. It is something she would like to feel she had accomplished. She also believes that the stud dogs mentioned here were, and are, dogs that possess the ability to produce with a variety of bitches, and will remain a part of today's Dobermans for some time. She knows there are always problems that go along with any breeding program, but, being honest and open, and always working to improve, will strengthen the lines. The quality of the animals far outweighs the problems.

CAROSEL: CAROL & ROSS PETRUZZO

Their names have been synonymous with Doberman Pinschers since the sixties, as having bred many Champions, WAC, ROM, Obedience and Schutzhund titled Dobermans, including Top 20, Specialty, Group and All-breed Best in Show winners, been DPCA Breeder of the Year and being the owners of a DPCA Brood Bitch of the Year.

Carol (Selzle) Petruzzo was introduced to the competitive Doberman community in 1960 by her now husband, Ross Petruzzo. Becoming interested in Obedience, she met Peggy Adamson at training classes, and was fortunate to be taken under her guidance. For years she helped Peggy with the breeding and raising of puppies and, during that time, she absorbed anything she could about this wonderful breed. Eventually she inherited many of the responsibilities, as Peggy's judging career soared. There came a time when almost every Damasyn Doberman had an Obedience title because of Carol. It wasn't too long before Carol was planning some of the Damasyn breeding. Today she is one of the USA's most respected breeders, thanks to the expert tutelage of one of the world's masters in the Doberman community.

Carol's first Dobermans were two lovely bitches, Damasyn the Tartika, CDX and Damasyn the Rocca Djil, UD, gifts from Peggy. Djil completed her UD before she was two years of age. The legacy of the Damasyn breeding program can be found in the Carosel pedigrees. As Carol became more and more interested in the conformation ring, she also became more skilled as a handler. Carol and Ross's success in this department is well known.

Among her favourite memories is her first success, Ch. Damasyn the Troycen. As a novice handler, Carol finished Troycen very quickly with back-to-back five-point majors. While shown sparingly as a Special, he had a ninety per cent Group placement record and was the sire of thirteen champions.

Ch. Damasyn the Limelight (Ch. Damasyn the Troycen x Ch. Damasyn the Legacy) was Carol's foundation bitch and DPCA Brood Bitch of the Year. She produced eight Champion get from three litters. From her breeding to Ch. Brown's B Brian came two notable dogs, Ch. Carosel B In A Hurry, CD, ROM and Carosel Be A Friend, known as Joe. He went on to become one of Australia's top sires and, even today, his quality and image is seen in his grandchildren.

Hurry became notable in his own right. Besides winning Best of Opposite Sex at the DPCA National Speciality, he captured the hearts of everyone who knew him and he had a long following. He was one of the smartest dogs one could imagine, and as gentle with children as he was a fierce guardian of the family. One of the true temperament aficionados of our breed, he was cited as having the ideal temperament for a Doberman. There will never be another Hurry.

From Limelight's breeding to Ch. Gra-Lemor Demetrius v. d. Victor came Ch. Carosel In the Spotlight, CD, ROM. Spotlight was the dam of five Carosel Champions and they, in turn, produced many Champion children and grandchildren. Of note was Ch. Carosel In the Mood of King Hill. She produced two Champions bred to Ch. Cabra's Dark and Debonaire, WAC. Moody is the grandmother to Ch. Carosel Make My Day, WAC, who continues to carry on the Carosel trademarks of quality in conformation and temperament. At this writing he is only four years old

Ch. Carosel in The Spotlight CD, ROM: The dam of five Carosel Champions.

Photo: William Gilbert.

Ch. Carosel Make My Day WAC: A highly successful show dog and now producing Champion offspring.

Photo: Jordan.

and is already the sire of sixteen Champions and many more started, or near completion. Basteque, as he is known, is a DPCA Top Twenty qualified for three consecutive years and a DPCA Top Twenty Winner (first year to qualify). He finished from the puppy class and is a multi-BOB, Group, Specialty, and All Breed Best in Show winner. He has been awarded the DPCA Superior Quality Specimen at the two nationals in which he competed.

The Carosel breeding program has been a fruitful one thus far, and Carol and Ross Petruzzo are looking forward to the next generation of Carosel Dobermans. There are eight Carosel-bred Champion/ROM Dobermans.

DOB MANN: EDD AND IRENE BIVIN

dob Mann Kennels is the property of Irene and Edd Bivin, with all breeding and dog maintenance done in a home environment. While Doberman Pinschers are the primary breed, the household also includes Smooth Standard Dachshunds and English Pointers.

The Doberman breeding was started by Irene (Nail) in the early 60s, but since 1978, when Edd and Irene were married, Edd's input and sharing has contributed immeasurably to the program. Both Edd and Irene are AKC approved Judges, who have officiated at shows all over the world. Edd's original breed was Pomeranians, which he bred very successfully through the 70s. Because both Bivins are judges and have bred multiple breeds, they bring a broad perspective into the dob Mann Kennel breeding program.

dob Mann Kennels originated in the early 60s when Irene Nail decided to add a Doberman Pinscher to the household for protection and for Obedience purposes. The Nails (Terry, Irene, Jesanne and Teresa) were already actively involved in purebred dogs, breeding primarily English Setters for gundog, Field and Obedience purposes.

The first Doberman was Jesanne's Greta Nail, UD, who lived for thirteen and a half years as a beloved companion, pet and Obedience dog. Her record in the Obedience ring was an outstanding one, with several perfect 200 scores recorded. In the mid-sixties they acquired for Teresa (the eight-year old), the bitch who was to become the real foundation of dob Mann Kennels. Purchased from the Azteca Kennels out of a litter that produced nine Champions, she was a red bitch, Ch. Azteca's Bellona, UD, better known as Shasta. She finished easily and was an excellent Obedience dog as well. Under the guidance and training of Teresa, she was High Scoring Dog at the National Specialty, with the, by then, ten-year-old Teresa handling. Bred sparingly, she produced several Champions and, thirty years later, still shows a marked influence on dob Mann Dobermans. She was sired by the famous stud dog, Ch. Ru-Mar's Morgansonne, UD, owned by Ruth Morgan Edwards of California.

dob Mann since that time has produced numerous Champions, with bitches down from Shasta. However, probably the most significant contribution of this kennel has been through their stud dogs. The first of these, C. Tolivar's Aristotle of Azteca, was sired by Bellona's litter brother, Ch. Azteca's Beacon. Bred very sparingly, Artistotle still produced twelve Champions and several were Group and BIS winners. He stamped his get with a specific type, sharp and sensible temperaments, and outstanding movement. He also passed along a tendency for longevity, as many of his get lived to be thirteen to fourteen years old.

Ch. Tolivar's Boo Radley dob Mann was his successor at the Kennels. He was an Ari son out of a von Tannenwald bitch. He produced over fifty Champions (both dogs and bitches), many of them BIS dogs, and was the sire, with three different bitches, of three successive DPCA Grand Prize Futurity winners. He was the top producer of Champions in the US for two years and was one year tied with his son, Ch. Gerent's Eldo Radley dob Mann, for that honor – an unprecedented achievement for a father and son.

Ch. Gerent's Eldo Radley dob Mann, sired by Boo and bred by Jerry and Rhoda Kelley, was out of a bitch from the Elexa kennels. This stud dog brought in an outcross going back to Ch. Edelhall Gigilo of Amulet, and he also appears in numerous pedigrees in the US today. He, too, is the producer of approximately fifty Champions, and resides in the Bivin household today at ten and a half years of age.

Ch. Tolivar's Boo Radley dob Mann: The top producer of Champions in the US for two years.

Bergman Photos.

Ch. Gerent's Eldo Radley dob Mann: A son of Ch. Tolivar's Boo Radley dob Mann, and sire of some fifty Champions.

Photo: Kohler.

The emphasis of dob Mann kennels has been sound temperament, a protective character, a pretty dog with a good head, and a dog who exemplifies the Doberman standard as the Bivins understand it.

The new, young, stud dog in the kennel, Ch. Texas Christian dob Mann, finished at fourteen months of age. Now only two, he is already showing promise of becoming another in the line of prepotent stud dogs from this kennel.

In recent years the dob Mann kennel name has been extended to dogs bred by daughter, Teresa Nail, and the stud dog there was Ch. Arco dob Mann, who is another top producer in the breed, as well as being one of the top winning Dobermans in the US for four years.

The Bivins live in Fort Worth, Texas, where Edd Bivin is a Vice Chancellor at the Texas Christian University.

ELECTRA: JUDITH BINGHAM

Judith has been breeding Dobermans for twenty-five years and is proud to be the breeder of Ch. Electra's The Wind Walker, the top producing sire in US history, with ninety-five AKC Champions to his credit. Six of his get went on to become all-breed Best in Show winners. The daughter that really started his stud career was the very showy Ch. Royal Tudor's Wild as the Wind, co-bred by Judith and Beth Whilhite, who, as already mentioned, went on to become the top winning bitch in the history of the breed and Best in Show at Westminster KC.

Ch. Electra's The Wind Walker: Top producing sire in US history.

Judith has used two of his daughters, Ch. Chehalem Double Mint and Ch. Kai Esa's Santa Ana Wind, to continue her breeding program since his death. She has always felt that a breeding program should be a long-term commitment and is continuously striving to improve her dogs to fit the standard for the breed, while trying to preserve the contributions of the great ones which appear in her pedigree.

JULMAR: JULIO AND MARIA REGUEIRO

The Julmar Kennel name means dedication and loyalty to the Doberman breed. Although the Regueiro's started showing Dobermans in 1975, their first show litter was not born until 1983. Their Can. Am. Ch. Zeitlin's V.K. Modesty Blaze x Ch. Toledobes Master Card, produced their first BIS dog, Ch. Toledobes Jaquar v Julmar. The same year, their Ch. Marienburg Comanche Firebird was accidentally bred, and this unplanned litter produced a good one, Ch. Julmar's

*Ch. Julmar's Rio:
No. 1 Doberman in
1987.*

*Photo: Earl
Graham Studios.*

*Ch. Banchee's
Navajo of Julmar:
A prolific winner
in the show ring.*

*Photo: Chuck and
Sandy Tatham.*

Malaga, dam of Ch. Derringer's Ricochet v. Derby. They bred their Comanche twice to Ch. Cabra's Dark and Debonaire, WAC, and she produced six champions: Ch. Julmar's Rio, No. 1 Doberman 1987, Ch. Julmar's Fiesta, Ch. Julmar's Flamenco, Ch. Julmar's Copacabana, Ch. Julmar's Rodolfo Valentino and Ch. Julmar's Jeronimo.

Comanche, bred to Ch. Agape The Lion of Judah, produced three more Champions. Ch.

Julmar's Eres Tu, Ch. Julmar's Guantanamera and Ch. Julmar's Siboney. Among his Champions, Siboney produced Ch. Carosel Make My Day. These lines have proven to be top-producing ones and Julio and Maria are proud of their heritage.

Among his Champions, Jeronimo produced the top BIS Australian bitch, Ch. Celestion Comanche Moon.

Currently his son, Ch. Banchee's Navajo of Julmar, has already been signalled by top breeders incorporating him in their breeding program. Navajo was a Champion at twelve months and continues to win in the Breed and Group rings. His correctness in conformation and movement are quickly making him stand out. He has a litter on the ground out of Ch. Dabney's Hot Enchilada of Le-High, better known as Chile.

Julio and Maria are proud of the fact that they have not bred many litters, but that the lines created by their breedings have been recognized as important building blocks. They feel their years of dedication have been rewarded by the recognition and respect given to the Julmar name.

KYJUR: TAMA JOHNSON

Tama went to her first DPCA National in 1973, having only been showing dogs for a few months. The topic of the week was "standard size". It was to take first priority in her book. With Tama's competitive horse background, and her intense love of the Doberman Pinscher, Kyjur began. Today, with forty-five Champions to her credit, she feels that she has succeeded in breeding the kind of Doberman that suits her needs – good-looking enough for an owner/handler to win in the conformation ring; intelligent enough to win in the Obedience ring; a short-bodied, round-muscled, standard-sized athlete who can run fast, jump high and hit a Flyball box hard; an enthusiastic four-legged pal to compete with in Agility games, and a solid, protective pet, with a temperament to do all of the foregoing.

In 1989 Ch. Kyjur Crystal Hi Heel Sneaker, WAC was awarded the DPCA Top Producing Dam of the Year and she tied Tama for 1989 DPCA Breeder of the Year. Just twenty-five and a half inches tall, she had a total of fourteen living puppies. Ten became Champions, four were ROMs. Her legacy and prepotency continued through her daughter, Ch. Kyjur Christmas Stocking, ROM, for in 1993 Chris, as she is known, was honored with the 1993 DPCA Top Producing Dam award. Second generation!

At the Houston Nationals in 1989 approximately one hundred and thirty Specials were present. Eleven of these were Kyjur Dobermans. Eight were Sneakers' pups and six made the cut, with Mrs Peggy Adamson judging.

Sneakers has get, grandget and great-grandget competing in all sorts of areas. Her son, Ch. Kyjur Jumpin Jack, ROM, Agil II, just completed his Flyball Championship. Her grandson, Kyjur Last Boy Scout is doing agility and Flyball, and soon to go into the Obedience and show ring. A great grand-daughter, Kyjur Ruby Slipper, has several points from the puppy class.

Tama says she can't imagine life without her Dobermans: they are the "Porsche" of the canine world, and her best friends.

MARIENBURG: MARY RODGERS

The Marienburg Kennel was established by Mary Rodgers in 1963. In thirty-one years there have been ninety-nine American Champions produced by this kennel.

Mary obtained her first Doberman, a red male, in 1961. In 1962 a black female, Ch. Zigeuner's Fiesta (all Rancho Dobe background) was added. She was the dam of Mary's first litter in 1963 and figures prominently in her early breeding program. Her second female was purchased later in that year as a six-week old puppy, the black Ch. Sultana von Marienburg, whose quality and show presence enabled her to break many existing show records and become the top winner of the late sixties. Sultana's show record included thirty-seven all-breed Best in Shows. Although she didn't produce any top winners, her black granddaughter, Ch. Marienburg's Mary Hartman, out of Mary's top producing bitch, Ch. Marienburg's Only One, broke her grandmother's show records during the late seventies, by winning forty-four all-breed Best in Shows and Top Dog all-breeds 1978.

During the mid-seventies another Doberman great came from Marienburg – the red male, Ch. Marienburg Sun Hawk. He lived for barely nine years but sired eighty-five American Champions as well as many Champions in other countries. He had a profound influence on the Doberman breed in America during the late 70s and 80s. Hawk and/or his sister, Ch. Marienburg Apache Warbonnet, figure prominently in the backgrounds of such noted American Dobermans as Marienburg's Mary Hartman, Marienburg's Lone Eagle, Sherluck's L. B. Jake, Eagle's Devil D, Lemil's Firecracker and Carosel Make My Day.

Sun Hawk died in 1982. In 1985 Mary brought a black male puppy to the US from the Franckenhorst Kennels in the Netherlands. Dexter vom Franckenhorst had a great influence on the Marienburg Dobermans from the mid-eighties to the present. Although primarily used on Marienburg females and not widely accepted by American breeders, Dexter sired outstanding qualities which blended well with any line he was bred to. His name is included in the pedigrees of several of the current 1993-94 Top Twenty US winners, including the 1993-94 No. 1 Doberman. Dexter has sired twenty-five or more American champions.

Forty, fifty and more years ago, Dobermans from Europe, mainly Germany and the Netherlands, were the major influence contributing to the American Doberman. Since then, few were brought in or bred to, and then only sporadically, until Dexter began to be used. Mary made several trips to Europe after that, attending shows and visiting breeders, noting, with a few exceptions, that the breeders both in the US and in Europe don't look beyond their own boundaries to enhance and broaden the scope of the total Doberman.

SHERLUCK: FAYE STRAUSS
Sherluck began in 1973 with the acquisition of the eight-week old black puppy bitch, Ch. Moraga Hill's Desert Wind. Her dam, Ch. Hy-lo's Joan of Arc, and sire, Ch. Von Lieb's London, were both sired by Kay Hill line-bred Dobes. Kay Hill was a significant line in the 1960s.

In 1975 Sherluck acquired Desert Wind's red half-sister, Ch. Moraga Hill's High Fashion, WAC. Her sire was Ch. Encore's Black Rites. This gave the kennel another bitch who was strongly line-bred on Kay Hill. Fashion was very sound with bone and substance, and became a top-ten Doberman in 1979. She was a multi-group and Specialty winner. Most memorable was BOS at the DPCA National. Blessed with a tremendous foundation, Sherluck has now produced sixty-six Champions in twenty-one litters, including the foundation of many successful breeding programs and top show dogs.

Desert Wind produced thirteen Champions in three litters and was the top producer in 1980, 1981 and 1983. The first litter, sired by Ch. Wessynton's Moloch CD, produced Am. Can. Ch. Sherlucks Duke of Earl (sire of six Champions and foundation of Linda V. Dobes) and Am. Can. Ch. Sherlucks Crimson N. Clover (a BIS winner who produced a DPCA Grand Prize Futurity and was foundation bitch of top winning Simca Dobes, homebased in Canada.)

Desert Wind was then bred to renowned sire Ch. Marienburg's Sun Hawk and produced ten Champions. Most notable was Ch. Sherluck's LB Jake, multi BIS winner, DPCA top Specialty winner in 1983, and DPCA top-ten 1981 to 1983. He produced thirty-plus Champions and OTCH Obedience dogs. Ch. Sherlucks Falcon v Marienburg and Ch. Sherlucks Caroline v. Marienburg, to mention a few, were also outstanding. Ch. Moraga Hill's High Fashion produced nineteen Champions (there were thirty puppies from four litters) making her the top producing female in the history of the breed. She was DPCA top producer from 1984 to 1986. Bred to LB Jake twice, most notable was top-ten Dobe Am. Can. Sherlucks Barney Miller, Wingate foundation bitch Ch. Sherlucks Private Benjamin (DPCA top producer in 1990 with seven Champions), and Ch. Sherlucks Flamingo Road (producer of eight Champions for Sherluck).

Fashion was then bred to noted sire Ch. Tolivars Boo Radley. dob Mann offspring included Ch. Sherlucks Drum Fire (the number-one Doberman in 1989 and sire of thirty-plus Champions) for K-Rite, Ch. Sherlucks Prairie Breaker (sire of nine-plus American champions), and Ch. Sherlucks Casalaria (DPCA Grand Prize Futurity, BIS winner and dam of thirteen Champions).

Ch. Sherlucks Flamingo Road produced an all-champion litter, sired by Ch. Arco dob Mann. There were four outstanding bitches: top-twenty BIKS winner Ch. Sherlucks Primrose Lane, Ebony's champion producer Ch. Sherlucks Hollywood Blvd., Arista foundation Ch. Sherlucks Sunset Blvd., and multi-champion producer Ch. Sherlucks Yellow Brick Road, Mystique's foundation.

Ch. Sherlucks Flamingo Road was then bred to Ch. Sherlucks Prairie Breaker. Notable offspring includes multi-group and DPCA merit award winner Ch. Sherlucks High Finance, and multi-BIS winner, Can. Ch. Sherlucks Financial Wizard, Sterling Dobermans' multi-champion producer, Ch. Sherlucks Ruffian V. Keenland, and champion producer Sherlucks Brandywine.

Ch. Sherlucks Casalaria, DPCA top producing dam in 1989, was bred to LB Jake. The offspring included BIS winner Ch. Sherlucks True Grit, top-twenty Dobe Ch. Sherlucks Diamond Lil, and multi-champion sire, Ch. Sherlucks High Noon. In a litter of ten, eight became Champions.

Ch. Sherlucks Slew o Gold, Casalaria's sister, was DPCA top producer in 1990. Sired by Ch. Gerent's Eldo Radley dob Mann, there was Addox Dobermans' Champion producer Ch. Sherlucks Good Golly Ms Molly. Sired by prominent sire, Ch. Electra's the Windwalker, there was Am. C. Sherlucks High Roller (seven international titles), and multi-group and Specialty winner, Ch. Sherlucks Good as Gold, and Ch. Sherlucks New York Minute, sire of ten Champions.

The past twenty years have been very rewarding for this kennel. Sherluck is proud of all their dogs, including those not mentioned. Their breeding philosophy is to breed only the best, honestly evaluating the dam and finding the stud that will improve her. Sherluck dogs are kept in condition through free-running in wooded surroundings. Their dogs are Gary and Faye's constant companions, sharing their bed, car and life.

TOLEDOBES: PATRICK & JUDY DONIERE & SUE BROWN

Toledobes, officially began in 1955 with the purchase of a black bitch who ended up being pet quality. In 1957 we were fortunately able to obtain a bitch with a pedigree worth its weight in gold. She became Ch. Wahlmar's Baroness CD (a double Ch. Damasyn Dictator, Ch. Alcor v. Millsdod granddaughter), the foundation of Toledobes. She produced six champions and several of her sons and daughters became multi-champion-producing sires and dams. By her litter to Ch. Alamaps Checkmate, she produced Champions Toledobes Barbiturate, Checkmates Chessman, Chancellor, Toledobes Classic Cameo and Covergirl Girl. Barbiturate was the dam of over six Champions and the foundation of many a kennel's startup in Dobes. Chessman sired several, including Fred Curnow's Vaness'a Little Dictator V. Tavey. Covergirl Girl produced the Best of Breed winner at the 1966 DPCA National, Ch. Toledobes Linebacker. Cameo produced Ch. Toledobe's Jail Bait, Jim Dandy and Jethrine, and Quarterback (1966 DPCA Grand Futurity winner), and was the grandam of Ch. Damasyn Carly of Jerseystone, co-owned with Peggy Adamson. Baroness also produced Ch. Toledobes Filibuster, by Ch. Browns Dion, who sired many

Champions. A great many Champions and many non-Champions, who themselves proved to be top producers, came from Toledobes. One of our best was the non-Champion bitch, Toledobes Generation Gap, who produced around ten Champions, all by Ch. Andelane Indigo Rock.

Many years have passed and a lot of top dogs and bitches have come down from these great dogs. All dogs still being produced at Toledobes are directly descended from Baroness, and I will just list some of the more recent ones.

Due to the weekly judging commitments of Pat and myself, raising puppies was impossible until Sue Brown came into the picture. She bought a bitch from me, who had an injury which make her unable to be shown, but I wanted puppies out from her pedigree. So started a wonderful relationship, as a friend and business partner. Pat, Sue and I select a suitable stud, Sue raises the litters, I usually am the one who puts some training into them, and we both sell the puppies to show and pet homes, and expenses are shared by all. Several times we place a good bitch on a co-breeding arrangement with other people, and they also become part of the team.

This happened with Mary Hernandez. We placed a lovely Windwalker daughter with her, Toledobes Riviera. She ended up, to date, producing eleven Champions in four litters, all sired by different studs. The first was Ch. Sheer Force of Equinoxx (sold to Brazil). The others are: Am. & Can. Ch. Toledobes Sheer Ice, Sheer Chaos and Sheer Madness. By Ch. Primary Caught Redhanded are Champions Caughtcha Looking (Top 20), Caught Cheating (multi-group winner), Caught in the Act, Caught on Fire, and a lively bitch in Obedience, Caught the Brass Ring, CDX. By Ch. Carosel Make My Day are Champions Makin Georgia, Group winner and Top 20, Make N A Statement, Group winner, Make N New Waves, BOB winner (Make N Impression died needing only a major to finish).Toledobes have bred and owned more than one hundred Champions and are one of the older breeders in the country who are still active. We breed only one litter a year, or occasionally co-breed two, with the co-breeder raising the puppies. We feel you can only do justice, and get the right homes, when breeding on a very limited basis.

Our puppies are whelped in the spare bedroom of our homes and are raised with children, other pets and lots and lots of love. We will not sell to homes without complete fenced yards, nor to kennels or dealers, or to homes where they are left alone more than four hours at a time. We have strict buying policies, but then these dogs are like our children and we feel they must be raised and socialized properly. We seldom sell our dogs out of the country unless we know personally the people who want them, and the facilities they have for raising a Toledobe pup.

Few of our own dogs are campaigned in the Specials ring, unless the owners want to proceed with the showing after finishing their Championships. Our purpose is to breed the best puppies we can, usually line-breeding unless we need to add a particular trait. We then outcross to a closely line-bred dog, and then come back into our own line again. We usually produce multiple Champions from each litter. If a litter contains only one pup good enough to finish and the rest are not so hot, I consider it a poor litter. This, of course, is if the puppies are placed in homes that will show them. Some of our dogs are Champion quality, but we may have placed them into homes where, for one reason or another, the new owners do not want to show. This is usually when someone has had one of our dogs for years and, due to their death, wants to replace that dog. I will give them a beautiful puppy because I know the care and love that dog will receive.

We have seen exhibitors and breeders come and go over the past forty years and have made many, many friends. Our National Specialty is our vacation time to renew old friendships and make new ones. We have missed only one National since 1955 and, if you have never attended the Doberman Pinscher Club of America National Specialty, you are missing the best educational, fun experience in the world.

DOBERMANN BREEDERS DIRECTORY

IRELAND
ASSISI
Angela & Desmond McNally
59 Knockcairn Road, Dundrod, Crumlin, Co Antrim, N. Ireland BT29 4UE.
Tel: 01232-825265
Dogs at Stud/Puppies Occasionally for Sale/Boarding Facilities Available.

WALES
HALSTATT
Mr R. D. & Mrs F.I. Lloyd, 1 Pant-y-Dwr, Cwm Taff, Merthyr Tydfil, Mid Glamorgan CF48 2HS.
Tel: 01685-377946
Dogs at Stud/Puppies Occasionally for Sale.

SOUTH EAST
DAVWAY
J. & I. Battershell, Hillview, Froxfield, Petersfield, Hants GU32 1BZ.
Tel: 01730-827348
Dogs at Stud/Puppies Occasionally for Sale.

DOBERMORAY
Mrs Alison Dougherty, Our Pad, Shepherdswell Road, Eythorne, Dover, Kent CT15 4AD.
Tel: 01304-830529
Dogs at Stud/Puppies Occasionally for Sale.

LONDON & HOME COUNTIES
POMPIE
Hilary Partridge, Devon Villas, 37 Quarry Hill, Grays, Essex RM17 5BT.
Tel: 01375-379885
Dogs at Stud/Puppies Occasionally for Sale.

TAZOKHA
Mrs Val Willis, 385 Ongar Road, Brentwood, Essex CM15 9JA.
Tel: 01277-231568
Dogs at Stud/Puppies Occasionally for Sale.

KAYALA
Debbie & Shaun Gamble, Elmdale, Sedge Green, Roydon Hamlet, Essex CM19 5JR.
Tel: 01992-448296
Dogs at Stud/Puppies Occasionally for Sale.

SWNYDWR DOBERMANNS
CH. SWNYDWR STORM BEARER J.W. – d.o.b. 27/1/89

8 CCs,
6 Reserve CCs

*(Ch. Crossridge
The Jazzman x
Stevelys Black
Jezabel)*

We had no intentions of keeping MIKE. We had kept his litter sister, SWNYDWR PAMPERO, and he left us for his new home, but at seven months we had to have him back as he would not settle. Unfortunately PAMPERO was tragically killed at 14 months and we were then unable to part with him, so he lives with his full brother from a previous mating, SWNYDWR MAHOGANY MAESTRO, who did very well in the ring, gaining 3 reserve CCs, but we found it very hatrd showing two brown males, so ROBBIE retired.

CH. SWNYDWR CELEBRATION J.W. – d.o.b. 20/6/90

*(Ch. Crossridge
The Jazzman x
Stevelys Black
Jezabel)*

CHARLIE is big and beautiful, being a very boisterous, outgoing character who made her presence felt in more ways than one. CHARLIE did quite well at Championship shows and Open shows, gaining her Junior Warrant in eight weeks. CHARLIE lives with her two brothers and her mum, the Old Queen herself, STEVELYS BLACK JEZABEL (Ch. Halsbands Helmsman x Ritlo Amazing Grace). ABBIE did not mean to be a show girl, but what a brood bitch! She was faithful to CH. CROSSRIDGE THE JAZZMAN, producing three superb litters to him.

All are owned and loved by JEAN & MILTON QUIGLEY
Swn Yr Dwr, Pant Glas, Talywain, Gwent NP4 7TX Tel: 01495-772009

SWNYDWR DOBERMANNS

CH. SWNYDWR ME AND MY GIRL AT ROCKSEA – d.o.b. 1/8/93

3 CCs
1 Reserve CC

(Ch. Holtzburg Mayhem x Swnydwr Celebration)

SAM has been consistently placed at most Championship shows and has won many B.O.Bs at Open shows. Some of SAM'S recent wins include Crufts '95, Birmingham National, Three Counties & East of England. Many thanks to everyone who has thought so highly of "My Girl". So look out, SAM'S ABOUT!!!

SAM is loved every minute of the day by S. LYONS & M. ROCKEY Tel: 01222-794825

SWNYDWR THE GOOD LIFE AT DARRAMARG J.W. – d.o.b. 1/8/93

(Ch. Holtzburg Mayhem x Swnydwr Celebration)

MARGO came into our life a beautiful brown Dobe puppy. A pet is all we wanted, but MARGO decided to give us much more, a super show girl gaining many places in both Championship and Open shows, and always a lady. We are so proud of her. She is one special girl. We cannot thank Jean and Milton enough for letting us have her, and we thank Charlie (Swnydwr Celebration), her mum.

**P.M. & S.M. Wiggins, Greystones, Pant Hirwaun, Hoel y Cyw, Mid Glam CF35 6HH
Tel: 01656-861649**

KEYALA

CH. & IRISH CH. BILSAM THE THRILLER J.W.
– introducing "BUGSY", the first-ever Brown & Tan Dobe to achieve both English and Irish crowns

KEYALAS ICE MAN J.W., Res. C.C.
CLYDE, our up-and-coming youngster, is making his mark in the ring, along with BUGSY's many offspring.
BUGSY and CLYDE have both been H.D. & C.S. screened and are at stud to approved bitches only.
Our breeding policy is to achieve quality not quantity, soundness and most importantly temperament. With this
in mind, we feel our puppies can live a happy and contented life in show and pet homes.
STUD & PUPPY ENQUIRIES to: DEBBIE & SHAUN GAMBLE
Elmdale, Sedge Green, Roydon Hamlet, Essex
Tel: 01992-448296 – Mobile: 0836-640107